Behold and See Sc
A Catholic and Hands-on Ap

MW01484835

MICHAEL J. SPEAR

LIFE SCIENCE

CATHOLIC HERITAGE EDITION

Catholic Heritage Curricula

1-800-490-7713   *www.chcweb.com*
P.O. Box 579090, Modesto, CA 95357

ISBN: 978-0-9913264-0-2

Original edition © 1998 Helene Spear

Catholic Heritage Edition © 2014 Theresa A. Johnson

Interior Design: Lauren Woodrow
Image credits may be found on pages 274-275.

Printed by Sheridan Books Inc., Chelsea, Michigan
April 2014   Print code: 358301

For more information:
Catholic Heritage Curricula
P.O. Box 579090
Modesto, CA 95357
www.chcweb.com

Ancillary Materials to this Course

Student Workbook provides student-friendly exercises, research assignments, experiments, formal labs, keywords for memorization, diagram and label exercises, tests, and a complete answer key.

Daily Lesson Plans: This course is designed to be completed in one year, but it can also be taught over two years to allow more time to discuss and investigate topics of interest. Daily lesson plans to assist in teaching this course are available at Catholic Heritage Curricula (*www.chcweb.com*).

A Catholic and Hands-On Approach to Science

Firmly grounded in the belief that faith and reason are inseparable, the science materials published by Catholic Heritage Curricula teach up-to-date scientific knowledge within the context of our Catholic faith. Scientifically excellent, these texts allow students to progress rapidly in their understanding of scientific discoveries and the scientific method. More importantly, they gently but compellingly demonstrate God's active and foundational role in creation, and reflect on the proper use of scientific knowledge for the glory of God.

The *Behold and See* series is distinguished by an emphasis on conceptual understanding rather than just memorization of facts. Straight-forward explanations allow students to master concepts as simply and easily as possible, while the series' hands-on approach allows students to actually *do* science instead of just reading about it. Learn more about the science programs offered by Catholic Heritage Curricula by visiting *www.chcweb.com*, or request a free catalog by calling 1-800-490-7713.

⚠ Please note: Although every effort has been made to ensure the safety of all experiments within this program, users are responsible for taking appropriate safety measures and supervising children during experiments. Catholic Heritage Curricula disclaims all responsibility for any injury or risk which is incurred as a result of the use of any of the material in this program.

Question the beauty of the earth,
the beauty of the sea,
the beauty of the wide air around you,
the beauty of the sky;

question the order of the stars,
the sun whose brightness lights the day,
the moon whose splendor softens the gloom of night;

question the living creatures that move in the waters,
that roam upon the earth,
that fly through the air;
the spirit that lies hidden,
the matter that is manifest;
the visible things that are ruled,
the invisible things that rule them;

question all these.
They will answer you: "Behold and see, we are beautiful."

Their beauty is their confession of God.
Who made these beautiful changing things,
if not One Who is beautiful and changeth not?

—Saint Augustine

CONTENTS

Chapter 1: Introduction, *2*

Chapter 2: Measurement, *10*

Chapter 3: Collections, *18*

Chapter 4: Basic Chemistry, *26*

Chapter 5: Cells, *36*

Chapter 6: Simplest Cells, *44*

Chapter 7: Protists: A Microscopic Menagerie, *54*

Chapter 8: The Fungi, *62*

Chapter 9: Plant Classification, *70*

Chapter 10: Plant Structure and Response, *82*

Chapter 11: Plant Growth and Reproduction, *92*

Chapter 12: Animals, *100*

Chapter 13: Chordates, *116*

Chapter 14: Nutrition, *126*

Chapter 15: Testing for Nutrients, *136*

Chapter 16: Introduction to Systems, *144*

Chapter 17: The Skeletal and Muscular Systems, *152*

Chapter 18: The Digestive System, *158*

Chapter 19: The Circulatory System, *166*

Chapter 20: The Respiratory System, *174*

Chapter 21: The Excretory System, *182*

Chapter 22: The Endocrine System, *188*

Chapter 23: The Nervous System, *198*

Chapter 24: Disease: The Fight for Life, *210*

Chapter 25: Animal Behavior and Reproduction, *226*

Chapter 26: Ecology, *238*

Appendix I: Word Roots, *251*

Appendix II: Plant Uses, *252*

Glossary, *255*

Dedication

To my girlfriend,

my bride,

the mother of my children,

Helene,

and all the members of my family,

who daily give me an interest in,

and an enthusiasm for,

LIFE.

Special Thanks

Daniel, Elena, Emily, Gabriele, Jane, John, Rachel,

Mr. and Mrs. Elmer J. Spear, Mr. and Mrs. John M. Spear,

Mrs. Lynn Harter, Brigette Olejniczak,

Spear Printing Company, Inc., Washingtonville Pediatrics

Dear Young Scientist:

As a teacher, I like to begin with prayer. Isaiah 44:24 is especially appropriate when discussing the life sciences:

> Thus says the Lord, your redeemer,
> who formed you from the womb:
> "I am the Lord who made all things,
> who alone stretched out the heavens;
> when I spread out the earth,
> who was with me?"

This verse just about says it all when discussing life science and the current issues involved with life. It explains the origins of life as well as the origin of the entire universe. Personally, I think it explains why God would go to all the effort of creating such a marvelous place for us to live and why He would bother with human beings at all. Note the question posed by God's words, "Who was with me?" If you or I or even an atheistic scientist were to make something even half so wonderful as a simple, one-celled organism, the urge to tell others would be overwhelming. I think that God is so pleased with His heavens and earth that He formed each of us in our mother's womb just to share the beauty of creation with us. By reading an author's novels you may come to know the person behind the pen. By studying life science, I have discovered that you come to know the Author of Life.

The vocabulary in *Life Science* has not been filtered to remove words you might not know and understand. As you read, many words take on meaning from their use in the text. Do not skip words you do not know. Look up words new to you and learn them! Key terms which should be memorized are written in CAPITAL letters in the text. If the scientific names are difficult to pronounce, you can get friendly and just use their initials. Study hard, work harder, and learn plenty. It is my hope that you will keep this program and use it again and again.

—Michael J. Spear

Michael J. Spear was a native of Washingtonville where his interest in nature grew from the farms, ponds and fields of Orange County, New York. Mr. Spear's Bachelor's degree in Forest Biology was earned at the College of Environmental Sciences and Forestry in Syracuse, New York. A concurrent degree in Biology was awarded by Syracuse University. His Master's degree was earned through private and public colleges in the Hudson River valley.

Mr. Spear taught every level of science for grades 7 through 12. He helped guide the interests of young boys and girls for more than two decades at science and outdoor living camps in New York State. Mr. Spear was active in the pro-life movement, a member of the Nocturnal Adoration Society, an active member of his parish, and founder of a private Catholic high school.

Mr. Spear was married to Helene Spear and is the father of seven children: Emily, John, Daniel, Elena, Gabriele, Jane and Rachel. He died in an automobile accident on his way to work in February 1999.

INTRODUCTION

Wonder is the seed of knowledge.

—Francis Bacon

FIGURE 1.1. PINUS LONGAEVA
Bristlecone pine trees grow at high elevations in extremely harsh conditions. They are some of the oldest trees in the world, many living for almost 5000 years.

INTRODUCTION

Life Science

Life science is an attempt to understand the varied world of living things, of which you and I are a part. A world inhabited by invisible creatures—some able to kill the strongest among us, some giving us an advantage over the killers! A world in which the tallest living thing is higher than you standing on top of me and seventy-six of your friends on top of that! (Figure 1.2)

Life science includes the study of a tremendous variety of living things, all with their own unique characteristics. To study and understand the wonderful world of each living **ORGANISM**, we must begin by defining our subject matter and learning the study skills necessary for success.

BIOLOGY, the study of living things, will require an ability to measure and to organize information. As biologists we will use a microscope to view one-celled plants and animals and we will collect specimens to study the variety of living things. Our experiments and studies will show us that you, the giant blue whale, the tiny amoeba, and the ancient bristle cone pine—all so different!—share the same basic life functions. Living things both great and small, plant and animal, all carry out eight life functions.

FIGURE 1.2. SIZES
Here is the size of Average Arnold, your every day, all-around dad, as compared to one of the coast redwoods, the tallest organisms on our planet! The tallest redwood is located in Redwood National Park, California and is 380 feet tall! For comparison, the largest animal, the giant blue whale, only grows to be about 100 feet long—still much larger than a human being!

1. **TRANSPORT** includes the absorption and distribution of chemicals. The blood in your circulatory system does the job of transport in your body.

2. **IRRITABILITY** may also be called response or regulation. Irritability is displayed when an organism reacts to a stimulus. For example, you look toward the door when you hear a knock.

3. **NUTRITION** includes the process of **PHOTOSYNTHESIS** in plants and the processes of **INGESTION**, **DIGESTION**, and **ABSORPTION** in animals.

4. **RESPIRATION** within living cells provides the energy for life through the **OXIDATION** of food. It also maintains the proper temperature for life. Respiration within the cell is accompanied by external respiration, which in animals is called breathing.

5. **EXCRETION** is the putting out of wastes. Excretion prevents the pollution of an organism's internal environment.

6. **SYNTHESIS** is the process by which a creature makes useful chemicals for secretion, regulation, repair, and growth.

7. **GROWTH** is an increase in the size or number of cells. You started life as a single cell; now you are trillions and trillions of cells all working together!

8. **REPRODUCTION** is a life function necessary for the species but not for the individual. In the life process of reproduction a new individual of the same organism is created.

Somehow, all of these life functions are blended together in each of God's creatures. The sum total of all eight life functions is called **METABOLISM**.

We will study life science for these reasons: to prevent disease; to eat correctly and live a healthy life; to know and understand our fellow passengers on spacecraft earth; and to preserve life for those as yet unborn.

1. TRANSPORT
Red blood cells passing single file through a capillary

2. IRRITABILITY
Venus flytrap snapping closed on a fly

3. NUTRITION
Chipmunk eating sunflower seeds

4. RESPIRATION
A swimmer's cells use oxygen to produce energy.

5. EXCRETION
Stomata, small holes in a leaf, excrete oxygen.

6. SYNTHESIS
The adrenal glands synthesize, or make, adrenalin.

7. GROWTH
This newborn baby will grow into an adult.

8. REPRODUCTION
Ducks reproduce by laying eggs.

FIGURE 1.3. METABOLISM
The sum total of all eight life functions is called metabolism.

The Scientific Method

As part of this course, we will practice using the scientific method, an organized way of solving questions and problems. The steps of the scientific method are:

1. Define the question or problem.

2. Collect data (information) through research.

3. Formulate a **HYPOTHESIS**—that is, an educated guess—to answer the question.

4. Experiment using a **CONTROL** (to provide a basis for comparison) and a variable group (a group subjected to the variable factor being tested).

5. Interpret the results of the experiment and draw a conclusion that supports or rejects the hypothesis.

6. Share your data through written compositions and oral reports.

Controlled Experiments

Science experiments are designed to solve a problem, to show relationships between observations, or to gather data for future research.

The hypothesis is a suggested explanation for something that has been observed. The hypothesis must be tested by a controlled experiment before it is accepted, rejected, or modified.

FIGURE 1.4. PLANTING A STRAWBERRY PLANT

A controlled experiment is an experiment in which most variables are controlled, that is, kept the same. A variable is anything that can change the results of the experiment. In a controlled experiment, one variable is purposely changed: for instance, the amount of fertilizer used to feed various strawberry plants. This variable is called the **INDEPENDENT VARIABLE**. The variable that will change because of the independent variable is called the **DEPENDENT VARIABLE**. For instance, the dependent variable in the strawberry plant experiment is how well the plants grow. The dependent variable depends on the changes that are made to the independent variable.

In order to be sure that the dependent variable is changing because of the independent variable, all the other variables in the experiment must be kept constant, or the same. For instance, you must plant the strawberry plants in the same soil, provide them with the same amount of water, and make sure they receive the same amount of sunlight. Otherwise, if strawberry #1 grows the best, you won't know whether it is because of the amount of fertilizer you used (the independent variable), or because of another variable such as soil, water, or sunlight.

Finally, in a controlled experiment there must be a control, or a similar test in which no variables are allowed to change. For instance, in the strawberry experiment, the control would be one or more plants which receive no fertilizer at all. The control allows us to confirm that the dependent variable is caused by the independent variable, and not by other, unknown factors.

In our experiments we will use an eight-part format:

I. Title—a word or phrase related to the content of the experiment;

II. Purpose—several concise sentences that clearly explain why the experiment is being done;

III. Materials—a list of items that will be used up during the experiment;

IV. Apparatus—a list of equipment that may be used again after this procedure has been completed;

V. Procedure—clearly listed, step-by-step instructions on how to do the experiment;

VI. Data—neatly organized information obtained by doing the procedure (charts, tables, graphs, calculations, observations, etc.);

VII. Questions—answers to any questions related to the lab, written neatly and in complete sentences;

VIII. Conclusion—a brief statement that sums up the results of the lab and indicates that the purpose has been fulfilled. For example, in a lab entitled "Testing for Fats," whose purpose is "to identify common foods rich in fats," a good conclusion might be: "Of the foods tested in this experiment, margarine and peanuts tested positive for fats."

FIGURE 1.5. SCIENTIST OBSERVING A GREEN LEAF WITH A MICROSCOPE

Graphing

Graphs are a way of showing data in a type of picture. For the experiments in your workbook, graphs will be provided for you to fill in the data. When you draw a graph on your own, follow these steps:

1. Draw the horizontal axis about 2 centimeters up from the bottom edge of your graph paper. Horizontal means from side to side (———), like the horizon! The independent variable is graphed on the horizontal axis.

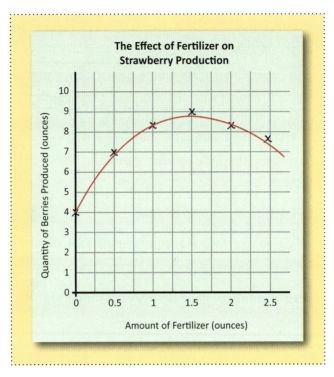

FIGURE 1.6. SAMPLE GRAPH

2. Draw the vertical axis about 2 cm from the left edge of your graph paper. Vertical means up and down (|). The dependent variable is graphed on the vertical axis.

3. Label the axes with numbers according to your data. For example, suppose there are 25 spaces on the horizontal axis and that the smallest piece of data is 3 and the biggest is 10. Divide the number of spaces by the largest piece of data to figure out how many spaces to use per unit of data: 25 / 10 = 2.5 spaces per unit of data. Use a number of spaces equal to or less than your answer to represent one unit of data. For the example, I would use two spaces for each number. Repeat the calculation for the vertical axis. Label both axes with a title and the units.

4. Plot the data with small X's so that the center of the X is at the correct point on the graph.

5. Connect the X's with a smooth curve of best fit.

6. Put a title on the graph. Put your name, date, subject and the page number or assignment on the heading.

Using This Text Correctly

The text is a tool for learning and study. Used correctly, your book will help you do your assignments faster and more thoroughly than "Haphazard Harriet." She's a student too smart for her teacher. When Harriet does her assignments she just "looks for the answers" without reading the assignment first, and without using the textbook tool fully. If you wish to save time and learn more easily, use each of the parts of the text correctly:

- The **title page** is the first page of a book, and includes information on the title, author, publisher, and place and year of publication. This information is necessary whenever you quote from a book for a report. You should always check the copyright date when using a book to look up any kind of current information. For example, in a history text published in 1988, you will find out that Ronald Reagan is currently president. However, even though he was extremely popular, Mr. Reagan is no longer president. You must use a book with a current copyright for current data.

- The **table of contents** provides an outline of the book with page numbers for each chapter. Use the table of contents to find a general topic in a book.

  A book's table of contents appears at the front of the book and gives an outline of the work. It is a good place to look to see what general topics the book discusses that interest you.

- The **body** is the main part of the book, which follows the outline of the table of contents. The body is where you go to read about a topic in depth. The body is pages 1 to 249 in this text.

- An **appendix** is a part of a text which is found near the end of some books. Appendices contain charts, maps, or other detailed information not included in the body. For example, see pages 251 to 253 in this text.

- A **glossary** is a micro-dictionary found near the back of a book. Use the glossary to define keywords when possible, since the meaning given there will fit the usage particular to the subject of the book. If a term is not in the glossary, then use a dictionary and choose the definition that best fits the use of the keyword in the text. In this book, the keywords which are most important to learn and on which you will be tested are printed in CAPITAL letters. All of these keywords are defined in the glossary on pages 255 to 272.

  Many words used in life science come from the same Greek or Latin "root" words. If you learn the meaning of the root word, then you will know the meanings of many words. For example, "biology" comes from two Greek roots: "*bio*," which means "life" or "living things" and "*-ology*," which means "the study of." Thus, biology is the study of living things. You may see the same root in many other words: biosphere, biologist, biodegradable, etc. The root words most important for becoming proficient in life science are listed in Appendix I on page 251.

 Worksheets: 1.1–1.5

 Formal Lab: 1.6

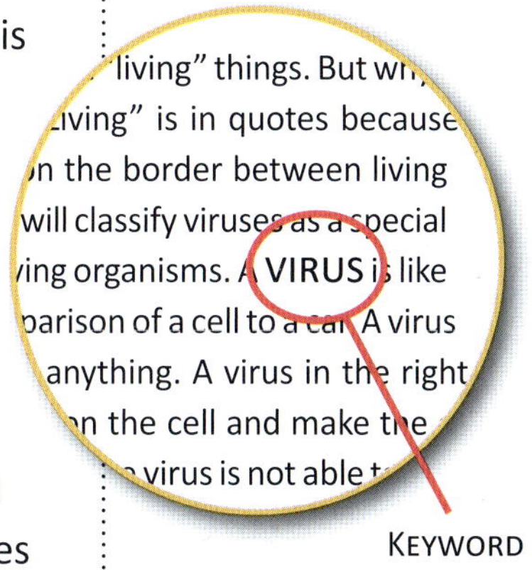

"living" things. But wh ...ving" is in quotes because ...n the border between living will classify viruses as a special ...ing organisms. A **VIRUS** is like ...parison of a cell to a car. A virus ... anything. A virus in the right ...n the cell and make the ... virus is not able t...

KEYWORD

FIGURE 1.7. EXAMPLE OF A KEYWORD IN THE MAIN BODY OF TEXT

MEASUREMENT

But You have disposed all things by
measure and number and weight.
For with You great strength abides always;
who can resist the might of Your arm?
Indeed, before You the whole universe is
as a grain from a balance,
or a drop of morning dew come down
upon the earth. . . .
And how could a thing remain, unless You
willed it;
or be preserved, had it not been called
forth by You?
But You spare all things, because they are
Yours, O Lord and lover of souls,
for Your imperishable spirit is in all things!

—Wisdom 11:20–12:1

FIGURE 2.1. RAFFLESIA KEITHII
Botanist measuring Rafflesia flower in Mt. Kinabalu National Park,
Sabah, Borneo

MEASUREMENT

The Metric System

You are probably used to using units of measurement such as feet, cups, and pounds in your everyday life. Now you will learn the skill of using the **METRIC SYSTEM**, a way of measuring objects based on the number ten. The metric system is used by industries and scientists throughout the world, because it is easier to convert measurements into other units in the metric system than in other systems. Learning to use the metric system is an important and necessary preparation for advanced science studies.

To measure the length of an object like yourself, use a meter stick. You are probably taller than one meter stick but not as tall as two. As a matter of fact, "Average Adam," your all-American, everyday boy of twelve years old,

FIGURE 2.2. A CENTIMETER RULER
This centimeter ruler is shown actual size for comparison of the units millimeter, centimeter, and decimeter. If you could divide the tiny millimeter, the smallest GRADUATION shown, into 1,000 equal parts, then you could visualize how small a μm (micrometer) is!

Decimeter: 10 dm = 1 m　　　**Centimeter: 100 cm = 1 m**
Millimeter: 1000 mm = 1 m　　**Kilometer: 1000 m = 1 km**

The metric system uses the unit kilometer instead of the mile. The kilometer is equal to 0.62 mile (about 5/8 mile).

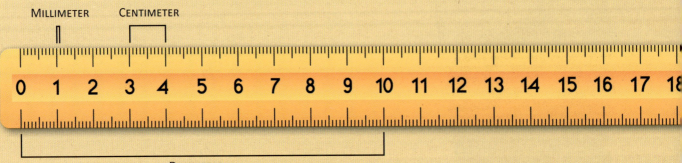

FIGURE 2.3. METRIC PREFIXES CHART

						Basic Unit							
Mega	—	—	kilo	hecto	deka	meter/liter/gram	deci	centi	milli	—	—	micro
M_	—	—	k_	h_	da_	m / l / g	d_	c_	m_	—	—	μ_

Greek prefixes mean bigger than one.   Latin prefixes mean smaller than one.

is exactly one and a half meter sticks tall. (His cousin, Haphazard Harriet, is actually a little taller than Adam now, but won't be in a few years.) The basic unit of measurement for distance is the **METER**. The instrument for measuring distance is the **METER STICK**. A smaller instrument is the centimeter ruler (see Figure 2.2). Note that a meter is divided into 10 parts called decimeters (dm), into 100 parts called centimeters (cm), and into 1000 parts named millimeters (mm). Meters, centimeters, and millimeters are units of measurement. Look up UNIT in the glossary to make sure you know its meaning. More importantly, be sure to **include units with every measurement you write down!**

There is one problem with the meter: sometimes it takes hundreds of them to measure a distance and sometimes it takes only a tiny, tiny fraction of a meter to measure an organism. Pauline Musters, the smallest woman on record, was only 0.59 meters (m) tall at 18 years old. But even that is big when compared to a bacillus bacterium that is only 0.000001 meters (m) long.

Having to write zero, point, zero, zero, zero, zero, zero, one meters (m) is a bit of a pain in the neck! As a result, the metric system has units that are based on the meter (m) but are bigger or smaller. It is more convenient to say one micrometer (1 μm) for the size of a bacillus, and it is much easier to write! "μ" is the Greek letter *mu*, pronounced MYOO (like the sound a cat makes).

Since the metric system is based on ten, you can change units simply by moving the decimal point. You can use the Metric Prefixes Chart (Figure 2.3) to convert from one unit to another.

For example, Average Adam is 1.5 m tall, but how many centimeters (cm) tall is Adam? Find the basic unit on the chart—meter (m)—then count the number of steps you must move to get to centimeters (cm). Note that you move two places to the right. Now move the decimal point in your initial quantity, 1.5 m, two places to the right:

$$1.50 \longrightarrow 150$$

Now write this number with the correct units as your answer: Average Adam is 150 cm tall. Pauline Musters was 0.59 m tall; how many centimeters is this?

You must know the correct abbreviations for the different units. The centimeter (cm) is approximately as wide as the average pinky finger. Centimeters are used to measure hand-sized things. Kilometers (km) are used to measure distances between cities. Micrometers (μm), also called **MICRONS**, are used to measure microscopic objects.

You already know the basic unit of length is the meter (m), but what are the units for liquid volume and mass? Soda bottles come in one or two **LITER** (l) sizes and candy bars are often measured in **GRAMS** (g).

Mass (g)

The triple beam balance is used to measure **MASS** in the unit grams. Do not confuse mass with weight. Mass is the amount of matter present. Weight is a measure of the force of gravity on an object. One thousand grams equals one kilogram, which is approximately 2.2 pounds (on earth). The kilogram is approximately the mass of seven baseballs.

Notice that the metric system uses the same prefixes even when we are measuring mass instead of distance. Just as 1000 meters equals one kilometer, so 1000 grams equals one kilogram. The basic unit is different but the prefixes are the same.

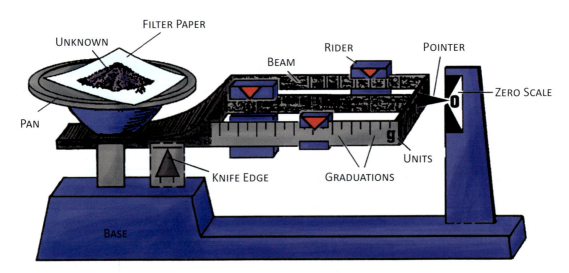

FIGURE 2.4. THE TRIPLE BEAM BALANCE
The triple beam balance is used to measure the mass of an object. To find the mass of a solid object, place the object gently on the pan. Move the largest rider over until the pointer moves downward. Move the largest rider back one notch. Repeat with the medium sized rider, then with the smallest rider until the pointer is at the exact position on the zero scale that it was pointing to before you began. Now add the amounts indicated by each of the three riders and write your determination of the mass with the unit grams (g).

Robert Wadlow, the tallest man on record, was 7 feet, 1 ¾ inches tall when he was thirteen years old. At that time, his mass was 115,666.05 grams (g), which certainly sounds like a lot! But the gram is approximately the mass of one, medium-sized paperclip. A better unit for Robert's mass would be kilograms (kg). Use the **Metric Prefixes Chart** to figure out Robert's mass in kilograms. Start at the basic unit, grams (g), and count the steps to kilograms (kg). Since you move three places to the left on the Metric Prefixes Chart, you should move the decimal point three places to the left: one place, 11566.605; two places, 1156.6605; three places, 115.66605! This is the magnitude of your answer. Round this off to a reasonable number of places and add the correct units for your final answer. Thirteen-year-old Robert Wadlow had a mass of approximately 115.7 kg.

For comparison, the average twelve-year-old girl's mass is about 39.7 kg, and Average Adam would be roughly 1.45 kg less than that. As big as Robert Wadlow was, it would take over one thousand two hundred (1,200) thirteen-year-old Robert Wadlows to have a mass equal to one blue whale (139,255.2 kg). What is the mass of this blue whale in megagrams (Mg)?

FIGURE 2.5. ROBERT WADLOW

You really must remember the metric prefixes in order with the blank spaces included. The prefixes used for values greater than one are Greek: **MEGA** (1,000,000), —, —, **KILO** (1,000), **HECTO** (100), and **DEKA** (10).

Latin prefixes indicate values less than one: **DECI** (1/10), **CENTI** (1/100), **MILLI** (1/1,000), —, **MICRO** (1/1,000,000). All of the prefixes are based on the number ten.

Area (cm²) and Volume (cm³ and cc)

Wow—510,070,000! Is that big! Is that big?

Measurements must always include the units. If the above is in square millimeters (mm²) then it is only 510 square meters (m²), just two-thirds the area of a baseball field.

But when we write 510,070,000 with the units square kilometers (km²), now that is big! The surface area of the entire earth is approximately 510,070,000 square kilometers (km²). To compare, Average Arnold (Average Adam's average-sized dad) has a skin surface area of about 1.86 m²—that is, a surface area of 0.00000186 km².

Let's try to "see" the basic idea of **AREA**. Use a centimeter ruler to measure the rectangle in Figure 2.6. This rectangle is 2 cm on one side and 3 cm on the other side. If we mark off small squares that measure one

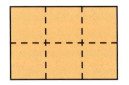

**FIGURE 2.6.
A RECTANGLE**
Area is determined
by multiplying the
length times the
width: (3 cm) (2 cm).

centimeter on each side, we find that six of these little "square centimeters" will fit on the 2 cm by 3 cm rectangle. The unit "cm × cm" is called square centimeters (cm²). You must memorize the general formula for rectangular area:

AREA = LENGTH × WIDTH

When doing an area calculation, always write the formula, then substitute the numbers with their units; finally, box your answer with the correct units. For example:

$$A = L \times W$$

$$A = (3\ cm)\,(2\ cm)$$

$$\boxed{A = 6\ cm^2}$$

Whenever additions or subtractions are done with units, the units must be the same. For area or volume problems the units must also be the same. For example, what is the area of the front of Figure 2.7?

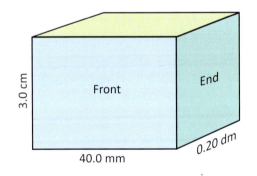

FIGURE 2.7. A BOX

Almost everybody knows that the formula for area is length times width, but we must change centimeters or millimeters before we multiply. Note that the answer is written in square centimeters.

$$A = L \times W$$

$$A = (40.0\ mm)\,(3.0\ cm)$$

$$A = (4.00\ cm)\,(3.0\ cm)$$

$$\boxed{A = 12.0\ cm^2}$$

This same idea, that units must be the same, also applies to rectangular volume calculations:

VOLUME = LENGTH × WIDTH × HEIGHT

For example, the volume of the box in Figure 2.7 can be calculated using the above formula. Before we can multiply, we must change all the units to one kind.

$$V = L \times W \times H$$

$$V = (40.0\ mm)\,(3.0\ cm)\,(0.20\ dm)$$

$$V = (4.00\ cm)\,(3.0\ cm)\,(2.0\ cm)$$

$$\boxed{V = 24\ cm^3}$$

Note the units in the answer. Metric **VOLUME** is measured in cubic centimeters, abbreviated cm³ or cc. You may have seen a baby bottle marked in cubic centimeters or a motorcycle that is 80 cc. The cubic centimeters marked on the bottle measure the volume of liquid it can hold. The cubic centimeters on the motorcycle measure the volume of its cylinder; the more cubic centimeters, the bigger the piston, and thus the more power.

Liquid Volume (l)

Liquid volume is measured in liters. The milliliter is approximately eight drops of water. When you memorize the volume formula you must also remember this fact:

One milliliter = one cubic centimeter

1 ml = 1 cc

So we could say that a two-liter soda bottle is 2,000 ml. That is the same as 2,000 cubic centimeters.

Temperature (°C)

In the metric system, temperature is measured in **CENTIGRADE** degrees, °C. Centigrade refers to the 100 graduations, or degrees, from freezing to boiling. This temperature scale is often called Celsius after its inventor, Andre Celsius. Temperature is how hot or cold something is compared with a standard. Room temperature is about 20 °C and the human body temperature is 36.5 °C.

Each measurement of temperature must include the correct units. You may be familiar with Fahrenheit degrees (°F), which are used in our weather reports. In chemistry and physics courses you will be using the absolute scale measured in Kelvins (K).

The fixed points for water are its freezing and boiling points. Pure water freezes at 0 °C, 32 °F, and 273 K. At one atmosphere of pressure pure water boils at 100 °C, 212 °F, and 373 K. Which is colder: 0 °C or 32 °F or 273 K?

Heat (cal)

A calorimeter is used to measure heat in the unit calories. Try not to confuse temperature with heat. Temperature is how hot or cold something is compared to a standard. Heat is a measure of the amount of energy available for transfer to another object. (That is, heat is a measure of the kinetic energy of the molecules in an object.)

FIGURE 2.8. CENTIGRADE AND FAHRENHEIT DEGREES
"Does the temperature ever fall below zero where you live?" Can you figure out the problem with this question? That's right! It doesn't include any units. Although you might be able to guess whether the questioner is referring to zero degrees Fahrenheit or zero degrees Centigrade, there is no way to tell from the question itself. As you can see from the thermometer in the photo, 0 °F and 0 °C are very different temperatures, so including the unit makes a big difference.

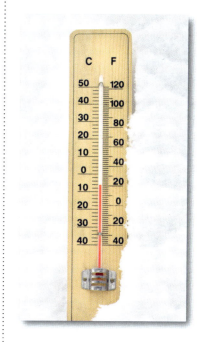

 Worksheets: 2.1, 2.3–2.5

 Diagram: 2.2

Microscope: 2.6–2.7

COLLECTIONS

All the sciences which study the works of creation tend to the glory of their Author; they are praiseworthy in themselves and holy in their goal; to know the truth, is to know God.

—Fr. Armand David

FIGURE 3.1. MOTHS AND BUTTERFLIES IN AN INSECT COLLECTION

COLLECTIONS

I found the nest of a phoebe (FEE-bee), a soft nest of moss lined with delicate hairs and fibers. This nest, however, was different! Never have I found another like it. This nest still had the tiny skeletons of the baby birds in it! "What had happened to the mother bird?" I wondered. Thirty years later I still have that and many other nests. I've enjoyed the fun and exercise of finding nests in the fall of each year. (Why the fall?) I learned about the birds that made each nest. I came, like Longfellow's Little Hiawatha, to learn of ". . . every bird its language, learned of them and all their secrets, where they built their nests in summer, where they hid themselves in winter . . ." Since then, hundreds of other children have enjoyed seeing my collection. They have studied the way each nest is made—each as different as the species of bird that constructed it.

Collections are made to learn from, to enjoy, to preserve specimens for later, and for the beauty of the objects. Collections are especially important to life scientists, since discovering and classifying different plants and animals is one of the best ways to learn about all creatures great and small. For this life science course, you will collect either leaves or insects. Of course you may collect both on your own, but choose one for this assignment. Seeds and seashells are other interesting objects to collect on your own! For your collection you must have at least ten different specimens.

When you have finished reading the chapter, you may get started on your own collection! Begin by deciding whether you will collect leaves or insects, and then follow the instructions in the chapter to complete your collection.

FIGURE 3.2. Each species of bird builds its own, unique type of nest.

Leaf Collections

For each specimen, look for one or two medium-sized leaves. Never take more than two or three leaves from any one branch. Be sure to ask permission before collecting from an ornamental (a tree in someone's yard)! Remember **not** to collect poison ivy, poison oak, or poison sumac. As you collect the leaves, be sure to record information about the tree or bush from which you took the leaf. This will help you to identify the leaf later on. Key features to record include the shape of the tree, the texture of the bark, the shape of the leaf, the spacing of the leaves on the branch, the site of the tree, and the type of fruit produced by the tree. See the chart below for the basic features of trees.

To preserve your specimens, place each leaf between two sheets of newspaper along with a card showing:

1. the date collected;

2. the name of the leaf (if known);

3. special notes about where the leaf was collected;

4. the name of the person who collected the specimen.

FIGURE 3.3. As you collect specimens from different trees for your leaf collection, make notes about the shape, bark, branches, and location of each tree. These notes will help you to identify the leaves later on.

BASIC FEATURES OF TREES

Crown shape:
- Round
- Triangular
- Oval
- Feather Duster

Site:
- Deep woods (full shade)
- Fence line (partly sunny)
- Open field (full sun)

Site moisture: • Wet   • Dry

Bark:
- Smooth
- Grooves
- Rough

Leaf type:
- Alternate
- Opposite
- Evergreen (keeps its leaves all year)
- Deciduous (loses its leaves in the fall)

Leaf shape:
- Whole leaf
- Lobed leaf

Edge shape:
- Serrated edge
- Smooth edge

Fruit:
- Cone
- Nut
- Bean
- Berry
- Helicopter

POISON IVY

POISON SUMAC

POISON OAK

FIGURE 3.4. Do not collect poison ivy, poison oak, or poison sumac. In the fall, these plants have red and yellow leaves. In the spring and summer, their leaves are green.

Do not allow the leaves to overlap in the newspaper. Put several layers of newspaper between the sheets with leaves on them. Place the stack of newspaper and leaves in a dry, warm place with several large, heavy books on top of it. After a week the leaves will have dried out. Remember that they are now fragile and will crumble instead of bend.

Identify each of the leaves in your collection, using a standard field guide to trees along with the information you recorded when you collected the leaves. Cut out a 2 cm by 4 cm label for each leaf. On each label, write:

1. the name of the tree;

2. the date collected;

3. the place collected (town and state);

4. the collector's name.

Mount the leaves and labels with a clear-drying glue. Spread a thin layer of glue over every part of the back of each specimen and place it carefully on a stiff piece of paper. Be sure no excess glue is on the edges or coming through the leaf.

Glue the label near the leaf. Put a sheet of newspaper over the leaf and label and then place them both under a heavy book. Immediately lift the book and paper to check if any glue has come out from under the edges of the leaf or label. If it has, clean it up and use a new sheet of newspaper. Put the book back on top and allow the glue to dry. Store your collection in a **dry** place.

Insect Collections

There are more kinds of insects on earth than there are of all other members of the animal kingdom put together. Insects reproduce rapidly. They may be found almost anywhere. Especially good places to look for insects include on flower blossoms, in old logs and stumps, near ponds, and around outdoor lights. Spiders, because they have more than six legs, are **not** insects. Do not collect them. Use **caution** if you collect bees or wasps.

Collect the live or dead insects in a plastic container. **Do not use glass** jars. This author has the scars on his right hand to clearly indicate why no glass jars should be used! You must note **where** (town and state) and **when** (the date) each specimen was collected and **who** collected it.

Insects are killed by putting them in a killing jar. The killing jar should be glass and it should stay put in one place. Be sure to keep it out of reach

Father Armand David

Armand David (1826–1900) was a Vincentian priest and a talented naturalist who collected hundreds of wild animals, plants, rocks, and fossils from China, including previously unknown species like the Giant Panda. Fr. David originally went to

FIGURE 3.5. FR. ARMAND DAVID

China as a missionary, but he was such a talented naturalist that scientists in France asked that he be allowed to devote himself to collecting the plants and animals of China. His superiors agreed because Fr. David's scientific work would help gain support for the Chinese missions.

Now, Fr. David loved science, but he had spent all his life dreaming of being a missionary. Another person might have been disappointed at being told to give up this dream. Not Fr. David! In his humility, he knew that it did not matter whether the Chinese were evangelized by himself or by another missionary. He simply did his best in the job his superiors had assigned to him. Although he would not be directly involved in evangelizing the Chinese, Fr. David understood that by supporting his fellow missionaries, he would still be a missionary.

Fr. David's life as a naturalist certainly was not an easy one! He traveled thousands of miles through the wildest regions of China, enduring poor nutrition, dangerous terrain, climate extremes, illness, fatigue, and encounters with bandits and hostile natives. What gave him strength to persevere through these trials? Fr. David revealed his secret in his diary: "[the Christian's] feet touch the ground, but his heart is in heaven, which he never loses sight of and towards which he still works. Whether in the quiet of a monastery or in the whirlwind of earthly affairs . . . the Christian lives calmly and walks with a firm step towards his goal by the conscientious fulfillment of his duties." Fr. David became a great scientist because he did everything for the glory of God.

FIGURE 3.6. GIANT PANDA

FIGURE 3.7. BEETLES, COCKROACHES, CRICKETS

FIGURE 3.8. GRASSHOPPERS, ETC.

FIGURE 3.9. TRUE BUGS
Note the triangle on the back.

FIGURE 3.10. BEES, FLIES, BUTTERFLIES, MOTHS

of small children! With adult supervision, soak a cotton ball with methyl acetate (or nail polisher remover) for use in the killing jar. ⚠ **CAUTION:** if a substance kills insects, it usually is not good for you to inhale! Clearly label the jar as a killing jar, even though methyl acetate is not considered highly toxic for humans.

Your insects should be pinned soon after killing. Once they dry out completely, the insects will be very fragile. Use a pinning board or a shoe box top. The red dots in Figures 3.7-10 show where to insert the pin for each type of insect. Regular straight pins rust and break off, so you will want to use size 3 insect pins. Put two labels on each pin, as shown in Figure 3.11. Make your labels 1.3 cm by 2.5 cm. Write on one label:

1. place collected (town and state);
2. the date collected;
3. who collected it.

On a second label include:

1. the name of the insect;
2. who identified it, if different from the collector.

Use the Simplified Key to Class Insecta to help you identify your specimens (Figure 3.13).

Store your collection in a small box. Glue two pieces of cardboard to the bottom of your box to hold the pins in place. Your collection should be scientifically accurate but also aesthetically pleasing. That is, you should carefully place the specimens and labels so that your collection is nice to look at!

Keep your collection dry and cool. Dermestid larvae, also known as carpet beetle worms, can ruin a beautiful collection. Keep the collection sealed tightly. Fumigate once or twice a year with a general household insecticide.

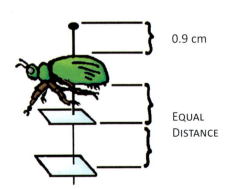

0.9 cm

EQUAL DISTANCE

FIGURE 3.11. LABELING AN INSECT SPECIMEN The back of each insect should be about 0.9 cm from the head of the pin, and the labels should be spaced equally below the specimen.

FIGURE 3.12. TINY INSECTS
Glue small insects such as mosquitoes onto a mini triangle of stiff paper.

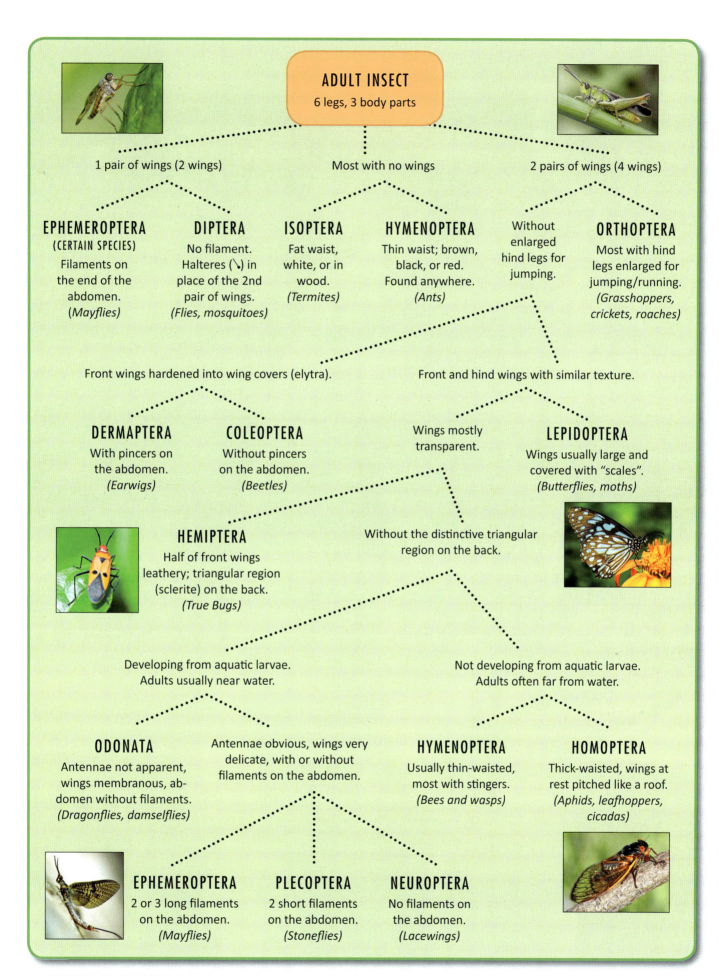

ADULT INSECT
6 legs, 3 body parts

1 pair of wings (2 wings)

Most with no wings

2 pairs of wings (4 wings)

EPHEMEROPTERA
(CERTAIN SPECIES)
Filaments on the end of the abdomen.
(*Mayflies*)

DIPTERA
No filament. Halteres (↘) in place of the 2nd pair of wings.
(*Flies, mosquitoes*)

ISOPTERA
Fat waist, white, or in wood.
(*Termites*)

HYMENOPTERA
Thin waist; brown, black, or red. Found anywhere.
(*Ants*)

Without enlarged hind legs for jumping.

ORTHOPTERA
Most with hind legs enlarged for jumping/running.
(*Grasshoppers, crickets, roaches*)

Front wings hardened into wing covers (elytra).

Front and hind wings with similar texture.

DERMAPTERA
With pincers on the abdomen.
(*Earwigs*)

COLEOPTERA
Without pincers on the abdomen.
(*Beetles*)

Wings mostly transparent.

LEPIDOPTERA
Wings usually large and covered with "scales".
(*Butterflies, moths*)

HEMIPTERA
Half of front wings leathery; triangular region (sclerite) on the back.
(*True Bugs*)

Without the distinctive triangular region on the back.

Developing from aquatic larvae. Adults usually near water.

Not developing from aquatic larvae. Adults often far from water.

ODONATA
Antennae not apparent, wings membranous, abdomen without filaments.
(*Dragonflies, damselflies*)

Antennae obvious, wings very delicate, with or without filaments on the abdomen.

HYMENOPTERA
Usually thin-waisted, most with stingers.
(*Bees and wasps*)

HOMOPTERA
Thick-waisted, wings at rest pitched like a roof.
(*Aphids, leafhoppers, cicadas*)

EPHEMEROPTERA
2 or 3 long filaments on the abdomen.
(*Mayflies*)

PLECOPTERA
2 short filaments on the abdomen.
(*Stoneflies*)

NEUROPTERA
No filaments on the abdomen.
(*Lacewings*)

FIGURE 3.13. SIMPLIFIED KEY TO CLASS INSECTA

BASIC CHEMISTRY

I tell my students to try to know molecules
so well that when they have some question
involving molecules, they can ask themselves,
What would I do if I were that molecule?

—George Wald

FIGURE 4.1. THE FATHER OF MODERN CHEMISTRY
Antoine-Laurent de Lavoisier in his laboratory

BASIC CHEMISTRY

Before beginning to study the smallest living creatures, we must first study atoms and molecules, the tiny building blocks of matter which make up all creatures. Chemistry is the study of how atoms and molecules interact with each other. Living things are powered by interactions between atoms and molecules, so it is important to understand the basics of chemistry before studying life science.

Atoms

An **ELEMENT** is a simple substance that cannot be broken down by ordinary chemical means—for example, carbon, oxygen, and sodium. An **ATOM** is the smallest part of an element that still has all the properties of the element. Atoms are extremely tiny, so we always have many of them even in a small piece of material. An element is made up of many atoms of the same kind.

An atom is so tiny that even using the best compound microscope on earth, you can't come close to seeing one. With a special electron microscope, which uses a beam of electrons instead of light rays to "look" at things, you can actually magnify objects 10 million times. At that power atoms can be seen, but they appear to be indistinct, hazy dots.

FIGURE 4.2. ASSORTED CHEMICAL ELEMENTS
Both metals and non-metals are included here, as well as solids, gases, and liquids. In the gas jars are hydrogen and oxygen. Sulfur (yellow) and carbon (black) are solid non-metals. Mercury (in dish) is a metal that is liquid at room temperature. The three metals at bottom are: lead (foil, lower right), tin (rods, lower left) and copper (orange, lower left).

How big, or shall we say, how small are atoms? According to chemists there are approximately 1.5×10^{22} atoms in one drop of water. That's 15 billion trillion! That's 15,000,000,000,000,000,000,000 atoms in one drop of water!

A medium-sized atom is about 10^{-10} m (0.0000000001 m) in diameter. For comparison, you are about 1.5 m tall, which is ten billion times larger than an atom!

As tiny as an atom is, it is made of three main pieces even smaller yet (Figure 4.3). In the dense center region of an atom, the **NUCLEUS**, are **PROTONS** (with a positive electric charge) and **NEUTRONS** (which are neutral, that is, with no electric charge). Spinning crazily around the nucleus in **ENERGY SHELLS** are tiny particles called **ELECTRONS**, which have a negative electric charge and are much smaller than protons or neutrons. You should be familiar with electrons because they are electricity! These three pieces take up very little room, and most of the atom is empty space. Scientists often use Bohr models, such as those in Figure 4.3, to draw the parts of an atom. It is important to realize that Bohr models are not drawn to scale; the electrons in an atom are actually much, much smaller than the nucleus, and are much farther away.

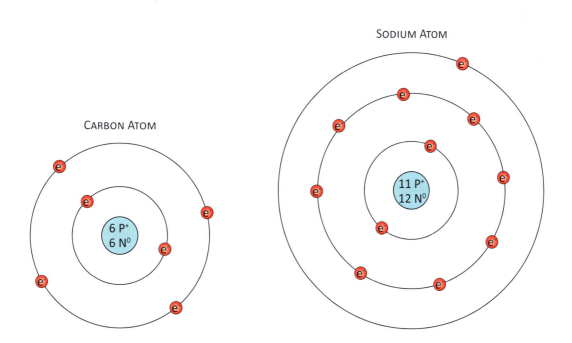

FIGURE 4.3. BOHR MODELS OF CARBON AND SODIUM ATOMS
The protons (+) and neutrons (0) are in the nucleus; the electrons (-) are spinning wildly in orbit in energy shells. Only two electrons may fit in the first shell, and only eight in the second energy shell. Most of the atom is empty space. The Bohr models above are not drawn to scale; if the nucleus of an atom were actually the size shown in the Bohr models above, the atom as a whole would be about the size of St. Peter's Basilica!

FIGURE 4.4. ELEMENTS MOST IMPORTANT FOR LIFE SCIENCE

SYMBOL	NAME	PROTONS	NEUTRONS	ELECTRONS	NOTES
H	hydrogen	1	0	1	Exists as H_2, an explosive gas. One of two elements in water. Needed for protoplasm. About 9.5% of you is H.
C	carbon	6	6	6	A black solid. Your pencil "lead" is carbon graphite. Approximately 18.5% of you is C. Organic compounds are C chains.
N	nitrogen	7	7	7	Exists as N_2, a stable gas. Air is 78% N_2. Needed to make protein. 3% of you is N.
O	oxygen	8	8	8	Exists as O_2, a gas needed for combustion. Air is 21% O_2. About 65% of you is O.

The four elements above make up almost all of the bodies of microbes, people, and the gigantic blue whale. The elements listed below are necessary in very tiny amounts.

Na	sodium (Latin: *natrium*)	11	12	11	Na is so active it is found only in compounds. Na is one element in table salt.
Mg	magnesium	12	12	12	A soft, silvery metal needed for muscle and nerve action.
P	phosphorous	15	16	15	An active non-metal needed for bones and teeth.
S	sulfur	16	16	16	A yellow solid needed for enzymes and protoplasm.
Cl	chlorine	17	18	17	Exists as Cl_2, a poisonous gas. Found in salt and stomach acid.
K	potassium (Latin: *kalium*)	19	20	19	A soft, active metal needed for muscle action.
Ca	calcium	20	20	20	A metal needed for bones and teeth.
Fe	iron (Latin: *ferrum*)	26	30	26	A metal needed in the blood to carry oxygen.
Cu	copper (Latin: *cuprum*)	29	35	29	A metal needed in tiny amounts for cells to work.
Zn	zinc	30	35	30	A metal needed in small amounts for tissues to work.
I	iodine	53	74	53	Exists as I_2, a purplish solid. Needed by the thyroid gland.

Atoms with the same number of protons in their nuclei are the same kind of atom. If two atoms with different numbers of neutrons and electrons have the same number of protons, they are still the same kind of atom. Of the more than 100 kinds of atoms, 92 may be found in nature. For life science, the 15 kinds of atoms shown in Figure 4.4 are the most important. Memorize the name and symbol for each.

Molecules

Just as an individual atom is a single piece of an element, a **MOLECULE** is one individual piece of a **COMPOUND**. A compound is a pure substance made of two or more elements. The different elements in a compound must be chemically joined in a definite ratio. For example, when atoms of hydrogen (H) and oxygen (O) combine in a two to one ratio, they form water (H_2O) molecules. This happens in a chemical reaction, which can occur quietly in your cells, or very loudly when hydrogen **GAS** explodes. We can write the equation for the chemical reaction like this:

$$2\ H_2\ +\ 1\ O_2\ \longrightarrow\ 2\ H_2O\ +\ energy$$

This chemical equation describes a chemical reaction that starts with two molecules of hydrogen gas (H_2) and one molecule of oxygen gas (O_2). First, the atoms of hydrogen in the molecules of H_2 gas separate, and the atoms of oxygen in the molecules of O_2 gas do the same. Then two atoms of hydrogen join one atom of oxygen to make water, H_2O. Gone are the explosive hydrogen gas and the oxygen gas needed for burning. In their place is the compound **WATER**, which when cooled is a **LIQUID**. Cooled below 0 °C, water becomes a **SOLID**.

Remember, atoms are pieces of elements and molecules are pieces of compounds. There are only 92 natural elements, but there are millions of compounds, because the elements can combine in thousands of different ways. In life science, we will concentrate on just a few of the millions of compounds.

About 60% of the human body is water. If you weigh 100 pounds (45.5 kg) almost 60 of those pounds (36.4 kg) is water! You might think I'm all wet; you'd be 60% correct. Most of the rest of your physical body is made of compounds with carbon in them, called organic compounds. A future chapter on nutrition will discuss the very large molecules in three groups of compounds: carbohydrates (sugars and starches); lipids (fats and oils); and proteins (hair, muscles, and enzymes).

There are several small, inorganic compounds that are also important for life science: NaCl is table salt; HCl is hydrochloric acid; and CO_2 is carbon dioxide.

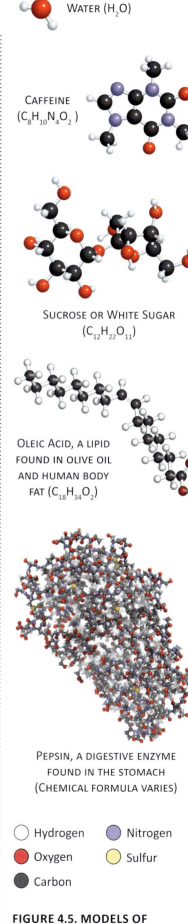

WATER (H_2O)

CAFFEINE ($C_8H_{10}N_4O_2$)

SUCROSE OR WHITE SUGAR ($C_{12}H_{22}O_{11}$)

OLEIC ACID, A LIPID FOUND IN OLIVE OIL AND HUMAN BODY FAT ($C_{18}H_{34}O_2$)

PEPSIN, A DIGESTIVE ENZYME FOUND IN THE STOMACH (CHEMICAL FORMULA VARIES)

○ Hydrogen   ○ Nitrogen
● Oxygen   ○ Sulfur
● Carbon

FIGURE 4.5. MODELS OF VARIOUS MOLECULES

Mixtures

A **MIXTURE** is formed when different kinds of compounds or elements are together but still keep their own properties. The liquid part of your cells (protoplasm) is a mixture of water and many other compounds. The liquid part of your blood (plasma) is also a mixture.

If you had to pick just one thing on earth most like your body's liquids, what would it be? Remember, you are mostly water. The 60% of you that is water is not pure water, though. In the water of your body are dissolved salts, oxygen and carbon dioxide gases, and organic compounds.

The one thing on earth most like your body's liquids is seawater! The oceans are mostly water but contain dissolved oxygen and carbon dioxide as well as organic compounds. As a matter of fact, when your life began inside of your mother, you were surrounded by a little ocean all your own, the amniotic sac. It is because of these similarities that some people think all living things must have come, way back in time, from something in the oceans. But life is much more than just seawater. Organisms, even the most simple, are very neatly organized and well planned.

FIGURE 4.6.

Are We Afraid of Chemicals?

Compounds which scientists use in chemical processes are often called chemicals. "Chemical" has become quite a negative word to many people, perhaps because of *chemical spills*, *chemical warfare* and *chemical dependency*.

One reason it can be hard to think positively about chemicals is because many people are unfamiliar with chemicals, or at least with their names. For example, do you have tetrahydrozoline hydrochloride in your home? You may recognize this chemical if I tell you it is one brand of non-prescription eyedrops.

Some chemicals are familiar, such as aspirin, rayon, gold, oxygen, and caffeine. It is when we hear a name like hydrogenated glucose syrup that many of us become uneasy, only to find out that this chemical is an ingredient in many sugarless gums.

Some people try to label chemicals as good or bad. They believe that bad chemicals cause tragedies. However, no chemical is bad or good. How they are used determines whether or not chemicals will be beneficial or harmful.

Many chemicals made by man are natural also. Hydrochloric acid is used in many industrial applications, but it is also produced in your stomach naturally! Do not fear chemicals, learn about and understand them.

Chapter 4

Antoine-Laurent de Lavoisier

Antoine-Laurent Lavoisier (1743–1794) was a Catholic scientist who is known as the Father of Modern Chemistry. His greatest contribution to chemistry was his insistence that science must be based on a strict observation of the facts.

For instance, in Lavoisier's day scientists believed that a substance called "phlogiston" was given off when materials were burned. The theory of phlogiston was a good hypothesis, but unfortunately scientists accepted it before it was proven by rigorous experiments.

Unlike many other chemists, Lavoisier did not think that the theory of phlogiston had been proved sufficiently, and he was right. After experimenting for a long time, Lavoisier showed that when materials are burned, they take a certain gas out of the air, instead of putting phlogiston into the air. Lavoisier called this gas "oxygen," the name that we still use today.

Lavoisier's careful experiments transformed chemistry into an exact science based on definite rules. He also classified everything that was known about chemistry at the time, giving elements the names which are still used today. His list of elements forms the basis for the modern Periodic Table of the Elements.

FIGURE 4.7. LAVOISIER AND HIS WIFE
Lavoisier's wife, Marie, assisted him in his scientific research and experiments.

Unfortunately, Lavoisier's scientific career was interrupted by the French Revolution, which condemned him to the guillotine because he had held a government position in the old French monarchy. Lavoisier's biographer writes, "Raised in a pious family which had given many priests to the Church, [Lavoisier] had held to his beliefs."

Periodic Table of the Elements

The Periodic Table of the Elements (see Figure 4.13) shows the symbols for all the known elements. The elements in the periodic table are arranged in order of increasing atomic number. An element's **ATOMIC NUMBER** is the number of protons which it has in its nucleus. For instance, the atomic number of carbon is 6, which means that it has six protons in its nucleus (Figure 4.8). The small numbers in the top right corner of each element represent the number of electrons in each energy shell. You can see from Figure 4.8 that carbon has two electrons in its first energy shell and four electrons in its second energy shell.

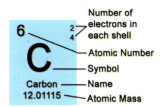

FIGURE 4.8. CARBON

FIGURE 4.9. POTASSIUM METAL
Potassium, like most **metals**, is highly reactive with air and water, so it is usually stored under oil. The black edges on these pieces of metal are evidence that the potassium has already begun reacting with the air.

 Worksheets: 4.1, 4.3–4.6

 Diagram: 4.2

 Microscope: 4.7

The eighteen vertical columns in the Periodic Table are called **groups** (Figure 4.13). Elements within a group have similar properties and contain the same number of electrons in their outermost energy shell. A horizontal sequence of elements is called a **period** (Figure 4.13). In a given period, the properties of the elements gradually pass from a strong metallic to a strong non-metallic nature, with the last number of a period being a noble gas.

Metals have only one or two electrons in their outer energy shells, which they can easily lose to bond with other elements. This makes the metals very reactive, so they cannot readily be found in a pure state. All metals are good conductors of electricity and heat and can be easily stretched and shaped (Figure 4.9). The **transition metals** are less reactive than the metals in Group 1 and Group 2, and many can be found naturally in a pure state (Figure 4.10).

Non-metals are poor conductors of heat and electricity, are brittle when in solid form, and cannot easily be stretched or shaped (Figure 4.11).

The **noble gases** are very stable because they have the maximum number of electrons in their outer energy shell, and hardly ever form compounds with other elements (Figure 4.12).

The **inner transition elements** include many synthetic and radioactive elements. Synthetic elements are those which do not occur in nature, but have been created by scientists in laboratories.

Hydrogen is a unique element and shares properties of metals and non-metals.

FIGURE 4.11. SULFUR
Sulfur is a **non-metal**, so it lacks the ability of metals to be stretched and shaped. Sulfur is used in fertilizers, insecticides, and gunpowder.

FIGURE 4.10. COPPER WIRING
Like all metals, copper is a good conductor of electricity. Since it is a **transition metal**, it is stable enough to be used commercially. Copper is the metal most commonly used in electrical wiring.

FIGURE 4.12. NEON SIGN
Many gases emit colored light when electricity passes through them, a property which can be used to make colorful lighted signs. Such signs are usually made with unreactive **noble gases** such as neon, because highly reactive gases would corrode glass tubing and electrical wiring.

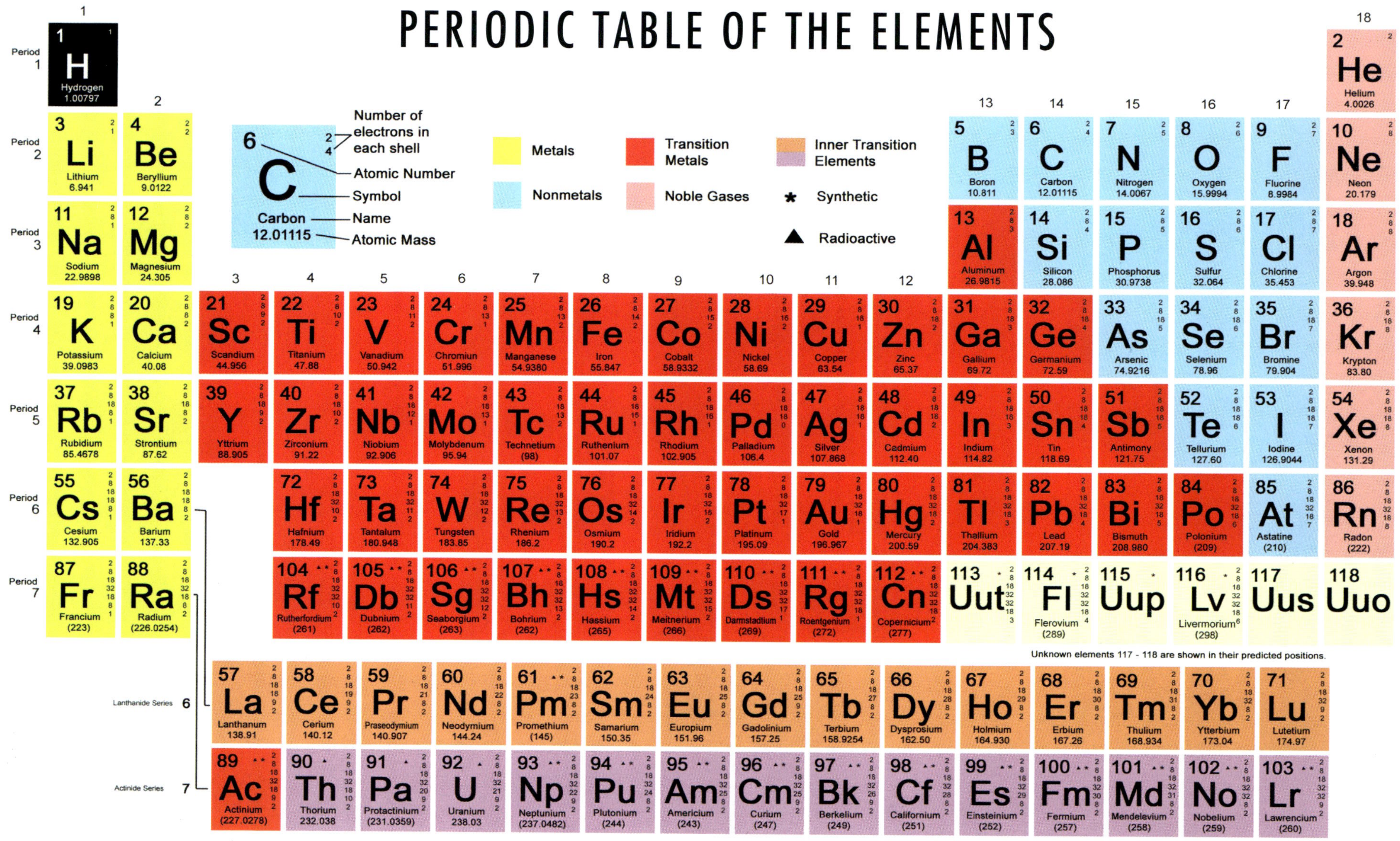

PERIODIC TABLE OF THE ELEMENTS

Legend / Key

Number of electrons in each shell
Atomic Number
Symbol
Name
Atomic Mass

6 → Atomic Number
C → Symbol
Carbon → Name
12.01115 → Atomic Mass
2, 4 → Number of electrons in each shell

Metals (yellow)
Nonmetals (blue)
Transition Metals (red)
Noble Gases (pink)
Inner Transition Elements (orange/purple)
* Synthetic
▲ Radioactive

Unknown elements 117 – 118 are shown in their predicted positions.

Lanthanide Series — 6
Actinide Series — 7

FIGURE 4.13. PERIODIC TABLE OF THE ELEMENTS

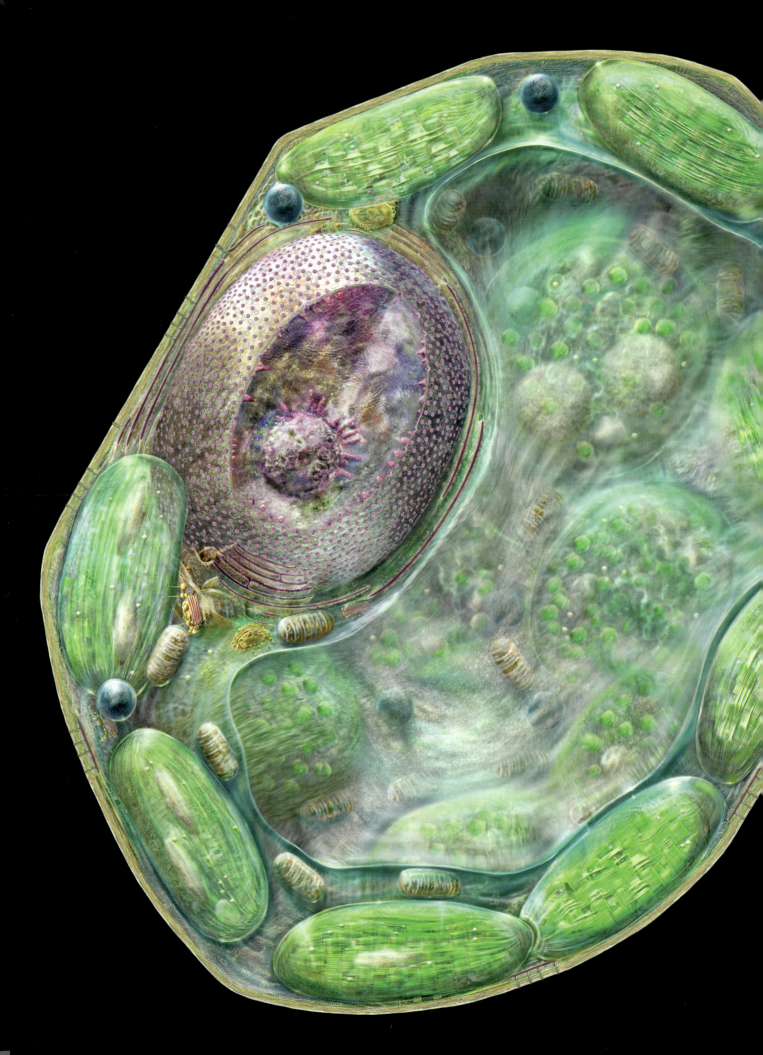

CELLS

Both religion and natural science require a belief in God for their activities. To the former He is the starting point, and to the latter the goal of every thought process. To the former He is the foundation, to the latter, the crown of the edifice of every generalized world view.

—Max Planck

FIGURE 5.1. ILLUSTRATION OF PLANT CELL
The cell wall (yellow) surrounds internal structures (organelles), including the nucleus (purple) and chloroplasts (green ovals). The nucleus contains the DNA that controls the cell's activity. Energy is generated by mitochondria (small brown cylinders). The large central vacuole (liquid and gas-filled space) is a storage area for food or wastes. The small blue spheres are peroxisomes and contain enzymes to break down harmful materials.

Cells

What would you plan to bring with you if you were going on a long submarine voyage (see Appendix I for the Latin roots the word "submarine")? What would you need if your vehicle were a spaceship? How about if you were just going into an underground cavern for a couple of days, what would you need to have?

To remain alive every creature, no matter how great or small, must have energy. With the energy that each organism takes in as food, almost all also take in oxygen gas. With that energy, living things grow and repair their bodies. With that energy organisms also get rid of waste products, including carbon dioxide gas.

What you would need on a submarine are the same things each part of your body must have: a source of energy (food), a way to use that energy, oxygen, raw materials to make new things from, and a way to get rid of carbon dioxide and other waste products. With a microscope and a drop of water from a pond or aquarium, you may observe tiny "submarines." Many of the **MICROORGANISMS** you may observe are made of just one **CELL**. Yet each cell, like a submarine or spacecraft, must obtain and use energy and remove wastes. Let's investigate the parts of a cell.

In 1665, Robert Hooke looked at a thin slice of cork and saw many empty boxes all packed closely together (see Figure 5.2). After peering at many other plant parts through his microscope, Hooke discovered that all were made of these small boxes, which he called cells. Cell means a very small room or compartment. Later biologists realized that each cell in a living plant is filled with living material, which they called **PROTOPLASM**. It was discovered that animals are also made of cells, but without the tiny, box-like **CELL WALL** found in plants. The cell wall helps support the plant's body.

FIGURE 5.2.
CELL WALLS OF CORK
For a science student, the word "cell" means the unit of structure in living things. This includes all the tiny parts neatly packaged into each living cell. In the photo below, taken by a scanning electron microscope, only the cell walls of the dead cork cells are visible. Magnification: 120x

Unlike animal cells, plant cells have tiny, green parts called chloroplasts. These parts are used in photosynthesis. Inside each **CHLOROPLAST** is an important green chemical called **CHLOROPHYLL** which is used by plants to capture sunlight.

Parts of Cells

Plants and animals are alike in that both are made up of cells. Your body is made of approximately 20 trillion individual cells each doing its own special job. Your cells are similar to all other cells in many ways. The thin **CELL MEMBRANE** encloses the cytoplasm and nucleus in every living cell. The **CYTOPLASM** is where cell activities take place. A dense structure that controls the cell, the **NUCLEUS**, is made of **NUCLEOPLASM** and a **NUCLEAR MEMBRANE**. With a good compound microscope you may be able to see some of the cell parts illustrated in Figures 5.6 and 5.8.

Osmosis

The cell membrane (or plasma membrane) is **SEMIPERMEABLE** and will only allow certain molecules to pass into the cell. This makes each of your cell membranes very special. Water, oxygen, glucose, and carbon dioxide are examples of compounds whose molecules can pass through the cell membrane. The cell membrane controls entry and exit from the cell.

Passive transport and active transport are two ways that molecules can move across the cell membrane. In passive transport, molecules move across the cell membrane without the use of energy by the cell. When there is a much greater concentration of a substance in one area, molecules in the substance naturally move away from each other and go toward the lower concentration. This movement from higher to lower concentration, without the use of energy, is called **DIFFUSION**. **OSMOSIS** is a special type of diffusion in which water passes through a cell membrane. The

FIGURE 5.3. DIFFUSION
Diffusion of the molecules from a tea bag illustrates how molecules move from higher concentration (inside the tea bag) to lower concentration (outside the tea bag).

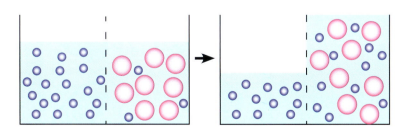

FIGURE 5.4. OSMOSIS
Osmosis causes water molecules (blue) to move through a semipermeable membrane (dotted line). The molecules move from the side with the greater concentration of water to the side with the least concentration of water. Osmosis can work even against gravity.

water molecules that pass through the cell membrane in osmosis move from a higher concentration of water to a lower concentration of water.

A cell can also move materials from lower to higher concentration, but this requires the cell to use energy. Movement across a cell membrane that requires the use of energy is called active transport.

More Parts of Cells

Plant and animal cells contain many different organelles, which are tiny structures in the cell, all with their own functions. The **MITOCHONDRION** is where the cell releases energy. Remember the "mighty mitochondria" as the powerhouses of the cell. The cytoplasm is in constant circular motion called **CYCLOSIS**. Cyclosis moves materials around the cell. **VACUOLES** may be empty (the word "vacuole" comes from "*vacuum*" which means "empty") or they may contain food or waste. The **ENDOPLASMIC**

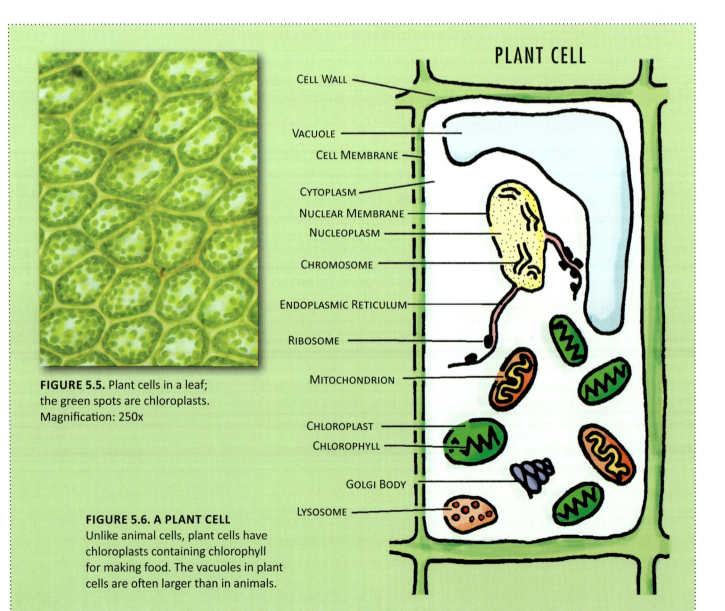

FIGURE 5.5. Plant cells in a leaf; the green spots are chloroplasts. Magnification: 250x

FIGURE 5.6. A PLANT CELL
Unlike animal cells, plant cells have chloroplasts containing chlorophyll for making food. The vacuoles in plant cells are often larger than in animals.

PLANT CELL

CELL WALL
VACUOLE
CELL MEMBRANE
CYTOPLASM
NUCLEAR MEMBRANE
NUCLEOPLASM
CHROMOSOME
ENDOPLASMIC RETICULUM
RIBOSOME
MITOCHONDRION
CHLOROPLAST
CHLOROPHYLL
GOLGI BODY
LYSOSOME

RETICULUM (en-doh-PLAZ-mik ray-TIK-yuh-luhm) is a tube-like organelle on which reactions take place.

The two, dot-like **CENTRIOLES** help animal cells make copies of themselves. Within the nuclear membrane, floating freely in the nucleoplasm, is a spherical shape called the nucleolus. Also inside the nucleus are **CHRO-MOSOMES**, long, thread-like chemicals that contain the instructions for operating the cell. The name chromosome comes from two Greek roots: "*chromas*," which means "color," and "*soma*," which means "body." The strands of chromosomes are named "colored bodies" because they absorb color very well when cells on a microscope slide are stained.

GOLGI BODIES, which look like stacks of pancakes, are storage centers for proteins. The **LYSOSOME** is a bubble-like digestion center. **RIBOSOMES** look like tiny dots on the endoplasmic reticulum. Ribosomes are important in making proteins.

 Worksheets: 5.1–5.5

 Experiment: 5.6

 Microscope: 5.7

 Formal Lab: 5.8

FIGURE 5.7. Smooth muscle cells; the red spots are nuclei. Magnification: 350x

FIGURE 5.8. AN ANIMAL CELL
All of the parts shown in this animal cell are also in a plant cell except for the centrioles. The vacuoles in an animal cell are usually smaller than in plants.

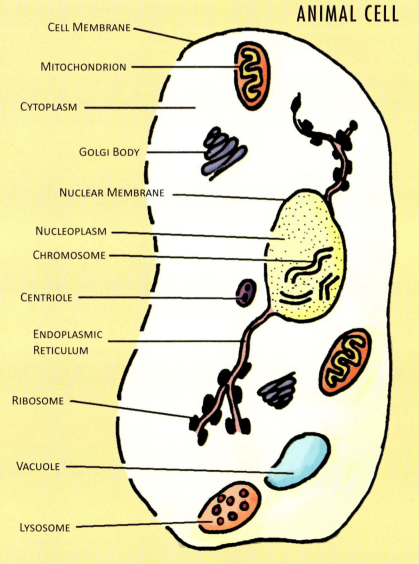

ANIMAL CELL

CELL MEMBRANE
MITOCHONDRION
CYTOPLASM
GOLGI BODY
NUCLEAR MEMBRANE
NUCLEOPLASM
CHROMOSOME
CENTRIOLE
ENDOPLASMIC RETICULUM
RIBOSOME
VACUOLE
LYSOSOME

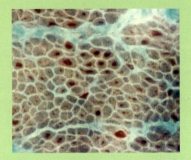

FIGURE 5.9. SMOOTH MUSCLE CELLS

FIGURE 5.10. PLANT CELLS

FIGURE 5.11. CELLS IN THE PEEL OF A RED CHERRY

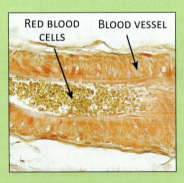

FIGURE 5.12. RED BLOOD CELLS IN A BLOOD VESSEL
Cells come in different shapes and sizes depending on the job they are designed to do. Red blood cells are among the smallest cells in the human body.

The Cell Theory

So many parts in just one tiny cell! Some living things are made of just one cell. Average Adam is made of trillions of cells, and a giant redwood tree is made of many, many more cells than that! The point is that **all creatures, great and small, are made of cells.** This idea is the cell theory. The cell theory has three main statements.

1. The cell is the unit of structure and function in organisms. This means that the activities we call "living" happen in each cell.

2. All living organisms are made up of one or more cells. This may be verified through use of the microscope.

3. Cells are made by other living cells. This statement seems obvious after studying life science in the laboratory, but it causes a problem. Where did the first cell come from? The cell theory cannot explain the very beginnings of life.

Your trillions of cells are now very organized and each has a special shape to help with its function in your body. However, your body began as just one cell!

The organization of your cells and how your one, original cell came to be are discussed in the chapter on systems (Chapter 16) and also in the chapter on animal reproduction (Chapter 25). For now, be able to recognize the parts of the cell and understand the function of those parts.

FIGURE 5.13. CELLS IN A PLANT BUD

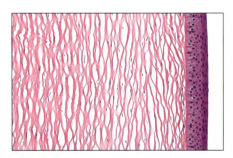

FIGURE 5.14. CELLS IN THE CORNEA OF THE EYE

Have you viewed plant or animal cells under a microscope before? You may have noticed that your samples looked less colorful than many of the micrographs (photos taken through a microscope) in the text. Microscope samples are often stained with special dyes so that their structure will be easier to see. For instance, the cornea cells in Figure 5.14 are purple because they were stained with hematoxylin and eosin. Similarly, micrographs taken by special types of microscopes, such as Figure 5.17, are originally black and white until they are colorized on the computer.

FIGURE 5.15. Each type of cell in this rice plant has its own special function.

Mitochondria and God's Design

Did you know that the world's largest mammal, the blue whale, can grow to 100 feet in length? (Stretch this whale across a basketball court, and he would be out of bounds on both ends!) On the other hand, a mature bumblebee bat is often less than an inch long.

What do these two creatures, one a krill-slurping ocean dweller and the other a cave-roosting plant eater, have in common? Both are warm-blooded mammals, give birth to and nurse their young, and were designed by the same Almighty God.

Yet, there are components of creation even smaller than the bumblebee bat. Organelles—tiny, specialized "organs," each with its own function—are found inside living cells. One of these organelles is the mitochondrion, a cell's "power-house." We can compare the energy-providing mitochondrion to a battery; tiny flashlights might utilize a single, tiny AAA battery, while a lantern might require a whole fistful of D batteries.

In somewhat the same way, our Intelligent Designer equipped body cells that require lots of "fuel" (like muscles) with an abundance of mito-chondria, while other cells with "low-energy" needs have only a few. "Low-energy-consuming" cells may contain only one mitochondrion, while "high-energy-consuming" cells may contain thousands!

How is it that each cell comes equipped with the right number of mitochondria to perform its designated function? (Think of how well that large lantern might function with only a single AAA battery rattling around inside.) Does the placement of mitochondria sound like a random accident, or the work of an Intelligent Designer?

My vote is with the Intelligent Designer!

FIGURE 5.16. The bumble-bee bat lives in caves in a small area of western Thailand and adjacent Myanmar.

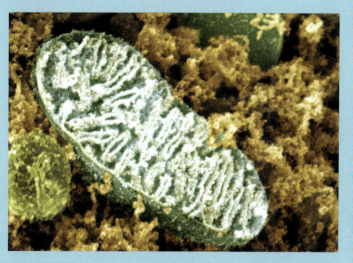

FIGURE 5.17. COLORED SCANNING ELECTRON MICROGRAPH OF A MITOCHONDRION
Mitochondria oxidize sugars and fats to produce energy in a process called cellular respiration. A mitochondrion has two membranes: a smooth outer membrane and a folded inner membrane where the chemical reactions to produce energy take place. Magnification: approximately 15,000×

FIGURE 5.18.
ILLUSTRATION OF BLUE WHALE (BALAENOPTERA MUSCULUS)
Blue whales are found through-out the world's oceans, feeding on small crustaceans called krill, which they filter out of the sea. It requires 3–4 tons of krill a day to support a blue whale.

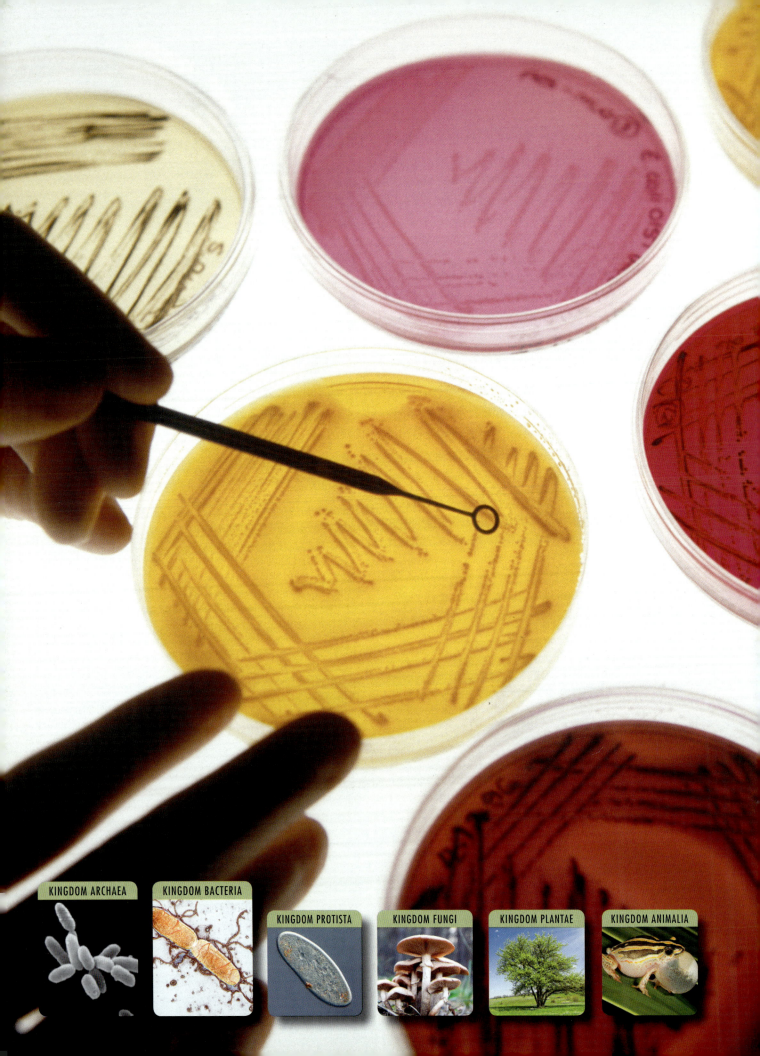

KINGDOM ARCHAEA

KINGDOM BACTERIA

KINGDOM PROTISTA

KINGDOM FUNGI

KINGDOM PLANTAE

KINGDOM ANIMALIA

Simplest Cells

And when with excellent microscopes I discern
in otherwise invisible objects the inimitable
subtlety of nature's curious workmanship . . .
I find myself oftentimes reduc'd to exclaim
with the Psalmist, How manifold are Thy works,
O Lord? In wisdom hast Thou made them all.

—Robert Boyle

FIGURE 6.1. PETRI DISHES CONTAINING DIFFERENT-COLORED NUTRIENT AGAR GELS AND DIFFERENT BACTERIAL STRAINS
Bacterial samples are smeared across the gels and microorganisms in the samples feed on the nutrients in the agar gels and multiply to form colonies. Microorganisms from these colonies can then be removed and analyzed. The technician in the photo is using a sterile loop to pick a single colony from one of the petri dishes.

SIMPLEST CELLS

The Necessities of Life

What are the necessary parts of an automobile? Its radio? No, we could get rid of the radio. We could eliminate many of the parts of a car and it would still work. Take out the air conditioner, the windows, the spare tire, even the seats, and the car can still operate. What are the necessities required for the car to still work?

A car must have gas in the tank, a source of energy. It must have an engine, a way to use the energy. It must have a transmission and wheels, a way to turn the energy into something useful. The car must have an exhaust to eliminate waste products. But all these parts won't work without a key, to turn on the car and make it start.

The car without a key does not work. But of course, a key by itself is not going to work either.

Compare the parts of a car to the organelles and parts of a cell. The gas in the tank would be the food molecules in a food vacuole. The engine would be the mighty mitochondrion where the cell combines oxygen with glucose to make **ATP** molecules. The transmission and wheels would be the endoplasmic reticulum and the ribosomes where the energy in the ATP molecules is put to use making proteins. The exhaust system would be vacuoles and the cell membrane, which eliminate carbon dioxide and other wastes. The key is somewhat like the **DNA** which forms the chromosomes in the nucleus. This deoxyribonucleic acid (DNA) turns on the cell and even tells the cell what to do.

Is the car alive then, just like a cell? No! The cell can do more than a car. A cell can grow. A cell can repair itself, which is part of the life function we call synthesis. A cell can reproduce more cells like itself, another of the life functions. A fourth life function cells can do, and cars can't, is irritability. Cells react to changes in the environment.

Viruses

Viruses are the smallest "living" things. But why the quotation marks? "Living" is in quotes because viruses are really on the border between living and non-living. We will classify viruses as a special group of almost living organisms. A **VIRUS** is like the key in our comparison of a cell to a car. A virus by itself cannot do anything. A virus in the right kind of cell can turn on the cell and make the cell produce more viruses. The virus is not able to transport materials, to move, to take in food, to use the food to release energy, or to excrete waste in order to grow. Of the eight life functions you learned about in Chapter 1, the only one that a virus can perform is reproduction. But a virus can't even do that without the aid of a host cell.

A virus is a piece of DNA (or RNA, ribonucleic acid) in a protein wrapper. The DNA is a set of instructions which can control a cell's metabolism. Viruses that take over bacterial cells are called **BACTERIOPHAGES** (literally, "bacteria eaters"). See Figure 6.2. We will study the effects of viruses on the human body when we study diseases.

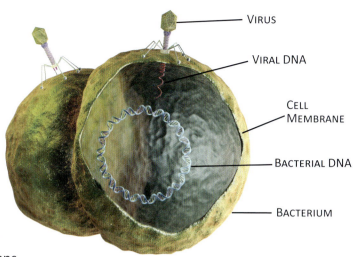

FIGURE 6.2. CUT-AWAY VIEW OF A VIRUS INVADING A BACTERIAL CELL
The virus attacks the cell by injecting its own DNA into the cell. The viral DNA takes over the cell's metabolism and forces the host cell to make more viruses.

Kingdoms Archaea and Bacteria

The simplest living things have no nuclear membrane and no organelles. All organisms with no nuclear membrane and no organelles are grouped into either Kingdom **ARCHAEA** or Kingdom **BACTERIA**. Unlike viruses, archaeans and bacteria carry out seven or eight of the life functions and may be called the simplest living things.

Organisms with no nuclear membrane and no organelles are called **PROKARYOTES** (Figure 6.3). Organisms that do have a nuclear membrane and organelles are called **EUKARYOTES**. Archaeans and bacteria are prokaryotes. Average Adam, the tiny amoeba, and the 275-foot-high giant sequoia are all eukaryotes. Every organism on earth is either a prokaryote or a eukaryote.

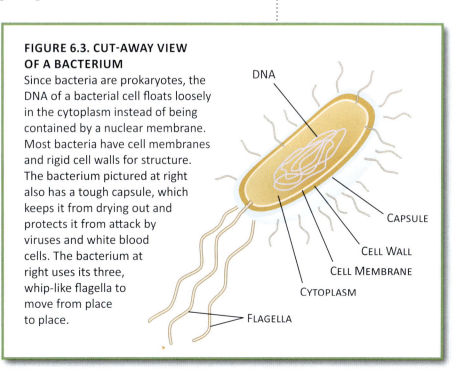

FIGURE 6.3. CUT-AWAY VIEW OF A BACTERIUM
Since bacteria are prokaryotes, the DNA of a bacterial cell floats loosely in the cytoplasm instead of being contained by a nuclear membrane. Most bacteria have cell membranes and rigid cell walls for structure. The bacterium pictured at right also has a tough capsule, which keeps it from drying out and protects it from attack by viruses and white blood cells. The bacterium at right uses its three, whip-like flagella to move from place to place.

FIGURE 6.4. <u>Halobacteria sp.</u> is an archaean that lives in highly saline lakes such as the Dead Sea.

Most of the organisms in Kingdom Archaea live in extreme conditions. For instance, some archaeans live in extremely saline water, such as the Dead Sea and the Great Salt Lake. Other archaeans thrive near deep-sea hydrothermal vents, where the temperature is well above the boiling point (100 °C or 212 °F). Thankfully, none of the archaeans cause diseases.

The Kingdom Bacteria contains a large variety of prokaryotes. Some types of bacteria have a **FLAGELLUM**, or even many flagella, for movement. At one time, bacteria were considered part of the plant kingdom because most have a cell wall. Many bacteria get their food from dead organisms (this is called **SAPROPHYTISM**), or by infecting living organisms (**PARASITISM**). Parasitic bacteria are the bacteria which cause diseases. Some bacteria get their energy by "eating" minerals. A few bacteria can produce their own food by using sunlight and a purple chemical similar to chlorophyll. **BLUE-GREEN ALGAE** are a type of bacteria that gets its energy through photosynthesis. The chlorophyll in blue-green algae is not in chloroplasts, but is simply floating in the cytoplasm. Blue-green algae and other bacteria are unicellular, but the single cells sometimes stick together in clumps or filaments (see Figures 6.5 and 6.11).

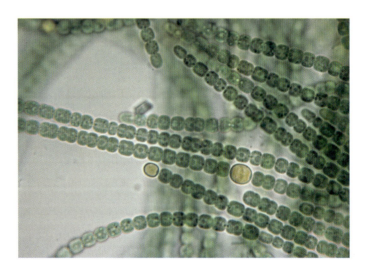

FIGURE 6.5. BLUE-GREEN ALGAE
Cyanobacteria (blue-green algae) grow in colonies to form long, algae-like filaments. Magnification: 175x

The most outstanding characteristic of a bacterium is its ability to reproduce. After growing to a maximum size, the single parent cell divides into two daughter cells. The process of splitting into two, called **BINARY FISSION**, may occur every thirty minutes under ideal conditions (Figure 6.7). That would result in over 1,000,000 bacteria in just ten hours from a single parent cell! This mass of bacteria, called a **COLONY**, can be seen without a microscope. Each type of bacteria forms a colony with a characteristic color and shape, which helps in identification (Figures 6.8–9).

AUTOTROPHS Make their own food energy		HETEROTROPHS Obtain food energy from other organisms		
CHEMOSYNTHETIC	PHOTOSYNTHETIC	SAPROPHYTIC	PARASITIC	MUTUALISTIC
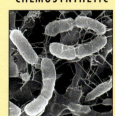		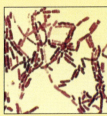		
Venenivibrio stagnispumantis produces food energy by breaking down chemicals in chemosynthesis.	Cyanobacteria (blue-green algae) use sunlight to produce food energy through photosynthesis.	Bacillus megaterium obtains food energy by decomposing dead organic material.	Borrelia burgdorferi is a parasite that gets its food from its host. It causes Lyme disease.	Escherichia coli lives naturally in the human gut, where it helps the body absorb vitamin K in return for nutrients.

The organisms in the Kingdom Bacteria can be divided into heterotrophs and autotrophs. Organisms which make their own food energy are called **AUTOTROPHS**. Blue-green algae, which produces food energy through photosynthesis, is a good example of an autotroph. **HETEROTROPHS** are organisms which cannot make their own food energy, and must obtain it from other organisms. Saprotrophic and parasitic bacteria are types of heterotrophs.

FIGURE 6.6. CHART OF AUTOTROPHIC AND HETEROTROPHIC BACTERIA

Bacterial colonies cannot grow forever because the necessities for life are used up as more bacteria are produced. Remember the necessities of life: a source of energy, a way to use the energy to make new chemicals, and a way to get rid of waste products. As a bacterial colony grows larger and larger, the source of energy is used up or the waste products build up to a point at which the bacteria can no longer grow and undergo binary fission.

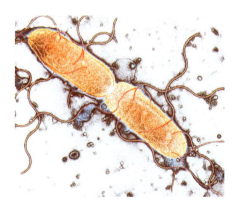

FIGURE 6.7. A single E. coli bacterium reproducing by binary fission. Magnification: approximately 48,000x

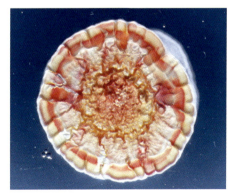

FIGURE 6.8. Close up of a colony of the soil bacterium Streptomyces lividans

FIGURE 6.9. Close up of colonies of typhoid bacteria (Salmonella typhi)

Bacteria of any of the three basic shapes (see Figure 6.10) must have the right conditions for them to perform their life functions. Five conditions that affect bacterial growth are:

1. **Food** as a source of energy.

2. **Temperature**, which allows the bacterial cell to carry out chemical reactions using the energy from the food. Very high temperatures kill bacteria (but some BACTERIAL SPORES may survive even boiling water). The cold temperatures of a refrigerator slow down bacterial growth but don't kill the microbes.

3. **Moisture** is needed for bacteria to grow. Drying out their food source slows the growth of bacteria. Too much salt or sugar in the bacteria's environment dries out the bacteria by osmosis.

4. **Light energy** can kill some bacteria. Most bacteria grow better in darkness.

5. **Oxygen** is necessary for the oxidation of food. (Oxidation is the process which releases the energy in food.) AEROBIC bacteria get their oxygen from the air. However, the tetanus bacterium (see the chapter on disease) and some others are actually killed by oxygen gas in the air. These ANAEROBIC bacteria get their oxygen from chemicals with oxygen atoms in them. Anaerobic bacteria must survive as spores until they end up where there is no free oxygen gas, such as in a deep wound.

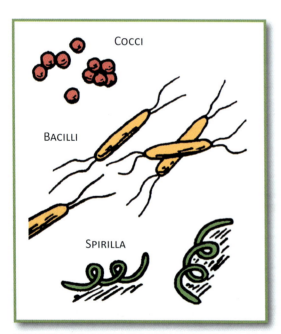

FIGURE 6.10. COCCI, BACILLI, SPIRILLA
Round, rod, and spiral types of bacterial cells may be seen under high magnification. See Figure 6.6.

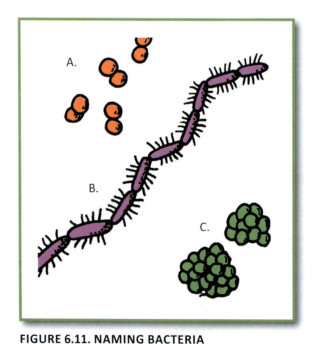

FIGURE 6.11. NAMING BACTERIA
Prefixes are used to describe clusters of cells.
A. A diplococcus is a cluster of two cocci.
B. A streptobacillus is a chain of bacilli.
C. A staphylococcus is a roundish clump of cocci.

50

Now you should understand better why most foods must be kept refrigerated after opening. Foods are kept from being decayed by bacteria through a manipulation of the bacteria's environment. Before the invention of refrigerators, many foods had to be "salted," and some were "sugared" to preserve them. Many foods, such as breakfast cereals, are dried. Canned foods are cooked first at high temperatures, then sealed up so that no oxygen is present. Canned foods may be good for many years. Frozen foods are kept at low temperatures but will eventually spoil. Heating milk at the dairy processing plant is a way to kill many of the bacteria in milk. This process, called **PASTEURIZATION**, is named after Louis Pasteur, a French

FIGURE 6.12. LOUIS PASTEUR

Louis Pasteur

When Louis Pasteur was born in 1822, scientists had seen bacteria under the microscope, but they did not know that these tiny creatures could cause terrible diseases such as anthrax, typhoid, and cholera. Since no one knew the cause of these diseases, doctors would often make their patients worse—unintentionally of course—by going from patient to patient without washing their hands.

Would you be surprised to learn that it was not a famous doctor, but a simple chemist who first discovered the role of germs in causing disease?

Louis Pasteur, a young French chemist, discovered that harmful bacteria could cause diseases when he was studying an insect disease that was killing off the silk worms in France. Even though he had not been trained as a biologist or doctor, Pasteur quickly realized how important his discovery was. In his own family, three of his five children had died from typhoid fever, a bacterial disease that today is easily prevented by immunizations.

Pasteur spent the rest of his life identifying disease-causing bacteria and devising vaccines to prevent those diseases. For instance, he discovered that the anthrax bacteria could be weakened by heat; once a person is inoculated with the weakened anthrax, they become immune to the full-strength anthrax. Pasteur received many honors during his lifetime, but his greatest reward was the knowledge of how many lives he had saved. One of his heroes was St. Vincent de Paul, the French priest who did so much to help the poor. Pasteur died at the age of 73, holding a crucifix in one hand and his wife's hand in the other.

FIGURE 6.13. NITROGEN-FIXING BACTERIA
Nodules of <u>Rhizobium leguminosarum</u>, the nitrogen-fixing bacteria, on the roots of the French bean, <u>Phaseolus vulgaris</u>. Photo shows actual size of nodules.

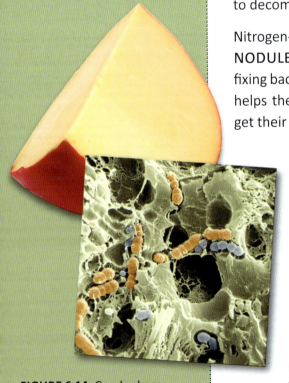

FIGURE 6.14. Gouda cheese consists of casein (milk protein) interspersed with fat globules and lactic acid bacteria. The bacteria shown in orange and blue are streptococci or lactococci.

chemist. Pasteur learned many of the things about bacteria that we use today to preserve food, and even save lives, from the attacks of bacteria.

Beneficial Bacteria

You may think that bacteria are the same as germs. This would be incorrect. True, some bacteria are germs which cause human, animal, or plant diseases, but life on earth would not continue without bacteria!

You recall the necessities of life: energy, ways to use it to rearrange chemicals, and a way to excrete wastes. Many millions of trillions of organisms have lived on earth. Their bodies contained the same oxygen, carbon, hydrogen, and nitrogen atoms needed in your body. If the dinosaurs and the forests of long ago never decomposed then the chemicals needed for life today would all be used up. In Chapter 26 you will learn that the earth's materials are used in cycles. The elements needed for life go in circles from existing in a biotic state (in living creatures) to existing in an abiotic state (in non-living materials) and back again.

Life is only possible because bacteria decompose dead organisms and their products. The **HUMUS** in topsoil is the result of this decay. Humus contains minerals and nitrates needed by plants. This is also the basic idea of a sewage treatment plant (Figure 6.15), where bacteria are cultured to decompose the raw sewage.

Nitrogen-fixing bacteria are a special group of bacteria that live in the **NODULES** of legumes such as clover and peas (Figure 6.13). Nitrogen-fixing bacteria take nitrogen gas from the air and "fix" it into nitrates. This helps the plants, which require nitrates to live. In return, the bacteria get their food, glucose, from the plants. Such a close relationship of two organisms, in which both live very close together and both benefit, is called **MUTUALISM**.

Bacteria are needed to provide many useful products including pickles, vinegar, sauerkraut, cheeses, tanned leather, and linen (Figure 6.14). They are used to change chopped corn into silage and to produce many kinds of chemicals out of molasses and sawdust. One of the newest uses of bacteria is in genetic engineering. In this process a piece of DNA from another organism is put into a bacterial cell. This causes the bacterial cell to produce a chemical that is usually made by the other organism. In the case of diabetes, the object of genetic engineering is to produce bacteria that make human insulin, which can be injected into the diabetic whose body can't make its own insulin.

FIGURE 6.15. Aeration tanks at a sewage treatment plant hold the sewage and bacteria while adding oxygen so that the decomposers can do their job. The bacteria break down organic compounds into simpler substances which may be added to the soil as fertilizer.

Figure 6.16 will help you organize some of the facts that you must remember from this chapter on prokaryotes, the simplest cells. In the next four chapters you will learn about the eukaryotes, which are grouped into Kingdom Protista, Kingdom Fungi, Kingdom Plantae, and Kingdom Animalia.

 Worksheets: 6.1–6.7

 Formal Lab: 6.8

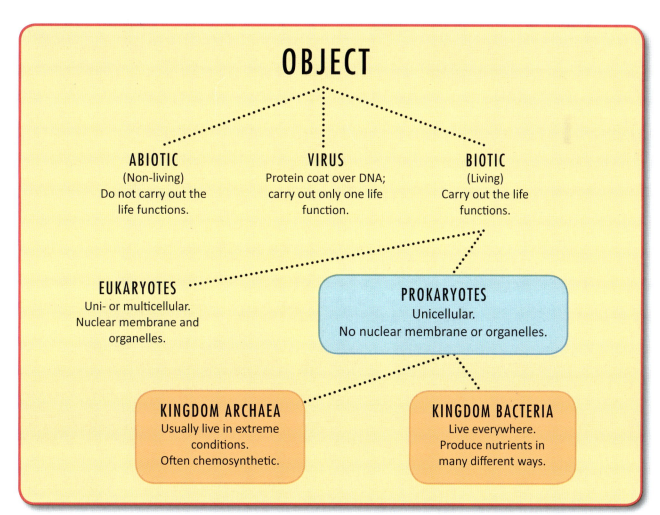

FIGURE 6.16. CLASSIFICATION OF PROKARYOTES: KINGDOM ARCHAEA AND KINGDOM BACTERIA

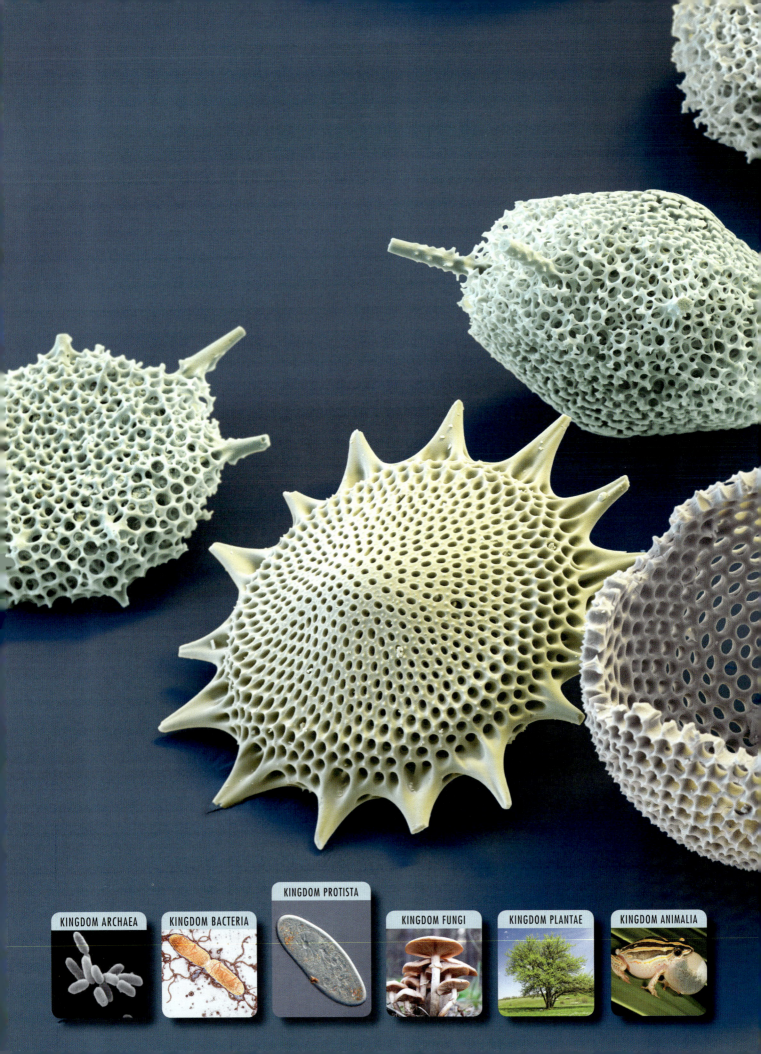

KINGDOM ARCHAEA

KINGDOM BACTERIA

KINGDOM PROTISTA

KINGDOM FUNGI

KINGDOM PLANTAE

KINGDOM ANIMALIA

PROTISTS: A MICROSCOPIC MENAGERIE

Is ditchwater dull? Naturalists with microscopes have told me that it teems with quiet fun.

—G.K. Chesterton

FIGURE 7.1. THE SHELLS OF VARIOUS RADIOLARIA
Radiolaria are single-celled amoeboids that are found in marine plankton. This color-enhanced scanning electron micrograph shows their silicate skeletons. A living radiolarian has pseudopodia (false feet, not shown) of protoplasm which project through the pores in its skeleton. As the radiolarian floats in ocean currents, its pseudopodia trap food particles on which it feeds. Magnification: 440x

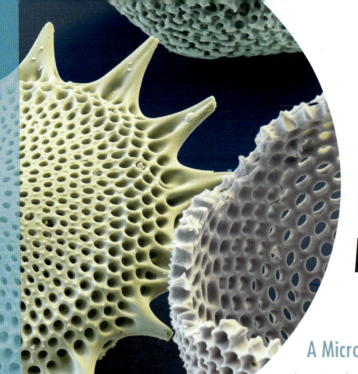

PROTISTS: A MICROSCOPIC MENAGERIE

A Microscopic Menagerie

The Kingdom Archaea and the Kingdom Bacteria contain pro-karyotes, organisms without a well-defined nucleus and without organelles. Prokaryotes are the simplest living things. Now we will investigate the Kingdom Protista, a group of microbes that are the first eukaryotes in the current system of classification. As you know, eukaryotes are unlike prokaryotes in that they have organelles and nuclear membranes.

You may see from Appendix I that the root of "Protista" is the Greek word "*proto*," which means "first." Thus, the first eukaryotes in our system of naming are called protists.

Taxonomy

Before we explore the microscopic world of Kingdom Protista, we must understand the worldwide system that is used to group, or classify, living things. Aristotle, a Greek philosopher who lived 350 years before Christ, gathered organisms from many parts of the world. He and his students tried to arrange the plants and animals into some kind of reasonable order. Aristotle is considered the founder of **TAXONOMY**. (The Greek word for "order" is "*taxis*.") Theophrastus, one of Aristotle's interested students, based his writings about plants on detailed study and careful classifications.

Almost 2000 years later, John Ray, an English botanist, classified nearly all of the plants around Cambridge, England. Because of Ray's work, the word "species" came to mean one kind of organism.

Building on John Ray's classification methods, Carolus Linnaeus developed the basis for the modern system of taxonomy. Just around the time when Linnaeus was studying living things, people began using a surname as well as a first name. Linnaeus decided

FIGURE 7.2. CAROLUS LINNAEUS

TAXONS	RED OAK (Quercus rubra)	HOUSE FLY (Musca domestica)	HUMAN (Homo sapiens)
Kingdom	Plantae	Animalia	Animalia
Phylum	Tracheophyta	Arthropoda	Chordata
Class	Angiospermae	Insecta	Mammalia
Order	Fagales	Diptera	Primates
Family	Fagaceae	Muscidae	Hominidae
Genus	Quercus	Musca	Homo
species	rubra	domestica	sapiens

FIGURE 7.3. SAMPLE CLASSIFICATIONS
Kingdoms are the largest taxons, or divisions, and contain varied organisms that only have a few characteristics in common. Species is the smallest taxon, containing only one kind of organism.

to do the same thing for plants and animals, and to use two names for each different kind of organism. This two-name system of naming is called **BINOMIAL NOMENCLATURE**. In 1735 Linnaeus published a book, *Systemae Naturae*, in which he named thousands of plants and animals. We still use most of those names today. The most important thing Linnaeus did was to use a seven-**TAXON** system with Latin names, the last two of which are called the scientific name.

The naming of organisms is important for many reasons, especially when we are trying to control diseases and pests or to preserve wildlife in our environment. Just think, with over 300,000 kinds of beetles, which are just one of the thousands of kinds of insects, there certainly could be confusion! Remember that any system of classification must separate well over a million known organisms.

All these creatures, from the great dinosaurs to the tiny bacteria, are put into just six, giant groups called **KINGDOMS**. A kingdom may be divided into smaller taxons called **PHYLA** (plural for "phylum"). In this chapter on protists and in the next chapter on fungi, we will not use the other five taxons. For our work on plants and animals, however, we will need to know that each phylum is divided into **CLASSES**, each class into **ORDERS**, each order into **FAMILIES**, each family into **GENERA**, and each genus into **SPECIES**. ("Genera" is the plural of "genus.")

For instance, the red oak is classified in Kingdom Plantae, Phylum Tracheophyta, Class Angiospermae, Order Fagales, Family Fagaceae, Genus Quercus, and species rubra (Figure 7.3). Thus, the red oak's scientific name is Quercus rubra.

FIGURE 7.4.
LUCILIA SERICATA
Common green bottle fly

FIGURE 7.5.
PTEROPUS VAMPYRUS
Malaysian flying fox

FIGURE 7.6.
CYANOCITTA CRISTATA
Blue jay

The genus and species of an organism, which together make up its scientific name, are always underlined. The first letter of the genus name is capitalized. The species name is always in lowercase. Sometimes you may see "Quercus sp." which indicates that there are several species referred to but all of them are oaks.

Perhaps a comparison will help you understand how the taxons work. Let our country be one of the kingdoms, then the states could be phyla, this county the class, this town an order, your street the family. Your home could be the genus and your room would be the species taxon. You can use the mnemonic in Figure 7.7 to memorize the taxon names in order.

How would you separate all living things from each other? Some creatures live on land, many can fly, a great number of organisms are herbivores (plant eaters). Shall we put everything found in the sky into the same group? That will put a housefly, a bat, and a blue jay all in the same small taxon! The wings of each organism are actually very different from the others. A fly's wings are a thin membrane; the bat's, a fold of furry skin; and a blue jay's is covered with feathers. These three organisms are very different (see Figures 7.4–6). We cannot correctly group organisms by where they are found, nor by what they can do, nor even by what they eat!

Think back to how we divided the prokaryotes from all the other living things. They have no nuclear membrane and no real organelles. Scientists use the structure of organisms for classification. Using structure as the basis of taxonomy indicates that killer whales are more like us than they are like fish! We will see in the chapter on Kingdom Animalia why this is true.

KINGDOM PROTISTA

To belong to the varied Kingdom **PROTISTA** an organism must have a nuclear membrane and organelles. But wait, you have those! Are you a protist? No. There is one more characteristic of protists: most of them are **UNICELLULAR** or very, very simple **MULTICELLULAR** organisms (Figure 7.8). Each cell of a protist does everything for itself, unlike in more complex organisms such as you or a fly or an oak, which have special cells for special jobs.

KINGDOM	PHYLUM	CLASS	ORDER	FAMILY	GENUS	SPECIES
6 of King	Phillip's	Classes	Ordered	Frozen	Grape	Sodas

FIGURE 7.7. TAXON NAMES
Use this mnemonic to remember the names of the taxons in order.

One simple way to classify the creatures in Kingdom Protista is to group them into plant-like, animal-like, and fungus-like protists (Figure 7.8). Based on differences in their structures, protists are divided by scientists into many different phyla (Figure 7.9). You will not be required to memorize all the long names in Figure 7.9, but you should be able to describe what all the phyla of the Kingdom Protista have in common: organelles, a nuclear membrane, and a unicellular body.

AMOEBA

A simple microorganism that has inspired many science fiction creatures is the amoeba. Actually there are many species in the Genus Amoeba. The name "amoeba" means "no shape" or "changing shape." This protist uses a **PSEUDO-POD** for locomotion (Figure 7.11). An amoeba ingests its food by engulfing it (Figure 7.10). Its contractile vacuole is a

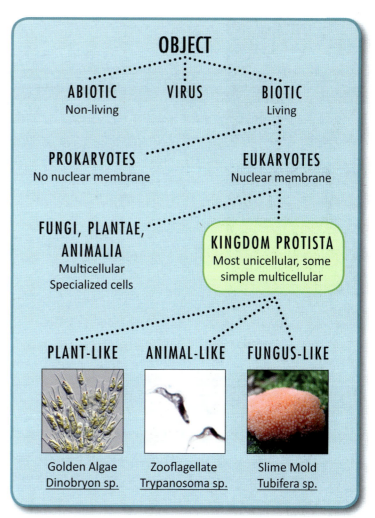

FIGURE 7.8. CLASSIFICATION OF KINGDOM PROTISTA
One way to organize protists is into plant-like, animal-like, and fungus-like protists.

	PHYLUM	COMMON NAME	DESCRIPTION	EXAMPLE
PLANT-LIKE	Euglenophyta	Euglenoids	Plant- and animal-like	Euglena sp. (Fig. 7.13)
	Chrysophyta	Golden algae	Have chloroplasts	Dinobryon sp. (Fig. 7.8)
	Dinoflagellata	Dinoflagellates	Two flagella	Ceratium sp.
ANIMAL-LIKE	Sarcodina	Amoeboids	Have pseudopods	Amoeba sp. (Fig. 7.10)
	Ciliophora	Ciliates	Move by cilia	Paramecium sp. (Fig. 7.12)
	Zooflagellates	Zooflagellates	Most are parasites	Trypanosoma sp. (Fig. 7.8)
	Sporozoa	Sporozoans	All are parasites	Plasmodium sp.
FUNGUS-LIKE	Myxomycota	Slime molds	Decay organisms	Tubifera sp. (Fig. 7.8)

FIGURE 7.9. MAIN PHYLA OF KINGDOM PROTISTA
There is a wide variety of organisms in Kingdom Protista, but all are unicellular or simple multicellular organisms with a nuclear membrane and organelles.

FIGURE 7.10.
THE ENGULFING PROCESS
Like the "blob" of science fiction fame, the amoeba flows over and around an unlucky cluster of algae! Magnification: 100x

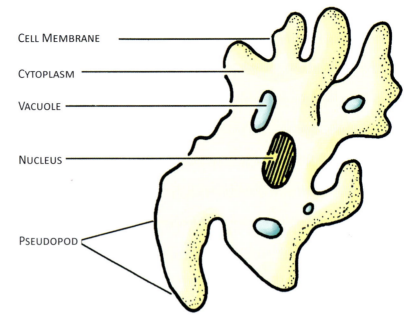

CELL MEMBRANE

CYTOPLASM

VACUOLE

NUCLEUS

PSEUDOPOD

FIGURE 7.11. AN AMOEBA
The amoeba moves by flowing its cytoplasm into one of its "false feet."

bubble-like organelle that squeezes excess water out of the amoeba. The amoeba reproduces through binary fission, splitting into two after making copies of the DNA in its nucleus.

PARAMECIUM

The paramecium is one of the most complex protists. If you take some sediment from the bottom of a pond with some pond water you may see both the amoeba and the paramecium. Add some grass to the culture as well. The paramecia will be on the bottom debris feeding on bacteria. The amoebas concentrate on the decaying grass. Figure 7.12 shows the slipper-like shape of the paramecium. Its unicellular body is covered with tiny, short, "hair-like" structures called **CILIA**, which it uses for locomotion. Unlike the ever-changing, shapeless amoeba, the paramecium has a rather stiff layer supporting the cell membrane called a **PELLICLE** with an oral groove in it. This complex little creature has two nuclei in each cell: one is a **MACRONUCLEUS** and the other a **MICRONUCLEUS**. The paramecium contains star-like **CONTRACTILE VACUOLES** used to excrete life's waste products. The paramecium often undergoes binary fission, splitting into two, or it may reproduce by **CONJUGATION**. The micronucleus is needed during conjugation, which is a type of sexual reproduction.

FIGURE 7.12. PARAMECIUM
The paramecium's contractile vacuole and cilia are visible in this micrograph.

60

EUGLENA

The euglena is a protist that has both plant and animal characteristics. It contains both chloroplasts for making food and a gullet for ingesting food. The euglena also has an **EYESPOT**. It has a soft pellicle with spiral-shaped thicker parts (Figure 7.13). The most noticeable part of the euglena is its one long flagellum which it uses to move from place to place in response to stimuli (Figure 7.15). The euglena reproduces by binary fission.

FIGURE 7.13. EUGLENA SPIROGYRA
The euglena's thin, clear flagellum is not visible in this micrograph. The spiralling stripes on the left end of the euglena are its pellicle. The red spot is its eyespot, which is able to perceive the intensity of light. Magnification: 225x

 Worksheets: 7.1–7.3, 7.5

 Diagram: 7.4

 Microscope: 7.6

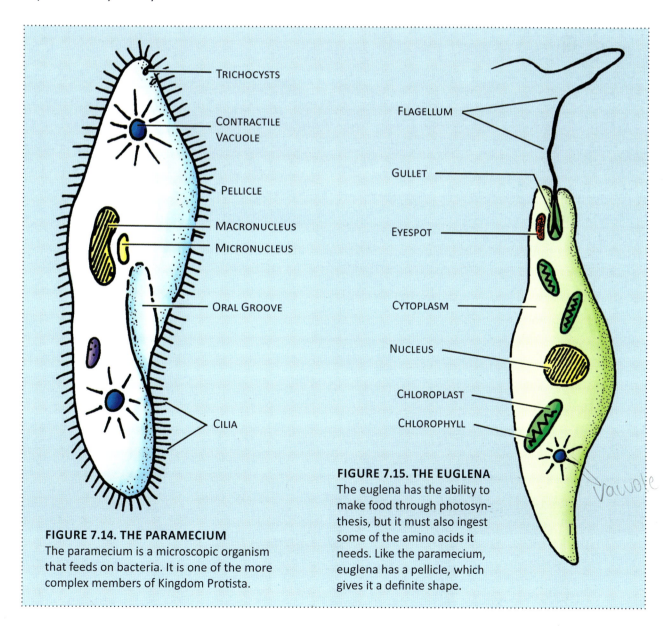

FIGURE 7.14. THE PARAMECIUM
The paramecium is a microscopic organism that feeds on bacteria. It is one of the more complex members of Kingdom Protista.

FIGURE 7.15. THE EUGLENA
The euglena has the ability to make food through photosynthesis, but it must also ingest some of the amino acids it needs. Like the paramecium, euglena has a pellicle, which gives it a definite shape.

KINGDOM ARCHAEA

KINGDOM BACTERIA

KINGDOM PROTISTA

KINGDOM FUNGI

KINGDOM PLANTAE

KINGDOM ANIMALIA

Chapter

8

THE FUNGI

Scientists do not create the world; they learn about it and attempt to imitate it, following the laws and intelligibility that nature manifests to us.

—Benedict XVI

FIGURE 8.1. FLY AGARIC (<u>AMANITA MUSCARIA</u>)
A poisonous but attractive woodland fungus with red cap and raised white spots

THE FUNGI

Almost Plants

Dead Man's Fingers, Witches' Snot, Destroying Angel, Death Cap . . . These almost sound like the names of rock groups Average Adam tells his friends not to listen to! Actually, they are the names of members of the Kingdom **FUNGI**. See Figure 8.5 on page 66.

Unlike the archaeans and bacteria, which are prokaryotes, fungi are eukaryotes with a nuclear membrane and organelles. Most fungi have a cell wall made of **CHITIN**. Unlike the protists, many fungi have specialized cells in a multicellular stage of their life cycle.

All the members of the varied Kingdom Fungi are heterotrophic, which means that they must obtain their food energy from other organisms or from decaying organic matter. Fungi digest their food externally by secreting digestive enzymes onto the food source. The enzymes break down the food so that the nutrients can be absorbed by the fungus.

You, like Average Adam, may not wish to become a **MYCOLOGIST**, but fungi are part of your life nonetheless! You should recognize mushrooms, puffballs, toadstools, mold, and yeast as fungi. You probably also know that fungi help in making bread and wine. You may have suffered from athlete's foot or

FIGURE 8.2. DEAD MAN'S FINGERS
Xylaria polymorpha, a woodland ascomycete, sometimes appears just like its name sounds. Unlike plants, fungi do not contain chlorophyll and must obtain their food energy from other organisms.

ringworm; the fungal parasites that cause these diseases are discussed in Chapter 24.

Helpful and harmful drugs are made from fungi. Like the bacteria, the fungi are extremely important for their role in decomposing organic chemicals into the simple substances needed to keep life going on earth.

The three main phyla of Kingdom Fungi are named according to how their members reproduce. (See Figure 8.5 on page 66.) The name Zygomycota is made of two words: "*zygo*," meaning "zygote" and "*mycota*," meaning "fungus." All the members of Phylum Zygomycota use conjugation to combine nuclear material and form a zygote. Black bread mold (Rhizopus sp.) is an example of these conjugation fungi.

FIGURE 8.3.
BLACK BREAD MOLD
Black bread mold (Rhizopus sp.) belongs to Phylum Zygomycota.

Most species of fungi are members of Phylum Ascomycota. Now, you already know that "*mycota*" means "fungus." "*Asco*" is from a root word that means "sack." The spores produced for reproduction are inside a microscopic sack called an **ASCUS**, and thus the ascomycetes are the "sac fungi."

Every time you eat a roll or bread you are ingesting yeast that was added live to the dough to make it rise. Yeast is an ascomycete that can also reproduce by **BUDDING**. Budding, a form of asexual reproduction, is similar to binary fission except that the cytoplasm is not evenly divided between the parent cell and the bud. See Figure 8.4.

Saccharomyces cerevisiae, a species of yeast, can convert grape juice into wine through a form of anaerobic respiration. The alcohol and carbon dioxide in the fermenting grape juice are actually the waste products that are produced when the yeast uses the glucose in the grape juice for energy.

In 1928 Dr. Alexander Fleming had an experiment that failed because his bacterial cultures were being killed by an ascomycete called Penicillium notatum. That failure turned into one of the greatest life-saving discoveries of all time. Dr. Fleming

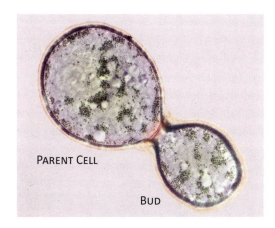

PARENT CELL

BUD

FIGURE 8.4. BUDDING IN YEAST
Budding is similar to binary fission except the cytoplasm is not evenly divided between the parent cell and the bud.

named the bacterial killing agent "penicillin." Today penicillin is produced using a mold of a different species, but the very same genus.

FIGURE 8.5. CLASSIFICATION OF KINGDOM FUNGI
A simplified key to Kingdom Fungi that leaves out technical details and some groups of fungi

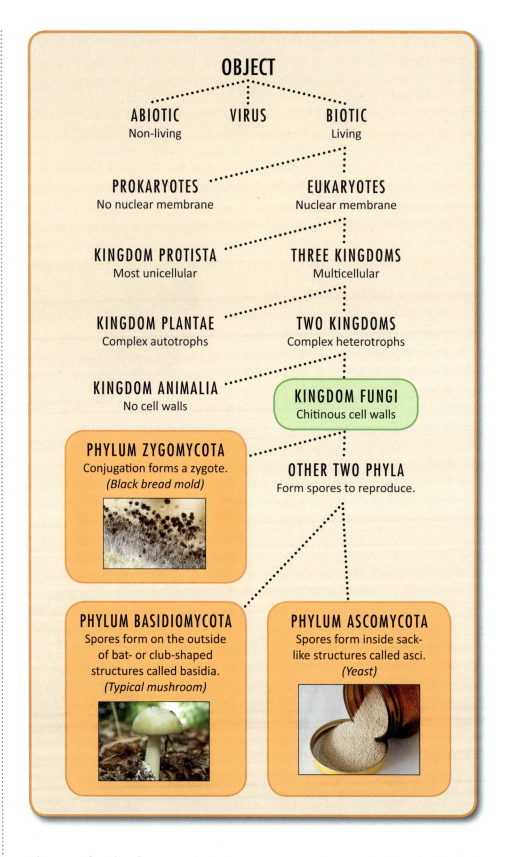

OBJECT

ABIOTIC
Non-living

VIRUS

BIOTIC
Living

PROKARYOTES
No nuclear membrane

EUKARYOTES
Nuclear membrane

KINGDOM PROTISTA
Most unicellular

THREE KINGDOMS
Multicellular

KINGDOM PLANTAE
Complex autotrophs

TWO KINGDOMS
Complex heterotrophs

KINGDOM ANIMALIA
No cell walls

KINGDOM FUNGI
Chitinous cell walls

PHYLUM ZYGOMYCOTA
Conjugation forms a zygote.
(Black bread mold)

OTHER TWO PHYLA
Form spores to reproduce.

PHYLUM BASIDIOMYCOTA
Spores form on the outside of bat- or club-shaped structures called basidia.
(Typical mushroom)

PHYLUM ASCOMYCOTA
Spores form inside sack-like structures called asci.
(Yeast)

The most familiar fungi produce tiny spores on microscopic "baseball bats" called **BASIDIA**. The Phylum Basidiomycota, or club fungi, are named that because of the shape of the basidia. The **SPORES** formed on the basidia are reproductive cells which will become new mushrooms.

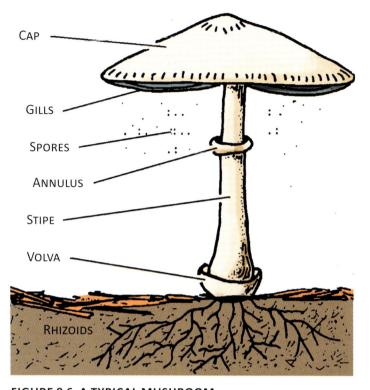

FIGURE 8.6. A TYPICAL MUSHROOM
Mushrooms are the best known members of Phylum Basidiomycota.
They serve an important ecological role as decomposers.

Mushrooms are basidiomycetes and the most obvious fungi of all. Next time someone gets a pizza with mushrooms, see if you can identify some of the following parts. See Figure 8.6.

First of all, the umbrella-shaped top is called the **CAP**. Underneath the cap are the **GILLS**, which are covered by microscopic, spore-bearing basidia. The stem is correctly termed a **STIPE**, and it often has a ring around it below the cap, called the **ANNULUS**. Sometimes there is a cup-like structure at the bottom called a **VOLVA**. These structures are all made of thin filaments of cells called **HYPHAE**. A mass of hyphae is called **MYCELIUM**. **RHIZOIDS** are root-like hyphae which break off when you pick a mushroom from the ground. Under the bark of a dead tree you may see a beautiful, fan-shaped **STOLON** formed of hyphae.

Not all basidiomycetes have gills. For instance, the stink

FIGURE 8.7. STOLON

FIGURE 8.8. A STINK HORN
Insects attracted to this sticky, and stinky, fungus help spread its spores. All fungi are heterotrophs and need a food source.

horn produces its spores interiorly and then exudes them in a sticky mass from the tip of its cap. The puffball is another fungus that produces its spores interiorly. You may have stomped on a mature puffball (<u>Lycoperdon sp</u>.) before and sent millions of spores into the air.

The gilled mushroom is Average Arnold's idea of a fungus. However, fungi come in many shapes and colors. Some people would call <u>Amanita phalloides</u> a toadstool because it is poisonous (Figure 8.9). Its nickname, Death Cap, clearly indicates the need to be an expert before deciding to eat any wild fungi. Figure 8.10 shows another unique basidiomycete, a bracket fungus used by artists.

FIGURE 8.9. <u>AMANITA PHALLOIDES</u>

Some basidiomycetes that cause plant diseases are called rusts and smuts. Wheat rust (<u>Puccina graminis</u>) and corn smut (<u>Ustilago maydis</u>) are two major fungal parasites of agricultural crops in America.

 Worksheets:
8.1–8.5

 Diagram:
8.6

 Experiment:
8.7

 Microscope:
8.8–8.9

FIGURE 8.10. ARTIST'S CONK
<u>Ganoderma applanatum</u> is a common type of club fungus which grows like a shelf on dead trees. The underside of the fungus turns dark brown when rubbed or scratched, so it can be used to draw pictures or write messages.

FIGURE 8.11. ALEXANDER FLEMING

Alexander Fleming and Antibiotics

How distasteful we find most fungi! Yet some molds (a type of fungus) not only add flavor to our foods, but also have the ability to cure bacterial diseases. For example, the mold that gives bleu cheese its distinctive flavor is closely related to life-saving penicillin.

The curative properties of this mold were discovered in 1928 by Alexander Fleming, who had been experimenting with bacteria. Returning from an extended vacation, Fleming discovered that, in his absence, some of the samples had been "contaminated" by an air-borne mold. Surprisingly, the bacteria nearest the mold had been destroyed, while those the farthest away continued to thrive. From this beginning, penicillin and other antibiotics were developed, saving millions of lives over the ensuing years.

Unfortunately, antibiotics are sometimes misunderstood and can therefore be misused. That is, antibiotics are effective against bacteria, but are ineffective in treating viral illness such as the flu.

Those who misunderstand this fact sometimes demand prescriptions for antibiotics even when inappropriate; this misuse has resulted in the creation of mutated bacteria which are antibiotic-resistant. (That is, the bacteria develop an immunity to antibiotics. These antibiotic-resistant bacteria cause infections which are difficult or impossible to cure!)

Alarmingly, these antibiotic-resistant strains are increasing at a rapid pace; perhaps you have heard of deaths caused by MRSA, or methicillin-resistant <u>Staphylococcus aureus</u>. Researchers are working at a feverish pace to produce newer strains of antibiotics to counter newer strains of bacteria, but can hardly keep ahead the bacteria's rate of mutation. The wise use of antibiotics can help alleviate this problem, as might an increase in pharmaceutical research and development.

The next time you grimace over a piece of moldy bread, or enjoy that bleu cheese dressing on your salad, think of all that Our Lord has set on His earth for us to discover and put to a godly use. Might you be the next Fleming?

FIGURE 8.12. COLONY OF <u>PENICILLIUM SP.</u> FUNGUS GROWING ON AGAR IN A PETRI DISH
This fungus produces the antibiotic penicillin, seen as small droplets on the surface.

KINGDOM ARCHAEA

KINGDOM BACTERIA

KINGDOM PROTISTA

KINGDOM FUNGI

KINGDOM PLANTAE

KINGDOM ANIMALIA

PLANT CLASSIFICATION

The beauty of the world is Christ's tender smile for us coming through matter.

—Simone Weil

FIGURE 9.1. FERN FROND
Ferns (Phylum Tracheophyta, Class Filicineae) reproduce by spores just as mosses do. Due to their vascular system, however, ferns can grow much taller than mosses (Phylum Bryophyta, Class Musci).

PLANT CLASSIFICATION

Plants

Take a moment to think of all the things you use that are made from, or result from, plants. Look at Figure 9.2 to remind yourself of some plant uses. Now turn to Appendix II in the back of your text to find a list of more than 150 uses we make of plants. As you can see, our lives are intertwined with the plant kingdom so closely that we could not live without plants.

All members of the Kingdom **PLANTAE** are autotrophs. That means they are "self feeders." Plants make their own food energy through photosynthesis. They make all of our food too, even though some plant food is changed into animal food before we eat it! If there were no plants, we could not enjoy beef, pork, fish, lobsters, clams, shrimp, or other animal products, because all these creatures depend on plants for their food.

You will learn more about how plants take sunlight and make food energy in a future chapter on nutrition. Right now our goal is to clearly answer: What is a plant? Then we will briefly outline the different kinds of plants.

Unlike archaeans and bacteria, plants are eukaryotes, so they have nuclear membranes and organelles. Unlike protists, the plants have multicellular bodies with special cells for special jobs. Unlike fungi, plants have cellulose cell walls and chlorophyll. Because plants contain chlorophyll, they can make their own food energy. See Figure 9.3 for an outline of the classification of Kingdom Plantae.

**FIGURE 9.2.
PLANT USES**
Plants and their products are a big part of any picture where people live and play. Can you identify three plant uses in this picture?

Algae

The plant kingdom contains a tremendous variety of creatures, some great, some small; but all are autotrophs with cellulose cell walls. There are three main phyla in the Kingdom Plantae. One, Phylum Chlorophyta, gets its name because of chlorophyll, the green chemical needed for photosynthesis. "Green algae" is a commonly used name for the plants in Phylum Chlorophyta. Some of these green algae are important starting points for the food chains in ponds and lakes.

One genus of green algae, Spirogyra sp., also called pond silk, is interesting to study under the microscope. Looking at Figure 9.4, you can identify the cell wall and the chloroplast. The ribbon-like chloroplast is in the shape of a spiral, thus the name—Spirogyra! With a compound microscope you can see for yourself the dense nucleus and sometimes a vacuole, as well as the cell wall and the spiral chloroplast.

A **PYRENOID** in Spirogyra is a storage area for starch. Pyrenoids (see Figure 9.4) are only visible if the algae has been exposed to sunlight for several hours before being viewed. In addition, to see the starch bodies, they must be stained with iodine first. The brown iodine solution turns blue-black when it reacts with starch molecules.

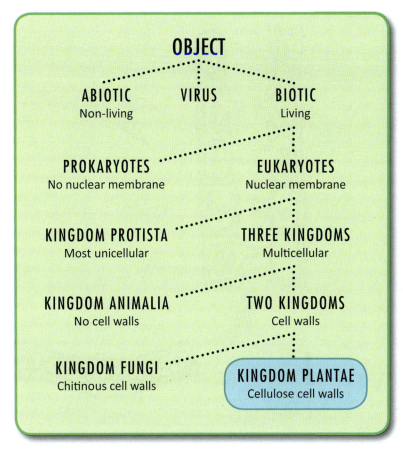

FIGURE 9.3. CLASSIFICATION OF KINGDOM PLANTAE
All members of the huge plant kingdom have important structural characteristics in common.

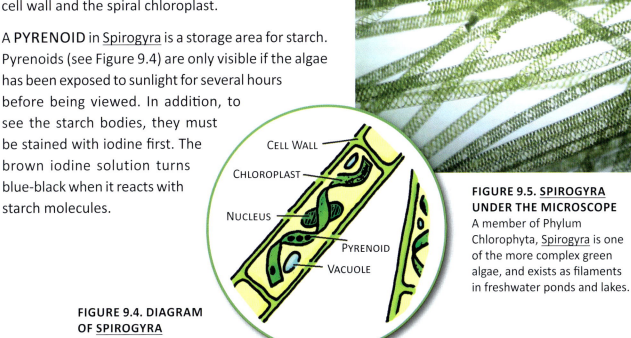

FIGURE 9.4. DIAGRAM OF SPIROGYRA

FIGURE 9.5. SPIROGYRA UNDER THE MICROSCOPE
A member of Phylum Chlorophyta, Spirogyra is one of the more complex green algae, and exists as filaments in freshwater ponds and lakes.

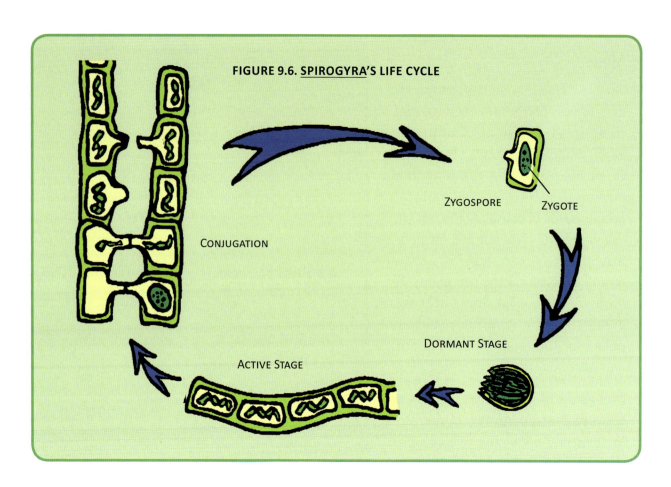

FIGURE 9.6. SPIROGYRA'S LIFE CYCLE

CONJUGATION

ZYGOSPORE   ZYGOTE

DORMANT STAGE

ACTIVE STAGE

Spirogyra reproduces asexually by binary fission, but it can at times reproduce sexually, as shown in the life cycle diagram (Figure 9.6). When _Spirogyra_ reproduces sexually through conjugation, two filaments join together. Cytoplasm from one of the cells fuses with cytoplasm in the other cell to produce a thick-walled zygospore. The zygospore, containing a zygote with a unique DNA, either germinates at once or lies dormant until the following spring, when it grows into a new filament of _Spirogyra_.

Chlorella sp. is another member of Phylum Chlorophyta. These tiny, spherical green algae have been studied intensely as scientists have tried to understand photosynthesis. _Chlorella_ gets its name from its one big chloroplast containing lots of chlorophyll. See Figure 9.7.

Protococcus sp. is a simple green alga that you may find almost anywhere (Figure 9.9). The green coloring on the north side of many tree trunks and on damp boards or even some rocks is due to millions of individual cells of _Protococcus_. This alga is so small that even with a good microscope you will only see its cell wall and chloroplast. But that's enough to know it belongs to Kingdom Plantae!

Fucus sp., brown algae in Phylum Phaeophyta, may be seen in the cool ocean waters off New York and New England (Figure 9.10).

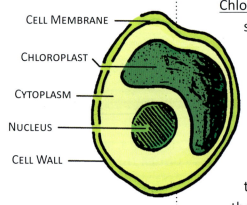

CELL MEMBRANE

CHLOROPLAST

CYTOPLASM

NUCLEUS

CELL WALL

FIGURE 9.7. CHLORELLA SP.

74

FIGURE 9.8. RED ALGAE

FIGURE 9.9. PROTOCOCCUS SP.

FIGURE 9.10. FUCUS SP.

FIGURE 9.11. SHIELD LICHEN Cetraria glauca can even be found on bare rocks, because the alga photosynthesizes food energy for both itself and the fungus, while the fungus provides the moist and shaded area the alga need to live.

FIGURE 9.12. REINDEER LICHEN. Reindeer lichen, Cladonia rangiferina, may be found as far south as New York State.

FIGURE 9.13. SOIL MAKERS British soldier lichen, Cladonia cristatella, with its poisonous red caps helps begin the formation of new soil on bare rocks.

Agar, used to make agar medium for culturing bacteria, is made from a red alga in the Phylum Rhodophyta. Members of Phylum Rhodophyta—for example, Irish moss (Chondrus sp.)—have chlorophyll just like other plants. But in red algae, red pigments cover up the green color (Figure 9.8).

Lichens

Some green algae live in very close association with fungi. The fungal hyphae provide a shady, humid environment for the algae. The algae make food for themselves, and are also used by the fungi as a food source. Two organisms living so closely for the benefit of both is called mutualism. You should recall learning about mutualism in Chapter 6, when we discussed nitrifying bacteria in the nodules on the roots of legumes.

LICHEN is a case of mutualism in which the two organisms are living so close together that many people think they are one creature. Lichens have even been classified and given scientific names as if they are one organism. For example, Cetraria sp. is a common grayish lichen that grows on boulders (Figure 9.11). The northern parts of North America, Europe, and Asia are covered by Cladonia rangiferina, known as reindeer lichen (Figure 9.12).

FIGURE 9.14. HORNWORT

FIGURE 9.15. LIVERWORT

FIGURE 9.16. MOSS
Haircap moss, Polytrichum commune, is a familiar member of Phylum Bryophyta, Class Musci.

FIGURE 9.17. BRACKEN FERN
Crushed up bracken fern is a natural insect repellant when rubbed on the arms, neck, and ankles.

Mosses

In the Phylum **BRYOPHYTA** are three classes, which include liverworts, hornworts and mosses. A common hornwort (Phaeoceros laevis) and the common liverwort (Marchantia polymorpha) are probably no more common to you than they are to Average Adam. These members of Phylum Bryophyta are small, green, and grow very close to the ground (see Figures 9.14–15). Because of their small size most people don't notice hornworts and liverworts.

Members of Phylum Bryophyta tend to be small since they have no **VASCULAR SYSTEM**. That is, bryophytes have no special tubes for moving liquids through their bodies. Bryophytes do not have true stems, roots, or leaves. Rhizoids are tiny, root-like structures that hold the mosses to the ground.

Bryophytes reproduce by alternation of generations. The sperm cells must swim through a film of water to reach the egg cell. The new organism is the single-celled zygote. The zygote grows and produces spores which grow into the part of a bryophyte that you can see easily.

The most familiar bryophytes are mosses (Figure 9.16). Like the liverworts and hornworts, mosses have no vascular system and need a film of water for reproduction. That explains why mosses are almost always found in the woods or under porches and in shady areas where it stays moist. That also explains why mosses get only a few centimeters tall. Without a vascular system, water cannot be raised very high above the ground.

Ferns

Ferns are often found where mosses and the other bryophytes grow. However, ferns are a very different kind of organism in one major way! Ferns have a vascular system.

All plants with vascular systems belong to the plant kingdom's Phylum **TRACHEOPHYTA**. The ferns, because they don't make seeds, are in Class **FILICINEAE**. Whisk ferns, club mosses, and horsetails are three other seedless classes in Phylum Tracheophyta (Figures 9.21–23).

The special, tube-like cells in the vascular system allow ferns to grow taller than mosses. Fossil evidence indicates that at one time there were forests of tree-sized ferns! These fern forests seem to have been abundant when the dinosaurs ruled the earth. Today, one of the tallest ferns you will find is Pteridium aquilinum, called common bracken (see Figure 9.17). The bracken fern grows up to two meters high, taller than Average Arnold, your average-sized dad!

FIGURE 9.18. A FERN FROND
The entire fan-like piece of this fern is the frond.

FIGURE 9.19. SORI
Sori of the western sword fern (Polystichum munitum): a low-power microscopic view of the fern's sori, the clusters of sporangia which contain the spores.

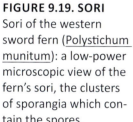

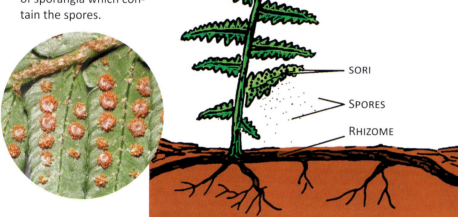

FROND

PINNA

SORI

SPORES

RHIZOME

FIGURE 9.20. A TYPICAL FERN
All the parts of a fern may be seen in this diagram of the New York fern. Its scientific name is Thelypteris noveboracensis. The plural form of "pinna" is "pinnae."

FIGURE 9.21. WHISK FERN

FIGURE 9.22. CLUB MOSS
Like the ferns this club moss cannot make seeds and must reproduce by spores. Unlike the mosses however, the club moss has a vascular system.

FIGURE 9.23. HORSETAIL
Northern giant horsetail (Equisetum telmateia)

Figures 9.18 and 9.20 show the **FROND** of a fern. Each frond is divided into sections which are sometimes mistakenly called leaves. The small parts of the frond are leaflets, correctly termed pinnae.

The undersides of some fronds are dotted with small brown bumps called **SORI**, made of clusters of **SPORANGIA** containing the spores (Figure 9.19). Some ferns have their sori on a separate stalk.

You may try to pull up a fern frond and find that it is attached to several neighbors by a horizontal, underground stem called a **RHIZOME**. The small, root-like rhizoids anchor the fern to the ground (Figure 9.20).

The ferns grow taller than the mosses because of their vascular systems, but they still need a film of water to reproduce. That is why ferns are found with mosses in wet, humid places.

Conifers

Similar to the ferns, and like the flowering plants that we will study, the conifers have a vascular system and are members of Phylum Tracheophyta. Unlike ferns, conifers and flowering plants do not need a film of water to reproduce. Instead, conifers and flowering plants produce seeds.

Plants with seeds are grouped in either Class Gymnospermae or Class Angiospermae. Plants with seeds **not** inside a fruit are all in the Class **GYMNOSPERMAE**. "*Gymno*" is a Greek root word meaning "naked," and "*spermae*" means "seed." That is, the seeds are "naked," not hidden. Look at a pine cone and you can see the seeds between the scales of the cone (Figure 9.25). Most gymnosperms are commonly called conifers, because they have cones.

The name **CONIFER** comes from two root words: "*coni*" meaning "cone," and "*fer*" from a Latin word meaning "to carry" or "to have." You should be familiar with the word "ferry" from the same Latin root. A ferry carries things. A conifer carries, or has, cones.

FIGURE 9.24.
A TYPICAL CONIFER
Picea pungens or blue spruce is very often planted as an ornamental tree on lawns. A vascular plant that bears its seeds on the scales of a cone, the blue spruce gets its species name from its sharp needles. The Latin word "*pungens*" means "sharp" or "to prick."

FIGURE 9.25. CONES

Most conifers are evergreens, meaning that some of their needles or scaly leaves stay on their branches over each winter. The conifers are the most important plants to both the lumber and the paper industries. The largest living creature on earth is a conifer (see Figure 1.2 in Chapter 1). The oldest tree is also a conifer: a bristle cone pine (Pinus longaeva) in California that began growing over 2,600 years before Christ was born (see Figure 1.1 in Chapter 1).

FIGURE 9.26. MAIN PHYLA AND CLASSES IN THE KINGDOM PLANTAE

FIGURE 9.27. GRASSES ARE FLOWERING PLANTS
Grasses, like many trees, have very tiny, often green flowers that are easily overlooked. Yet every flower, no matter how small, is a complex plant organ needed for the continuation of that species of plant.

 Worksheets:
9.1–9.2, 9.4–9.8

 Diagram:
9.3, 9.10

 Microscope:
9.9

Flowering Plants

Plants with seeds inside a fruit are grouped into the Class **ANGIOSPER-MAE**. *"Angio"* means hidden, so angiospermae means "hidden seed." Plants that have hidden seeds—that is, the angiosperms—are the flowering plants.

Every single plant food listed in Appendix II is a member of the colorful Class Angiospermae. The flowering plants are not only the most obvious plants on earth, but at this time are the most dominant plants. Flowers are special plant organs designed for reproduction that we will study in detail in Chapter 11. The flowers on an angiosperm may be easy to identify or almost unnoticeable (see Figure 9.27). If they are a gift for your mother be sure to get angiosperms with pretty, bright blossoms, such as those shown in Figure 9.28.

Class Angiospermae is easily divided into two subclasses based on the structure of the seeds. Plants in Subclass Monocotyledonae are called **MONOCOTS**, and plants in Subclass Dicotyledonae are called **DICOTS**.

COTYLEDON is the correct term for the special seed leaf used for food storage in a seed. You should already know from playing Monopoly that the prefix *"mono"* means "one." *"Di-,"* as in dissect, means "two." Now you can deduce that the word Monocotyledonae means "one seed leaf" and Dicotyledonae means "two seed leaves." The number of seed leaves is the main difference between monocots and dicots. The next time you have peas, beans, or even a few peanuts, be sure to remove the seed coat and you will see the two cotyledons that you are eating for their stored-up food!

Figure 9.29 outlines the other differences between monocots and dicots. For instance, every plant with one cotyledon has parallel veins in its leaves. Plants with two seed leaves have branching veins, and their vascular tissue is in a ring. These regular and consistent patterns of structure in monocots and dicots are evidence that these organisms were designed according to an intelligent plan.

FIGURE 9.28. AMERICAN FIELD DAISY
It is a lot easier to identify Chrysanthemum leucanthemum than it is to say its scientific name! There is an old movie called *Please Don't Eat the Daisies,* but actually daisies are one of the few composite flowers that are entirely edible!

MONOCOTYLEDONAE
Examples: corn, day lily, onion, wheat
DICOTYLEDONAE
Examples: peanut, daisy, apple
NUMBER OF SEED LEAVES (COTYLEDONS)
ONE
COTYLEDON
THE EMBRYO, OR TINY PLANT
TWO
THE EMBRYO, OR TINY PLANT
COTYLEDONS
VEINS IN REGULAR LEAVES
PARALLEL
BRANCHING
FLOWER PARTS IN MULTIPLES OF...
3'S OR 4'S
4'S OR 5'S
VASCULAR BUNDLES
SCATTERED
MICROGRAPH OF A MONOCOT STEM
IN A RING
MICROGRAPH OF A DICOT STEM

FIGURE 9.29. MONOCOTS VS. DICOTS

PLANT STRUCTURE AND RESPONSE

KINGDOM PLANTAE

KINGDOM FUNGI

KINGDOM ANIMALIA

KINGDOM ARCHAEA

KINGDOM BACTERIA

KINGDOM PROTISTA

FIGURE 10.1. THIGMOTROPISM
Because of thigmotropism, a plant response to touch, the tendrils of many climbing plants wrap around whatever they touch.

PLANT STRUCTURE AND RESPONSE

Cells to Systems

The organization of the beautiful and complex bodies of the gymnosperms and angiosperms begins with atoms. As you recall, a small number of different kinds of atoms make up many kinds of molecules. Those molecules make up the organelles which together form the cell.

Most cells of the archaeans, bacteria, protists, and fungi are generalized. That is, each cell does all the jobs that have to be done for itself. The shape of one cell and the next is very similar.

The cells of the members of the plant kingdom, especially the tracheophytes, are specialized. These cells have different shapes for different jobs, as illustrated in Figures 10.2–4.

A lot of cells with the same shape, all doing the same job, form tissue. Tissues working together to perform a life function are called an organ. A group of organs forms a system. All the systems of a creature, working together, form the organism.

No matter what their shape or function, all living cells must take in materials, carry out respiration, and excrete wastes. The specialized parts of the more advanced plants help them carry out the life functions better so that every cell may stay alive.

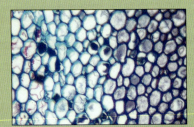

FIGURE 10.2. Cells for storage are fat and more or less round in shape. These are cortex cells in a fern.

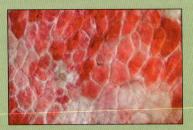

FIGURE 10.3. Cells for protection join together closely like the pieces of a living puzzle. These are epidermal cells in a cherry skin.

FIGURE 10.4. Cells for transporting liquids are shaped like soda straws. These are xylem and phloem cells in the stem of a cinnamon tree.

Roots

Figure 10.5 shows two types of root systems. One type is specialized for the storage of food materials; the other is especially good for absorption.

The familiar carrot **TAP ROOT**, very similar to the tap root shown in Figure 10.5, is a plant organ made of several tissues. The tap root's main function is the storage of food. Tap roots also have small side roots, called secondary roots, that help with absorption.

The thin **FIBROUS ROOT** system of plants such as grasses is better designed for absorption of water and minerals from the soil. Each tiny root can only store a little bit of food.

Either type of root system anchors the plant in the ground, and this helps prevent erosion. The role of plants in preventing erosion and maintaining water sheds is a plant use that is very important, but often overlooked.

A root system is a complex group of organs made of tissues. Unlike the rhizoids of ferns, the root systems of tracheophytes are true roots, designed for the transportation of water and food. The **XYLEM** (pronounced ZYE-lem) tissue transports water and dissolved minerals. Firewood is mostly dead xylem cells. The **PHLOEM** (pronounced FLOH-em) cells bring dissolved food down from the leaves to living cells in the roots.

Read this carefully: the phollowing may help you remember this phact—"**phood phlows in phloem.**" Once you remember that food is in the phloem, then you know the water is in the xylem.

Looking at Figure 10.6 you will observe a **ROOT CAP** which protects the tip of the root. Behind the root cap is the meristematic region, which is simply an area of cell division. All the cells in the meristematic region look nearly the same. Behind the meristematic region is the zone of elongation where the new cells grow longer and push the root cap through the soil. Behind the zone of elongation is the zone of differentiation. In the zone of differentiation, cells take on different shapes depending

FIGURE 10.5. ROOT SYSTEMS
On the left is a tap root designed for storage. On the right is a fibrous root system, especially good for absorption.

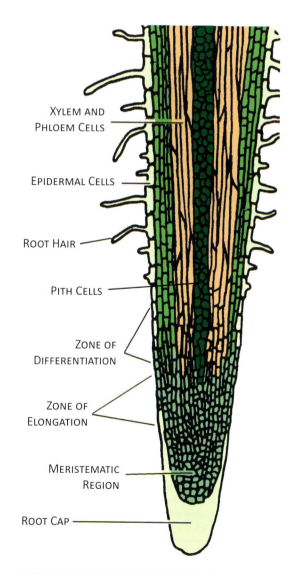

XYLEM AND PHLOEM CELLS

EPIDERMAL CELLS

ROOT HAIR

PITH CELLS

ZONE OF DIFFERENTIATION

ZONE OF ELONGATION

MERISTEMATIC REGION

ROOT CAP

FIGURE 10.6. A ROOT LONGISECTION
The complex structure of a true root shows different kinds of tissues organized to form the root. Cells in one kind of tissue tend to have the same shape.

on the function they will perform. **ROOT HAIRS** will also be seen from this point and beyond on healthy, fresh roots.

Root hairs are extremely important in the absorption of water and minerals from the soil. If you are going to transplant a tree or flower, it is critical that you keep the roots moist so that the delicate root hairs stay alive. If they dry out, the root hairs die. New root hairs grow as the root grows, but the old ones cannot be revived.

The **PITH** cells are large, loose cells designed for storing food. Pith cells are similar in shape to the cortex cells in Figure 10.2. The epidermal cells are tough and fit closely together for protection of the tissues underneath.

Stems

In plants that live for only one or two years, called annuals and biennials, the stems are soft. In perennials, which live for many years, the stems are often hard. The stems of annuals and biennials are called **HERBACEOUS STEMS** (Figure 10.7), and the hard stems of many perennials are called **WOODY STEMS** (Figure 10.8).

Stems are used for support, transport, storage and, if green, photosynthesis. Stems, like roots, have pith, xylem, and phloem tissues.

In Figure 10.9 the inside of a woody stem is magnified with the pith to the left. The thin circle of **CAMBIUM** is a special area of cell division between

FIGURE 10.7. HERBACEOUS STEMS
Timothy hay, Phleum pratense, has sweet, green, herbaceous stems that farm animals eat and Huckleberry Finn-types chew on.

FIGURE 10.8. WOODY STEM
Perennials can live for many years. This perennial's woody stem contains cells that formed long before you were born!

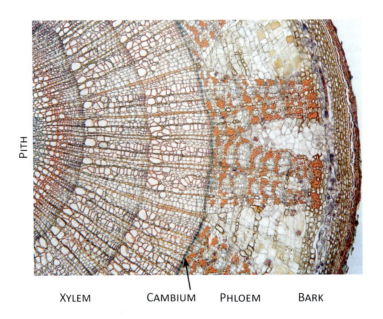

PITH

XYLEM   CAMBIUM   PHLOEM   BARK

FIGURE 10.9. CROSS-SECTION OF A WOODY STEM
The three-year-old stem of Tilia sp. shows the rings typical of a woody stem. The annual rings are due to a difference in the amount of xylem which grows in the spring and the xylem which grows in the dry summer. Magnification: 59×

the xylem and phloem. It is similar to the meristematic zone in the root. The rugged **BARK** is made of dead cells that protect the tissue underneath.

Some stems have become specialized to do one function more than others. The rhizome, **BULB**, **TUBER**, and corm (a bulb-like stem found in gladiolus and crocus plants), are all specialized stems.

Leaves

Leaves come in so many sizes and shapes that it is hard to believe they all have the same tissues and carry out the same functions. Green leaves are used to produce food and to exchange gases. Leaves are green because of the chlorophyll in their chloroplasts. The autumn colors of leaves show up when chlorophyll is no longer made in the leaf. In the chloroplasts, but hidden in the spring and summer by chlorophyll's green color, are two other colors. Xanthophyll is yellow and carotene is orange. The name "carrot" is related to the root word for carotene. The red pigment in some leaves is anthocyanin, located in the vacuoles. The brown color of dead leaves is caused by tannic acid.

The veins and shapes of leaves are used in taxonomy to name plants. A simple leaf has one blade on each "stem," or petiole (Figure 10.11). A compound leaf has three or more leaflets on a petiole (Figure 10.12).

The veins of a leaf may be palmate, like the outspread fingers of your palm; or pinnate, like a pinion feather; or parallel, with all the large veins

FIGURE 10.10.
SPECIALIZED STEMS
An onion bulb, Allium cepa, and a potato tuber, Solanum tuberosum, are underground stems used for food storage by the plant and for food by mankind.

PETIOLES

PETIOLE

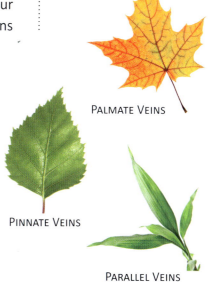

PALMATE VEINS

PINNATE VEINS

PARALLEL VEINS

FIGURE 10.11. SIMPLE LEAVES
A true leaf has a bud in the axil, or angle, of the petiole. Unlike the leaflets in Figure 10.12, the leaves shown above are true leaves.

FIGURE 10.12. COMPOUND LEAF
A leaf's "stem" is correctly termed its petiole. This compound leaf consists of many leaflets.

FIGURE 10.13. LEAF VENATION
The veins in a leaf may be arranged in several different ways. The arrangement of the veins in a leaf, called leaf venation, is an important clue for identifying the species from which the leaf came.

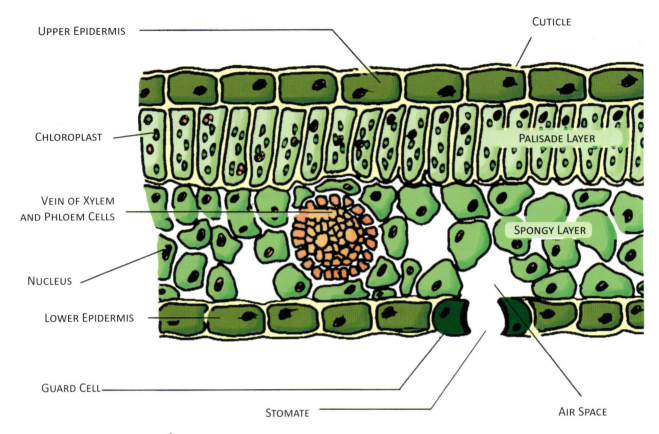

UPPER EPIDERMIS

CUTICLE

CHLOROPLAST

PALISADE LAYER

VEIN OF XYLEM
AND PHLOEM CELLS

SPONGY LAYER

NUCLEUS

LOWER EPIDERMIS

GUARD CELL

STOMATE

AIR SPACE

FIGURE 10.14. A LEAF CROSS-SECTION

FIGURE 10.15. GUARD CELLS
Stomates, openings in the lower epidermis of leaves, are opened and closed by guard cells. The green organelles in the micrograph below are chloroplasts.

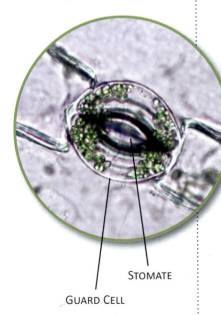

STOMATE

GUARD CELL

going the same direction, parallel to each other. The veins in a leaf are made of xylem and phloem cells, and are the ends of the vascular system that began in the zone of differentiation in the root.

Just like the root and stem, the leaf is a complex organ made of many different tissues. Study Figure 10.14 of a leaf cross-section. The most important function of leaves is to carry out photosynthesis. The palisade layer is where most of this food-making process takes place. The **PALISADE LAYER** got its name because under a microscope it resembles a wall or cliff, which is what a palisade is!

The **SPONGY LAYER** has lots of loose cells where oxygen and carbon dioxide are exchanged and water is released. The upper epidermis and the lower epidermis are protective layers on the top and bottom of the leaf. Some leaves have a waxy coating called a **CUTICLE** on their upper epidermis that helps protect the leaf. The cuticle also helps prevent the loss of too much water.

The lower epidermis has openings called **STOMATES**, which let water and oxygen out and carbon dioxide and oxygen in! A stomate is pictured in Figure 10.15.

Some plant stems have **LENTICELS** which are openings in the bark similar to stomates in the leaves (Figure 10.16).

An excellent example of how shape is related to function is the guard cells of a stomate. The job of guard cells is to regulate **TRANSPIRATION**, the evaporation of water from the leaves of plants. Guard cells are sausage-shaped and are situated on either side of the stomate, the opening in the leaf. The cell membrane on the side of the cell near the stomate is thicker than the cell membrane on the other side. See Figure 10.14.

When the guard cells become turgid with excess water they open the stomate. To see how this works, put a piece of tape on a partially blown-up balloon. The balloon must be a sausage-shaped one. Now, when you continue blowing up the balloon, it will bend because one side stretches more than the side with the tape. In the same way, the thicker side of the guard cell stretches less than the thin side, so the cell bends, opening the stomate.

As a plant dries out, the guard cells become flaccid and the stomate closes. This slows transpiration and keeps water in the plant. The reason most evergreens have needle-like leaves is because they must survive the winter when the ground water is frozen. The narrow needles of conifers do not transpire as much as broad leaves. This helps the conifers conserve water during the winter.

FIGURE 10.16. LENTICELS
The young stem of a water birch, <u>Betula occidentalis</u>, clearly shows the lenticels. The twigs of yellow birch, <u>Betula lutea</u>, a tree in the same genus, were the original source for the flavoring in birch beer soda.

Tropisms

Plants, unlike animals, have no muscular or nervous systems. For plants to react to their environment they must change the water pressure in their cells or grow in a new direction. **AUXINS** are special plant hormones that cause plant cells to grow more or less, depending on the cells. The amount of auxins in a cell depends on gravity, on the amount of sunlight, and on many other environmental factors. A plant **TROPISM** is a response to various environmental factors which is caused by the different concentrations of plant hormones in cells.

FIGURE 10.17. <u>Mimosa pudica</u> quickly folds its leaves when touched.

Like plant tropism, nastic movement is a response by plants to environmental factors. Unlike tropisms, which are caused by plant hormones, nastic movements are due to changes in the water pressure in plant cells. Nastic movements happen more rapidly than tropisms, which occur slowly as the plant grows in a new direction. For instance, the Venus flytrap captures its prey by nastic movement. Nastic movement is also what causes sunflowers to turn on their stalks throughout the day so that they are always facing the sun. The sensitive plant, <u>Mimosa pudica</u>, responds rapidly to touch because of nastic movement (see image above).

FIGURE 10.19. PHOTOTROPISM IN PLANTS

FIGURE 10.18. PHOTOTROPISM
The stem cells with more auxin are on the shaded side. When they grow longer the plant bends toward the light.

FIGURE 10.20. GEOTROPISM IN PLANTS
This bean plant tipped over. The part of the stem that was already mature could not change. The growing stem grew upward because of the greater concentration of auxins in the bottom side of the stem.

PHOTOTROPISM is a "light response" in plants. Sunlight causes the auxin in cells to move to the shaded side of the plant. The shaded side of a plant stem has a greater concentration of auxin. The cells on the shaded side grow longer than the cells on the sunny side. This unequal growth causes the plant to grow toward the light (Figure 10.18).

GEOTROPISM is a plant response to gravity. The word root "*geo*" means "earth," and geotropism is movement toward or away from the earth. The earth's gravity causes the concentration of auxin in a stem that has tipped over to be greatest on the bottom side (Figure 10.20). The greater concentration of auxin in the cells on the bottom side of the stem causes them to grow longer, and the stem turns upward.

Many of the fungi also respond to gravity. As you have learned, many fungi produce spores for reproduction. The spores must fall out of pores or out of the gills, so in order to reproduce, the fungus must grow with the correct surface facing downward. Geotropism allows fungi to reorient themselves if they are turned sideways. For instance, if a fungus grows on a dead tree and the tree falls over, geotropism allows it to reorient itself so that its spores can fall to the ground.

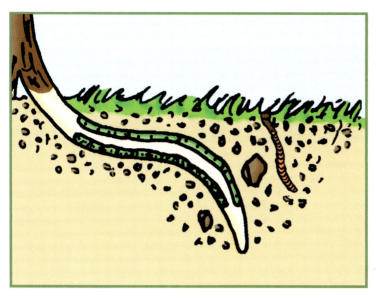

FIGURE 10.21. GEOTROPISM IN ROOTS
The effect of auxin on root cells is opposite to its effect on stems. In root cells, a greater concentration of auxin inhibits growth and the roots grow downward.

Worksheets:
10.1–10.4, 10.6

Diagram:
10.5, 10.7

Microscope:
10.8–10.10

The cells in plant roots respond to auxins in a way opposite to how the cells in the stems respond. In a root, more auxin causes less growth. The bottom side of a root has a greater concentration of auxin, so the cells don't grow as much as those on the top side. This causes the root to curve downward (Figure 10.21). If the root is exposed at the surface, the auxin moves away from the sunlight towards the bottom side of the root. The upper cells grow faster and longer. The root bends downward.

Hydrotropism is a plant response to water. This could be a problem where there are water or drain pipes that are cracked. The plant roots might grow toward and into the leaking pipes!

Thigmotropism is a plant response to touch. A familiar example of thigmotropism is the tendril of a bean plant or other climbing plant. The tendrils wrap around whatever they touch (Figure 10.22).

Chemotropism is a plant response to chemicals. The roots of plants may grow toward some chemicals but away from others.

Phototropism and geotropism would be interesting to investigate with an experiment of your own. Bean plants are good subjects for tropism experiments. You can buy the dried seeds in a grocery store.

FIGURE 10.22. THIGMOTROPISM
A plant displays thigmotropism when its tendrils wrap around a support.

KINGDOM ARCHAEA

KINGDOM BACTERIA

KINGDOM PROTISTA

KINGDOM FUNGI

KINGDOM PLANTAE

KINGDOM ANIMALIA

PLANT GROWTH AND REPRODUCTION

All my life through, the new sights of
Nature made me rejoice like a child.

—Marie Curie

FIGURE 11.1. YOUNG APPLE (<u>MALUS COMMUNIS</u>) ORCHARD IN KENT, ENGLAND, WITH A PINK POLLENIZER GRAFTED TO ONE TREE

PLANT GROWTH AND REPRODUCTION

Of all the life functions, reproduction is the only one an individual can live without. However, the species cannot survive if some of its individuals do not reproduce. There are basically two kinds of reproduction: asexual and sexual.

Asexual Reproduction

ASEXUAL REPRODUCTION involves only one parent. The offspring produced during asexual reproduction are genetically the same as that one parent. This means that the offspring will have all the same characteristics as the parent. As you will see, it is asexual reproduction that allows a farmer or scientist to grow types of seedless plants. It also ensures that a certain trait will be passed on from the parent to the offspring. Some methods of asexual reproduction, such as grafting, allow hybrids to be made that do not occur in nature. Asexual reproduction produces plants more quickly than sexual reproduction.

There are many types of asexual reproduction. Binary fission is the "splitting in two" of a cell. First the cell makes a copy of the chromosomes in its nucleus which contain the instructions to operate the cell. Then the parent cell divides its cytoplasm and nuclear material equally into two daughter cells. We mentioned in the section on classification that binary fission is the way many bacteria, algae, and protists reproduce. See Chapter 7 if you cannot name the protist shown in Figure 11.2.

Budding is similar to binary fission. Just as in binary fission, the cell makes a copy of the chromosomes in its nucleus. However, in budding the cytoplasm is not divided equally. The parent cell is larger and the daughter cell is smaller. Both cells have the same genetic information in their chromosomes, as in every case of asexual reproduction. Yeast cells, like those sold in food stores, reproduce by budding (see Figure 8.2 in Chapter 8).

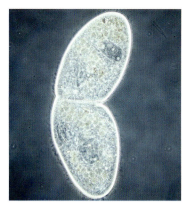

FIGURE 11.2. BINARY FISSION
The two daughter cells are exactly alike in terms of DNA. They are both genetically identical to the original parent cell.

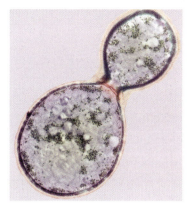

FIGURE 11.3. BUDDING
Yeast cells, used in making bread and wine, reproduce asexually by budding.

FIGURE 11.4. HYDRA BUDDING
Hydra are simple animals which can reproduce asexually by budding. In the image above, three daughter hydras are budding off from the sides of the parent Hydra.

Some of the less complex animals, such as the Hydra, also reproduce asexually by budding (see Figure 11.4).

Fungi and some plants reproduce asexually by **SPORULATION**. Figure 11.5 shows the fruiting bodies of mushrooms. The purpose of this part of a fungus is to produce spores that can produce new organisms in other locations. Each spore contains the same genetic information as the parent organism.

There are a great many different methods of **VEGETATIVE PROPAGATION**. All of them are types of asexual reproduction in which part of a plant (vegetable) is used to grow a new plant (propagation). The stems of some plants, such as geraniums, can be cut and kept alive until they form roots (Figure 11.7). Then the cutting may be planted.

In grafting, another type of vegetative propagation, the cut part is attached to another plant that is already growing. Grafting is the technique which allows farmers to grow seedless orange trees, a type of plant which otherwise would not be able to reproduce, since it does not have seeds.

Runners are special horizontal stems in strawberry and other plants that "run" along the surface and put down roots (Figure 11.8). If the runner is later cut, there will be two plants. Runners are a type of asexual reproduction by means of vegetative propagation.

Plants like raspberries may have stems that bend down to touch the ground. The stem takes root and can be cut

FIGURE 11.5. SPORULATION
Fungi and ferns reproduce by means of spores. The gills on the underside of a fungal cap are where the spores are produced.

FIGURE 11.6. GRAFTING
Fruit trees planted by seed usually take 7–10 years to bear fruit. This time can be reduced to as little as 2 years by grafting the seedling onto a mature tree.

**FIGURE 11.7.
GERANIUM CUTTING**
Geraniums are easily
propagated by cuttings.

FIGURE 11.8. RUNNERS
This strawberry plantlet was
formed when a runner from
the parent plant put down
roots.

to make two plants. This is called layering. Both plants will be genetically identical, just as in all the other types of asexual reproduction.

Two of the most familiar methods of asexual reproduction are bulbs and tubers (refer back to Figure 10.10). As you learned in Chapter 10, an onion bulb and a potato tuber are both specialized plant stems. You are probably familiar with the inside of an onion. The part you eat is actually a compressed stem and thick leaves. The "eyes" of a potato are actually new stems that can grow if given a chance. Bulbs and tubers yield plants genetically identical to the parent plant.

Sexual Reproduction

There is one, very important difference between asexual and sexual reproduction. In **SEXUAL REPRODUCTION**, the chromosomes in the nucleus of the new cell are a combination of genetic information from two parent cells. As you learned in Chapter 8, some fungi, called conjugation fungi, exchange nuclear material in a type of sexual reproduction. As a result, the new fungus is not exactly like either of the parent fungi. This often produces some individuals who are better able to live and survive under a given set of conditions. The most important advantage of sexual reproduction is this variation in the offspring.

Sexual reproduction in the more complex plants occurs through fertilization by two **GAMETES**. The gametes are the special cells formed just for reproduction. The male gamete is a sperm cell and the female gamete is an egg cell.

In angiosperms, the most advanced plants, the flower is a specialized organ for reproduction. Any flower that has the parts to make both sperm and egg cells is a complete flower (Figure 11.9). Some flowers, called incomplete, only produce sperm cells, while others only make egg cells.

Most flowers have a swollen base called the receptacle. The sepals grow from the receptacle and protect the flower bud before it opens. All the sepals together are called the calyx. The brightest and most obvious part of many flowers are the petals. Showy petals are found on flowers that need insects to pollinate them. The **COROLLA**, all the petals together, form bright patterns that certain insects fly toward. The corolla is like a target that attracts pollinators.

The Stamen

In studying the flower in Figure 11.9, note that the **STAMEN** is all of the parts needed to produce sperm cells. The filament is long and thin, just

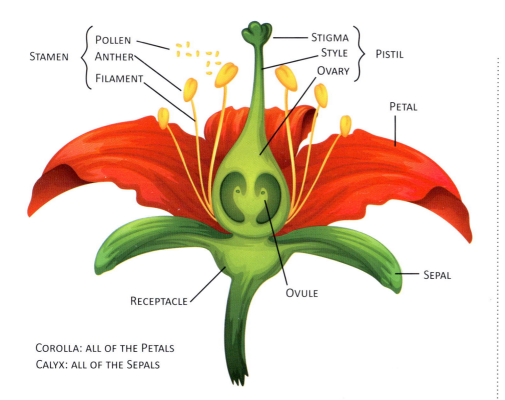

STAMEN { POLLEN, ANTHER, FILAMENT }

STIGMA, STYLE, OVARY } PISTIL

PETAL

SEPAL

OVULE

RECEPTACLE

COROLLA: ALL OF THE PETALS
CALYX: ALL OF THE SEPALS

**FIGURE 11.9.
A COMPLETE FLOWER**
This generalized flower has all the parts found in flowers and is called complete. A flower with only the male parts is incomplete and is called a staminate flower. A flower with only female parts is also incomplete and is called a pistilate flower.

what "filament" means! The anther is the correct "anther" to give when asked where the pollen is formed. The pollen produced by the anther contains the sperm cells. These parts make up "Stanley Stamen," the male part of a flower. Remember the word *men* in stamen to associate the stamen with the male parts. A staminate flower is an incomplete flower that contains only male parts: anther, filament, and pollen.

The Pistil

The central region of Figure 11.9 illustrates all the female parts of a flower, called the **PISTIL**. At the top is the sticky stigma whose function is to "grab hold" of the pollen. The style is slender and connects the stigma to the ovary. Remember, it is always in *style* to be slender. The enlarged part at the base of the pistil is the ovary. This is the part of a flower that becomes the fruit. Inside the ovary is the ovule, which contains the egg cell. The ovule eventually becomes the seed. "Patty Pistil" is all of the female parts of the flower. A pistillate flower is an incomplete flower with only female parts: stigma, style, ovary, and the ovule containing the egg cell.

Pollination

For sexual reproduction to occur, the pollen in the anther must get to the sticky stigma on the style. The process of pollen getting from the anther to the stigma is called **POLLINATION**. When pollen from a flower's anther reaches its own stigma, it is called **SELF-POLLINATION**. **CROSS-POLLINATION** occurs when wind, water, insects, or human beings cause the pollen from one flower to reach the stigma of a different flower.

MITOSIS: THE PROCESS OF GROWTH

Have you ever planted a garden and watched tiny seedlings grow into enormous pumpkins or sunflowers taller than yourself? Have you marveled at the tiny hands and feet of a newborn brother or sister—a brother or sister who might one day be taller than yourself? Let us praise God for the incredible process of growth!

In plants and animals, growth occurs by means of cell division in a process called **MITOSIS**. Think how many more cells there are in a full-grown sunflower as compared to a sunflower seedling! The millions of new cells that are formed as a sunflower grows to its full size are produced through mitosis. When a strawberry plant reproduces by vegetative propagation, it is the process of mitosis which allows the parent plant to grow the runner and the new plant. Your own growth is also due to "the mighty process of mitosis."

Mitosis is the normal process by which plants and animals produce new cells. In mitosis, a single parent cell divides into two smaller cells, which are called "daughter cells." The daughter cells are identical with the original cell, because they contain exactly the same chromosomes. Chromosomes, you remember, are double strands of DNA which contain the chemical instructions for operating the cell. Duplicating the chromosomes so that there will be one set for each daughter cell is the most important part of mitosis. During mitosis, the organelles are also duplicated and divided between the two new daughter cells.

The process of mitosis occurs in five stages, called interphase, prophase, metaphase, anaphase, and telophase. The diagram below will help explain the stages of mitosis.

To remember the stages of mitosis, use the mnemonic **IPMAT**.

I: Interphase contains the word "*inter*." "*Inter*" means "between" and interphase is when the cell is *between* divisions. During interphase the cell is working on growing larger, but not dividing. At the end of interphase, the cell produces a duplicate of each of its chromosomes.

P: Prophase contains the prefix "*pro*." "*Pro*" often means "first." What must happen *first* if a cell is to divide? First the chromosomes must organize themselves into pairs and the nuclear membrane must dissolve.

M: Metaphase begins with "m" for middle. The chromosomes and their newly made copies line up in the *middle* of the cell.

A: Anaphase begins with "a" for apart. The chromosomes move *apart* to each side of the cell.

T: Telophase begins with "t" for two. The cell, which now has a complete set of chromosomes on each side, divides into two. When mitosis is complete there are two cells, each with the normal number of chromosomes. Thousands of cells undergo mitosis daily in the human body.

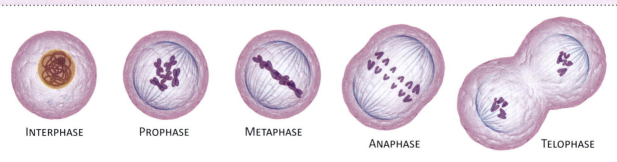

INTERPHASE   PROPHASE   METAPHASE   ANAPHASE   TELOPHASE

FIGURE 11.10. MITOSIS
The process of mitosis results in two daughter cells, both of which contain the same set of chemical instructions in their chromosomes.

Fertilization

It is only after pollination that fertilization can occur. **FERTILIZATION** is the process of fusion between two gametes: the sperm cell and the egg cell. Fertilization is the most important part of sexual reproduction. At the moment of fertilization a new combination of DNA (chromosomes) is produced. A new, unique organism is formed.

In order for fertilization to occur in a flower, the pollen grain stuck on the sticky stigma grows a long tube which reaches down through the style. The sperm cells contained in the pollen travel within this tube into the ovule, which contain the plant's egg cells. When the sperm and egg nuclei join together, fertilization occurs and a new plant's life begins. The single cell formed by the fusion of the sperm and egg cells is called the **ZYGOTE**. Because half the chemical instructions in the zygote comes from the sperm cell and the other half comes from the egg cell, the zygote is an individual! Even though it may be in a white flower, the zygote could produce pink flowers when it matures, because sexual reproduction has allowed genetic variation. The zygote will grow into an **EMBRYO**, or tiny organism in an early stage of its development. The ovule develops into the cotyledons and seed coat. The ovary becomes the fruit.

Seed Dispersal

The seeds inside the fruits of angiosperms and on the cones of gymnosperms are spread in several different ways. The shape of a seed is related to its method of **SEED DISPERSAL**. Figure 11.11 illustrates seed shapes and agents of dispersal.

Germination

The tiny, new plant inside its seed is alive but not actively growing. When the water and temperature become just right **GERMINATION** occurs. The seed swells, the seed coat splits open, and the embryo uses the food stored in the cotyledons to grow vigorously. If it is on a fertile spot the embryo will take root and grow into a mature plant. Eventually it will produce flowers, and the circle of life will begin again.

FIGURE 11.11.
SEED DISPERSAL
Seeds with wings or parachutes (A) are spread by wind. The coconut (B) is designed to float on water. Some seeds (C) stick to animals. Others (D) are used by animals for food and are carried away and buried. Even gravity can help in seed dispersal by pulling fruits and nuts downhill.

Worksheets:
11.1–11.4

Diagram:
11.5–11.6

Experiment:
11.7

Microscope:
11.8

FIGURE 11.12.
GERMINATION
Seeds will germinate if the environmental conditions are right for that species of seed.

KINGDOM ARCHAEA

KINGDOM BACTERIA

KINGDOM PROTISTA

KINGDOM FUNGI

KINGDOM PLANTAE

KINGDOM ANIMALIA

ANIMALS

One is constantly reminded of the infinite lavishness and fertility of Nature—inexhaustible abundance amid what seems enormous waste. And yet when we look into any of her operations that lie within reach of our minds, we learn that no particle of her material is wasted or worn out. It is eternally flowing from use to use, beauty to yet higher beauty; and we soon cease to lament waste and death, and rather rejoice and exult in the imperishable, unspendable wealth of the universe.

—John Muir

FIGURE 12.1.
Pelagia noctiluca is a jellyfish which can glow in the dark.

ANIMALS

Taxonomy Refresher

Carolus Linnaeus used Latin names and seven taxons to group plants and animals according to their structure. Because the gigantic sulfur-bottom whale (also called the blue whale) is multicellular, has no cell walls, and eats small, shrimp-like krill by the tons, this whale is in the Kingdom Animalia. Since it has a spinal cord in a backbone like fish, frogs, and flamingoes, the blue whale is a member of Phylum Chordata in Subphylum Vertebrata. But the big "blue" doesn't have scales like fish do, and its giant heart has four chambers, one more than a frog's heart. Further, Mrs. Sulfur-bottom gives birth to her little baby (about the size of two mini-vans!), unlike the flamingo, which lays eggs.

The facts that blue whales live in the ocean like fish and are good swimmers like frogs are not what is important in classifying them. Even if it were the pink whale instead of the blue whale, it would not be in the same class as the flamingo! **Animals are classified according to their structure.** Since a whale is warm-blooded and has hair, it is more like you than it is like a fish, frog, or flamingo. As a result, it is in the same taxonomic class as human beings: Class Mammalia.

The whale shares Order Cetacea with the very similar porpoises and dolphins, which all have flippers. The giant blue whale, like the other baleen whales, has no teeth and is in the Family Balaenopteridae. Figure 12.2 compares the taxons for several animals.

The object of the chart in Figure 12.2 is **not** that you memorize a lot of big names. There are four main ideas that the chart should help you to understand:

1. As two creatures have more and more structures that are similar, they are more alike and have more taxons in common.

2. No two species will have the same set of seven taxons.

	 BLUEGILL	 AMERICAN FLAMINGO	 HUMAN	 BOTTLENOSE DOLPHIN	 HUMPBACK WHALE	 BLUE WHALE
KINGDOM	Animalia	Animalia	Animalia	Animalia	Animalia	Animalia
PHYLUM	Chordata	Chordata	Chordata	Chordata	Chordata	Chordata
CLASS	Osteichthyes	Aves	Mammalia	Mammalia	Mammalia	Mammalia
ORDER	Perciformes	Phoenicopteri-formes	Primates	Cetacea	Cetacea	Cetacea
FAMILY	Centrarchidae	Phoenicopte-ridae	Hominidae	Delphinidae	Balaenopteri-dae	Balaenopteri-dae
GENUS	Lepomis	Phoenicop-terus	Homo	Tursiops	Megaptera	Balaenoptera
SPECIES	macrochirus	ruber	sapiens	truncatus	novaeangliae	musculus

FIGURE 12.2. EXAMPLES OF TAXONS

Since taxonomy is based on structure, how organisms are classified helps indicate which organisms are most closely related. Each species of organism has a unique set of seven taxons. No other species can share *all* of these seven taxons. Depending on how alike they are, species can share up to six of the same taxons. The greater the similarity, the more taxons the two species will share. For instance, the humpback whale and the blue whale share five taxons, which indicates that they are structurally very similar.

3. Organisms in the same phylum are also in the same kingdom, and organisms in the same class are also in the same phylum and kingdom. The same principle applies to organisms in the same order, family, or genus.

4. The genus and species names together form the scientific name for each kind of organism.

Animal Kingdom

Animals great and small, long and short, common and rare, all share several characteristics. The classification of animals begins with these characteristics of the Kingdom **ANIMALIA**:

1. Animals are **multicellular eukaryotes.** All of their many cells have nuclear membranes and organelles.

2. Animals are **heterotrophic.** Since they do not have chloroplasts, animals must ingest food.

3. Animals are made of numerous tiny cells with **no cell walls.**

The organisms in Kingdom Animalia are very diverse. For instance, the longest of all animals is over fifty-four meters long, which is as long as a line that starts on the front cover of this book and is drawn across the front and back of every page up to the glossary. This long sea creature, the ribbon worm, almost looks like a wide pencil line. Its scientific name, <u>Lineus longissimus</u>, means "the longest line."

Although the ribbon worm is long, it is not very impressive in terms of overall size. Neither is the most numerous type of animal, a marine nematode, which is nearly microscopic in size.

FIGURE 12.3.
CLASSIFICATION OF
KINGDOM ANIMALIA

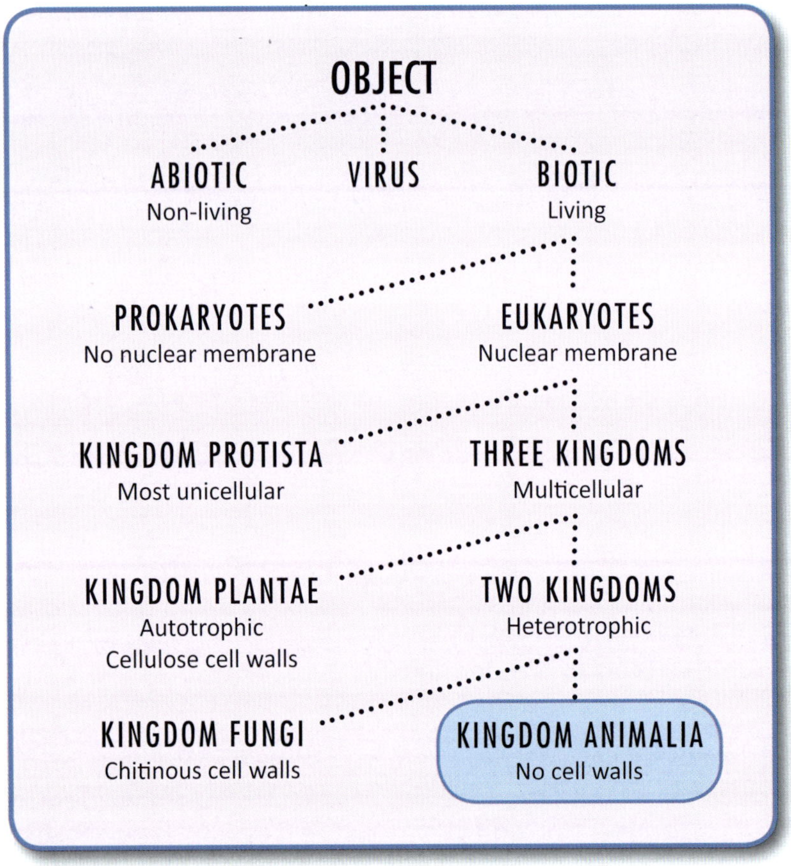

```
                    OBJECT

    ABIOTIC        VIRUS        BIOTIC
    Non-living                  Living

    PROKARYOTES              EUKARYOTES
    No nuclear membrane      Nuclear membrane

    KINGDOM PROTISTA         THREE KINGDOMS
    Most unicellular         Multicellular

    KINGDOM PLANTAE          TWO KINGDOMS
    Autotrophic              Heterotrophic
    Cellulose cell walls

    KINGDOM FUNGI            KINGDOM ANIMALIA
    Chitinous cell walls     No cell walls
```

The blue whale is the most massive animal ever to live. It would take approximately 1,900 Average Arnolds to add up to just one of these giant creatures! How many elephants do you think it takes to equal the size of just one blue whale? Don't just guess. Use this data to calculate your answer: it would take over 86 Average Arnolds to equal one elephant.*

There are ten main phyla of animals (Figure 12.5), and nine of them are described in this chapter. We will save the phylum to which human beings belong, Phylum Chordata, for the next chapter.

FIGURE 12.4. BLUE WHALE
This illustration shows the size of a blue whale in comparison to a human (see scuba diver in top right corner).

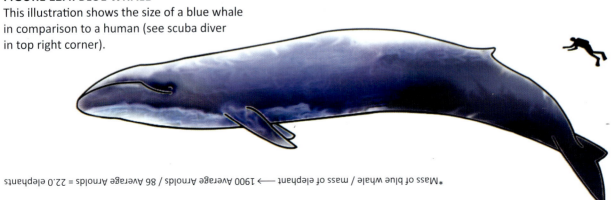

*Mass of blue whale / mass of elephant ⟶ 1900 Average Arnolds / 86 Average Arnolds = 22.0 elephants

FIGURE 12.5.
TEN MAIN PHYLA IN KINGDOM ANIMALIA

All the members of Kingdom Animalia are multicellular, heterotrophic eukaryotes with no cell walls. For a more detailed chart of the ten main phyla of animals, see Figure 12.30 at the end of this chapter.

PHYLUM PORIFERA Body full of pores *(Sponges)*	**PHYLUM CNIDARIA** Bag-like body *(Jellyfish)*

PHYLUM PLATYHELMINTHES Ribbon-like body *(Flatworms)*	**PHYLUM NEMATODA** Thread-like body *(Roundworms)*	**PHYLUM ANNELIDA** Many segments or rings *(Segmented worms)*	**PHYLUM MOLLUSCA** Muscular foot *(Mollusks)*
PHYLUM ARTHROPODA Chitinous exoskeleton *(Arthropods)*	**PHYLUM ECHINODERMATA** Spiny skin *(Starfish)*	**PHYLUM HEMICHORDATA** Stomochord *("Almost chordates")*	**PHYLUM CHORDATA** Dorsal nerve cord *(Chordates)*

Phylum Porifera (Sponges)

Do you remember learning that "conifer" means "cone-bearer"? The Phylum **PORIFERA** means "pore-bearer." A **PORE** is a small opening or hole. The porifera are the sponges, which, as adults, are full of holes. The adult sponge, full of pores, is **SESSILE**, which means it is attached by its base to one spot. The young sponge is a larva that swims around finding a place to settle.

There are no organs or systems in a sponge. A sponge's body plan is so simple that if it is cut into pieces, each piece will grow into a whole new sponge. This is called **REGENERATION,** and it is only possible in the lower animals. Your body is much too complex to regenerate anything except skin and small pieces of muscle.

Figure 12.7 is a photo of a sponge's skeleton. Their soft skeletons, made of a chemical called spongin, are useful in washing the family car! Sponges have no nervous system, and thus no eyes, ears, nose, or tongue. Many sponges live in the ocean, but Spongilla sp. is an example of a freshwater sponge.

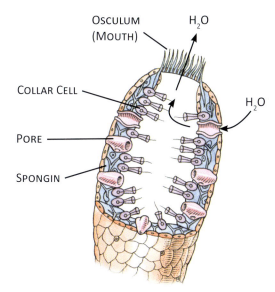

FIGURE 12.6. ADULT SPONGE ANATOMY
The collar cells which line the inside of the sponge beat their flagella to move water, containing food, into the pores and out of the osculum (mouth).

FIGURE 12.7.
SPONGE SKELETONS
The skeletons of sponges can be used for cleaning.

FIGURE 12.8. AZURE VASE SPONGE
Callyspongia plicifera

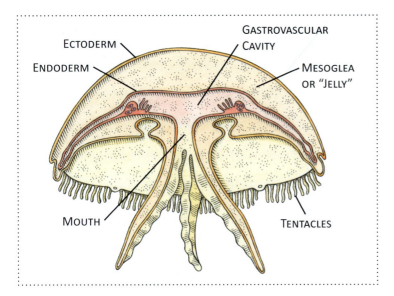

FIGURE 12.9. JELLYFISH ANATOMY

FIGURE 12.10. HYDRA SP.
Due to its many tentacles, Hydra littoralis is named after a mythological creature with many heads.

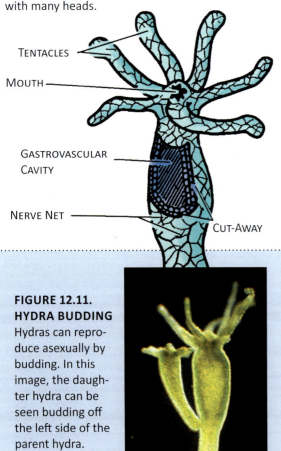

FIGURE 12.11. HYDRA BUDDING
Hydras can reproduce asexually by budding. In this image, the daughter hydra can be seen budding off the left side of the parent hydra.

Phylum Cnidaria (Jellyfish)

Hopefully you have never been stung by a jellyfish's nematocyst, a stinging cell on the end of a jellyfish's tentacles. Washed up on a beach, a jellyfish looks like a lump of clearish jelly. But in the water the graceful, bag-like body, with each **TENTACLE** waving in the currents, displays its **RADIAL SYMMETRY**. Most jellyfish are marine. They float freely with their mouth and tentacles downward.

Jellyfish have only two layers of tissue: the outer layer, called the ectoderm, and the inner layer, called the endoderm. The jelly-like substance in between the two layers of tissue explains why they are called jellyfish. Inside the bag-like body is the gastrovascular cavity where digestion occurs. Jellyfish belong to the Phylum **CNIDARIA**, which is the phylum of animals with bag-like bodies.

Hydra sp. is a freshwater cnidarian which is often sessile but can also move by a somersaulting action. Hydra sp. has no eyes, ears, nose, or tongue, but it does have sensitive skin with a nerve net (see Figure 12.10).

Hydras may reproduce asexually by budding to produce offspring genetically identical to the parent. Sexual reproduction occurs when testes and ovaries form in the ectoderm. Although a single hydra has both male and female characteristics during its lifetime, hydras never fertilize their own eggs because the testes and ovaries form at different times.

Phylum Platyhelminthes (Flatworms)

The Phylum **PLATYHELMINTHES** contains creatures that are more complex than those in Phylum Porifera and Phylum Cnidaria. Their common name refers to the platyhelminthes' ribbon-like body, with no segments. To remember the name, think "platy for flaty!"

The beef tapeworm (Taenia saginata) is actually quite complex when compared to Hydra sp. or Spongilla sp. (Figure 12.12). Beef tapeworms live as larvae in the muscle fibers of cows until the infected meat is eaten by humans. Like other parasitic flatworms, the beef tapeworm has a sucker-like head called a scolex, which it uses to attach itself to the human intestine. Since the USDA (United States Department of Agriculture) inspects meat that goes to market, Taenia saginata is no longer as common in humans as it used to be.

Planaria sp. is a small flatworm that looks cross-eyed (Figure 12.13). A planarian's two **DORSAL** eyespots are sensitive to light but are not like the eyes of more complex animals. A planarian's nervous system, which includes the eyespots, is much more developed than it is in poriferans and cnidarians, but not as developed as in higher animals.

Planarians and other flatworms have three basic layers of tissue, just as your body has. Between the outer and inner layers of tissue is a third layer, the mesoderm, which means "middle skin." The digestive system has only one opening, the mouth, which is on the **VENTRAL** side. The first part of the dead-end digestive tube is the pharynx.

Planarians are hermaphroditic! This is not as bad as it sounds, but it is interesting to understand where such a word came from. Hermes was a handsome Greek god and Aphrodite was the Greek goddess of love and beauty. "Hermaphroditic" means having both male and female characteristics. We could call the sponges and jellyfish hermaphroditic also because, like planarians, each sponge and jellyfish can make both sperm and egg cells.

Members of Phylum Platyhelminthes may be cut into two similar halves. This is a type of symmetry termed **BILATERAL SYMMETRY.** "Bi-," as used in "bicycle," means "two," and "lateral" means "side." Bilateral symmetry is found in most of the more complex animals.

Flatworms like Planaria sp. are still not too complicated to regenerate missing parts. In *Animals without Backbones* by Ralph Buchsbaum you can see a photograph of a five-headed planarian grown in the lab by partially cutting the head and allowing regeneration!

FIGURE 12.12. BEEF TAPEWORM
The typical flat shape and ribbon-like body of a flatworm is evident in the beef tapeworm above. Beef tapeworms can grow to be as long as 20 meters. Tapeworm larvae in infected meat are killed by properly cooking the meat.

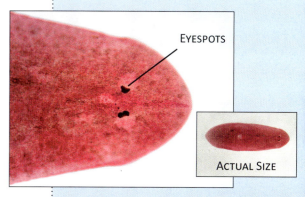

EYESPOTS

ACTUAL SIZE

FIGURE 12.13. A PLANARIAN'S EYESPOTS

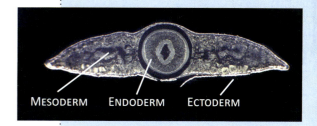

MESODERM   ENDODERM   ECTODERM

FIGURE 12.14.
CROSS-SECTION OF PLANARIAN
Planaria sp. and other members of the Phylum Platyhelminthes have three basic tissue layers.

FIGURE 12.15.
PSEUDOCEROS BIFURCUS
Marine flatworms, Genus Pseudoceros, come in a wide variety of colors and patterns, including stripes and polka dots.

FIGURE 12.16. NEMATODE
This parasitic nematode worm (Ascaris lumbricoides) inhabits the small intestine of its human host. An adult female, as seen here, may measure 35 cm in length.

Phylum Nematoda (Roundworms)

The most numerous animal of all is a little-known marine nematode, and there are more than 1,000,000 nematodes in each shovelful of garden soil. I'll bet you have never even heard of nematodes, let alone seen one! Hopefully you have never suffered from any parasitic nematodes.

NEMATODA means "thread-like," which is a good name for these tiny, round worms in the Phylum Nematoda. No respiratory or circulatory systems are present in nematodes, but they do have a complete digestive system with both a mouth and an anus.

Hookworm is a nematode which was once a common parasite in the southern United States. The nematode sticks to bare feet and bores through the sole of the foot. Inside its host, hookworms produce zygotes through sexual reproduction; the zygotes are then eliminated from the body with the solid waste. Shoes and sewage treatment plants have greatly reduced infestations of hookworm.

When Moses told the Jewish tribes not to eat pork, perhaps he was protecting them from Trichinella spiralis, a nematode that infests pork. In the U.S., thorough cooking of pork products has made pork worm less of a threat. Trichinella spiralis is still in most pork products, but is killed by the heat in well-cooked meat.

Phylum Annelida (Segmented Worms)

The segmented worms have bodies made of many rings. For example, the earthworm, Lumbricus terrestris, has the typical segmented body that is the outstanding structure of the Phylum **ANNELIDA**. The name "Annelida" comes from the root word "*annus*," which is Latin for "circuit" or "year." Our word "annual," meaning one circuit around the sun, has the same origin. We used the term "annulus" to name the ring around the stipe of some mushrooms. Annelida refers to the ringed bodies of the segmented worms.

FIGURE 12.17.
Earthworms help to mix the soil.

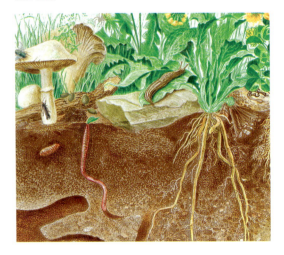

Earthworms have more important roles than just serving as fishing bait! In Chapter 9 you learned that we, and most other creatures, depend on plants for food, because they are the main autotrophs on earth. Plants, of course, depend on the soil to grow! Good soil is formed by the action of the earthworm. This lowly annelid adds organic matter to dirt particles. It opens the soil up for air and water to enter and mixes the soil.

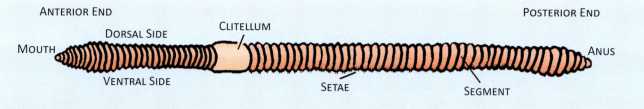

FIGURE 12.18. ANNELID ANATOMY
Lumbricus terrestris, the earthworm, has circulatory, digestive, nervous, and excretory systems, but no skeletal system.

Annelids are much more complex than the animals in the other phyla we have investigated so far. Refer to Figure 12.18 to see the parts of an annelid. Inside the third segment of Lumbricus sp. is a simple brain connected to a ventral nerve cord and many nerve cells throughout the body. There are five "hearts" connected to a ventral artery and to a dorsal blood vessel with valves. This blood system is a closed system, as is yours, which means that the blood is circulated through a network of blood vessels.

The worm's digestive system is the most complex yet of the phyla we have studied so far. Just like the nematodes, worms have both an **ANTERIOR** opening, the mouth, and a **POSTERIOR** opening, the anus. With no jaws or teeth, the worm uses its pharynx to draw in the food, which moves through the esophagus, crop, and gizzard. Finally, the food reaches the intestine at around the 19th segment.

Earthworms use their mucus-covered skin for breathing, and they are covered with stiff little bristles, called setae, for locomotion. Earthworms also have tubes called nephridia, used to excrete nitrogen compounds. The clitellum (see Figure 12.18) is a specialized region used for reproduction. Like poriferans, cnidarians, and platyhelminthes, annelids are hermaphroditic. However, they will not fertilize their own egg cells.

Phylum Mollusca (Mollusks)

Phylum **MOLLUSCA** contains soft-bodied animals with a muscular foot. The mollusk's body is muscular but not segmented. The soft body often has a hard shell.

Snails, with just one shell, are univalves. Clams and oysters are bivalves because they have two shells. The octopus and squid are both called cephalopods (SEF-uh-luh-pods), which literally means "head-foot." An important and, for many people, favorite, use of mollusks is as food!

**FIGURE 12.19.
CEPAEA HORTENSIS**
The white-lipped snail is a univalve mollusk.

**FIGURE 12.20.
OCTOPUS BRIAREUS**
The Caribbean reef octopus is a mollusk that does not have a shell.

FIGURE 12.21. MYTILUS EDULIS
The blue mussel is a bivalve mollusk.

Phylum Arthropoda (Arthropods)

"*Podos*" means "foot" in Greek. We used that root word in "pseudopod," the "false foot" of the amoeba; and in "cephalopod," the "head-foot" bodies of snails, octopuses, and squid. Crabs, spiders, thousand-leggers, and insects all belong to Phylum **ARTHROPODA**. "*Arthro-*" comes from a Greek word that means "jointed." Arthropoda means "jointed foot." The outstanding structure of Phylum Arthropoda is a chitinous **EXOSKELETON**. This skeleton on the outside, like a suit of armor, can only bend at the joints.

There are more kinds of these joint-footed animals than of all other kinds together. But wait. Didn't we say that a little-known marine nematode is the most numerous animal of all? We did, and that's correct! There are many more of that one kind of nematode than of any other species of animal. But there are more species of arthropods than of any other phylum of animals.

CLASS	STRUCTURE	EXAMPLES	NOTES
Arachnida (spiders, ticks, & scorpions)	Two body parts Eight legs	 ◀ Garden spider— Araneus diadematus Dog tick— Dermacentor variabilis	Spiders control pests. Ticks and mites are parasites and vectors.
Crustacea (crabs, lobsters, & crayfish)	Two body parts Four antennae Ten legs (two special)	 ◀ Sally Lightfoot crab— Grapsus Grapsus Eastern crayfish— Cambarus bartoni	Important food sources for humans.
Chilopoda (hundred-leggers)	Flattened body One pair of legs on each segment	 ◀ Amazonian giant centipede— Scolopendra gigantea	Hundred-leggers are carnivorous.
Diplopoda (thousand-leggers)	Rounded body Two pairs of legs on each segment	 ◀ American giant millipede— Narceus americanus	Thousand-leggers are herbivorous. "Di-" in "Diplopoda" refers to two pairs of legs per segment.
Insecta (insects)	Three body parts Six legs Two antennae	 House fly— Musca domestica ◀ Carpenter ant— Camponotus sp.	"Insecta" means "cut inward," referring to the three body parts.

FIGURE 12.22. CLASSES OF ARTHROPODS
All of the examples given above have exoskeletons.

The five main classes of the Phylum Arthropoda are compared in Figure 12.22. Just about everybody can find their most "unfavorite" creatures on this list, as well as pests that cause us to support a multi-billion-dollar chemical pest control industry. Also on this list are important natural "pest controls" that kill and eat pests which destroy our foods, and plant pollinators that give us bountiful fruit and vegetable harvests.

The arthropods can be as beautiful as a butterfly, as deadly as a scorpion, as nasty as a cockroach, and as interesting as a whirligig on a cool pond. Such great variety in this one phylum requires a closer look.

Phylum Arthropoda boasts species that can communicate with great precision. The figure-eight dance of the honey bee is still being studied to discover how the bee directs others from the hive straight to a food source. Phylum Arthropoda also includes insects with complex societies. Ants, for example, show division of labor and a type of caste system.

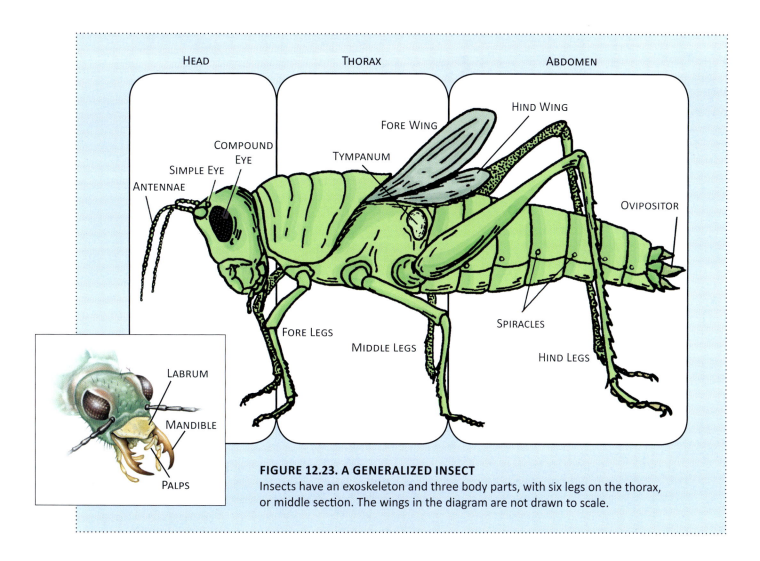

FIGURE 12.23. A GENERALIZED INSECT
Insects have an exoskeleton and three body parts, with six legs on the thorax, or middle section. The wings in the diagram are not drawn to scale.

Arthropods, insects in particular, are disease vectors of major importance. Diseases carried by flies, ticks, and mosquitoes have only been understood since the late 1800s. Some of these diseases carried by insect vectors are being investigated today. You will learn more about disease in another chapter.

Arthropods are often a person's favorite dish when they go out to eat at a restaurant. You have probably had lobster or crab for dinner, leaving

ORDER DIPTERA

Common greenbottle
(Lucilia caesar)

ORDER ORTHOPTERA

Eastern lubber grasshopper
(Romalea microptera)

ORDER COLEOPTERA

Stag beetle
(Lucanus cervus)

ORDER HYMENOPTERA

Potter wasp
(Katamenes arbustorum)

ORDER HEMIPTERA

Forest bug
(Pentatoma rufipes)

ORDER ODONATA

Southern hawker dragonfly
(Aeshna cyanea)

ORDER LEPIDOPTERA

Monarch butterfly
(Danaus plexippus)

FIGURE 12.24. SOME ORDERS OF INSECTS
Each order contains many families, each of which contains many genera and species of interest.

on your plate the chitinous exoskeleton that is the trademark of all the arthropods.

Class Insecta is huge in terms of number of species. Insects can be found almost anywhere on earth where there is life. The great variety of insect body shapes are illustrated in Figure 12.24.

Insects change their shapes during different stages of their lives. The process of changing shape to reach adulthood is called **METAMORPHOSIS**. In complete metamorphosis, the insect goes through four stages: egg ⟶ larva ⟶ pupa ⟶ adult. Sometimes an insect **LARVA** is referred to as a caterpillar. The **PUPA** of a butterfly is called a chrysalis and that of a moth is a cocoon.

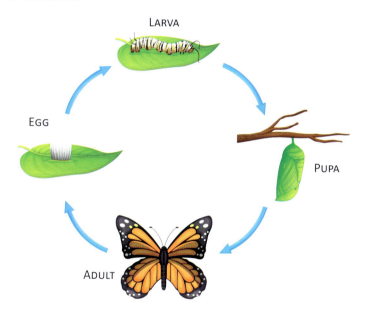

LARVA

EGG

PUPA

ADULT

FIGURE 12.25. COMPLETE METAMORPHOSIS
This diagram of the four stages of complete metamorphosis represents the life cycle of the monarch butterfly, Danaus plexippus.

The familiar red-legged grasshopper, Melanopus femurrubrum, undergoes what is called incomplete metamorphosis in which the young, called a **NYMPH**, looks almost like the adult. After hatching from the egg, a nymph grows and molts until it reaches its adult size.

Phylum Echinodermata (Starfish)

Starfish, and their marine relatives the pretty sand dollars and prickly sea urchins, are animals with spiny skin and radial symmetry. The phylum name **ECHINODERMATA** (pronounced ee-KYE-noh-der-mah-tah) means "spiny skin." We've seen the root word "*derma*" for skin in several terms: the lower and upper epi**dermis** of leaves, the ecto**derm** or outer layer of tissue in animals, the endo**derm** or inner layer of tissue, and the meso-**derm** or "middle skin" in all animals from the flatworms to you!

FIGURE 12.26. SAND DOLLAR
A living sand dollar trying to bury itself in the sand.

FIGURE 12.27. TILED STARFISH
Fromia monilis

FIGURE 12.28. RED SEA URCHIN
Strongylocentrotus franciscanus

Echinoderms display radial symmetry, which means that they have a shape which can be cut into similar pieces like a pizza. Each ray of a starfish has tube feet on the ventral side, while the mouth is located at the center on the ventral side. On the top is a round dot near the center. This dot is used to filter water, and is called the sieve plate.

Clams and other mollusks are favorite foods of the starfish, so you can imagine how unpopular starfish are with fishermen who raise mollusks. People used to try to kill starfish by chopping them up and throwing the pieces back into the sea. By regeneration each piece of the starfish would grow back its missing parts! By not understanding the life science of a starfish, the fishermen were actually helping these pesky echinoderms reproduce asexually.

Phylum Hemichordata (Marine Worms)

Phylum Hemichordata, the "almost chordates," are a small group of animals similar in some ways to echinoderms, and in other ways like the most complex animals—the chordates. The phylum is characterized by bilateral symmetry and a stomochord. All are marine; the acorn worm is an example. For now, we will omit the hemichordates, just as we have skipped some of the less well-known phyla of the animal kingdom.

Worksheets:
12.1–12.2, 12.5–12.6

Diagram:
12.3–12.4

Experiment:
12.7

FIGURE 12.29. ACORN WORM

PHYLUM PORIFERA

Body full of pores
Skeletons made of spongin
(Sponges)

PHYLUM CNIDARIA

Bag-like body
Radial symmetry
(Jellyfish)

PHYLUM PLATYHELMINTHES

Flat, ribbon-like body
Three tissue layers
(Flatworms)

PHYLUM NEMATODA

Round cross-section
Complete digestive system
(Roundworms)

PHYLUM ANNELIDA

Many segments or rings
(Segmented worms)

PHYLUM MOLLUSCA

Soft-bodied with muscular
foot; often a hard shell
(Mollusks)

PHYLUM ARTHROPODA

Chitinous exoskeleton
Jointed body
(Arthropods)

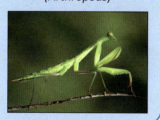

PHYLUM ECHINODERMATA

Spiny skin
Radial symmetry
(Starfish)

PHYLUM HEMICHORDATA

Bilateral symmetry
Stomochord
("Almost chordates")

PHYLUM CHORDATA

Dorsal nerve cord
Internal skeleton
(Chordates)

SUBPHYLUM VERTEBRATA
Backbone (vertebral column)
(Vertebrates)

CLASS AGNATHA

CLASS CHONDRICHTHYES

CLASS OSTEICHTHYES

CLASS AMPHIBIA

CLASS REPTILIA

CLASS AVES

CLASS MAMMALIA

FIGURE 12.30. MAIN PHYLA IN THE KINGDOM ANIMALIA

KINGDOM ARCHAEA

KINGDOM BACTERIA

KINGDOM PROTISTA

KINGDOM FUNGI

KINGDOM PLANTAE

KINGDOM ANIMALIA

13

CHORDATES

There is a hierarchy of life in the universe
and the life of man is higher than any other
life, not because he has nutritive powers
like a plant, not because he has generative
powers like a beast, but because he has
thinking and willing powers like God. These
constitute his greatest claim to life and in
losing these he becomes like to a beast.

—Archbishop Fulton J. Sheen

FIGURE 13.1.
The Indian peafowl (Pavo cristatus) is a member of Class Aves in Phylum
Chordata.

CHORDATES

Chordates

All animals in the Phylum **CHORDATA** possess a dorsal nerve cord, an internal skeleton and, at some point in their development, gill slits. Chordates have complex bodies with bilateral symmetry. The name "Chordata" refers to the notochord which grows along the dorsal side of chordates while they are embryos and which develops into the backbone. There are several chordates in special subphyla whose notochords do not develop into backbones. You, and most familiar animals, belong to the Subphylum **VERTEBRATA**. Each piece of the backbone is a vertebra, thus the subphylum name is Vertebrata (Figures 13.2–3).

The Phylum Chordata, Subphylum Vertebrata is divided into seven main classes.

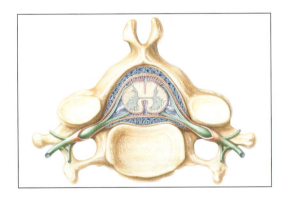

FIGURE 13.2. VERTEBRA
Cross-section of spinal column showing how vertebrae in the backbone protect the spinal cord.

FIGURE 13.3. SKELETON
The spinal column, or backbone, is plainly visible in this illustration of a crocodile skeleton. The spinal column is made up of many individual vertebrae which protect the bundle of nerves called the spinal cord.

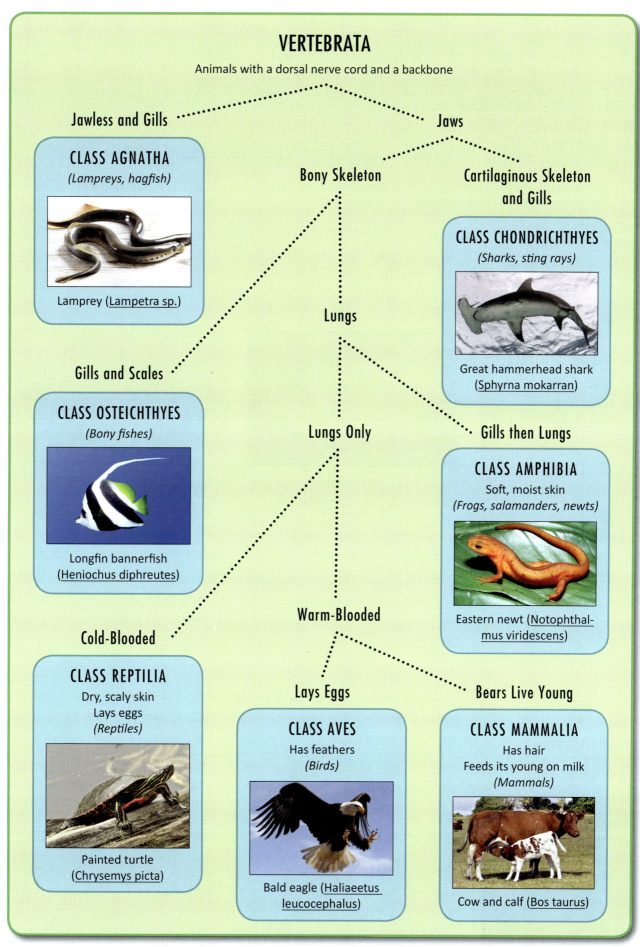

FIGURE 13.4. MAIN CLASSES IN THE SUBPHYLUM VERTEBRATA

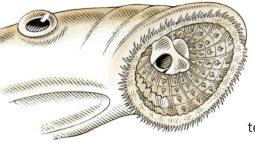

FIGURE 13.5.
ICHTHYOMYZON CASTANEUS
Instead of jaws, the sea lamprey has a toothed, funnel-like mouth.

Lampreys

Class **AGNATHA** contains **COLD-BLOODED**, jawless animals with gills. Lampreys and hagfish are jawless fish (Figure 13.5). Like other cold-blooded animals, a lamprey or hagfish cannot maintain its body temperature independent of its environment.

Sharks

Class **CHONDRICHTHYES** is the class of cold-blooded fish with jaws and **GILLS**. Sharks and stingrays are called cartilaginous fish because their skeletons are made of cartilage instead of bone. These fish have gill slits with no cover over them (Figure 13.6).

FIGURE 13.6. BLACK TIP REEF SHARK
This shark's gill slits are clearly visible.

FIGURE 13.7. RAINBOW TROUT

Fish

Class **OSTEICHTHYES** contains cold-blooded animals with gills and scales and with a skeleton of bone. The word root "*ichthyes*" means "fish." So an ichthyologist is a person who studies fish, and osteichthyes ("*osteo*" means bone) are the bony fish (Figure 13.7).

The gills of the bony fish are covered by flaps called opercula, unlike the exposed gill slits of the model used to film the horror movie *Jaws*. The great white shark is **not** a member of Class Osteichthyes because its skeleton is **not** bone.

FIGURE 13.8. HYPEROLIUS
MARMORATUS
Painted reed frog

Amphibians

Class **AMPHIBIA** contains cold-blooded animals with a moist, soft skin (Figure 13.8). The young have gills; the adults breathe with **LUNGS**.

Can you determine the meaning of the word "amphibia"? It is made of two root words: "*amphi-*" and "*bio*." You may know what an amphibious airplane is, or perhaps you are ambidextrous. An amphibious plane can land on water or solid ground. If you are ambidextrous, you can write with both your left and your right hands. "*Amphi*" (or "*ambi*") means "double"

or "both." "*Bio*" means "life." Class Amphibia is so named because its members live both in water and on land.

A female frog, with lungs, lays her eggs in water. The tadpoles that form have gills and live in the water. As they grow, the tadpoles develop lungs and are able to leave the water. See the newt, another amphibian, pictured in Figure 13.4 at the beginning of the chapter.

In winter frogs **HIBERNATE** in the mud of ponds and streams. In the summer, if the weather gets too hot and dry, the frogs may **ESTIVATE**. Estivation, like hibernation, is when an organism's metabolism slows down and the animal survives without eating. Estivation occurs in the summertime, hibernation in the winter.

At one time people believed that frogs could form automatically out of mud. This mistaken theory of spontaneous generation may have been caused in part by the habit of frogs to estivate. In 1668 Francesco Redi of Italy proved that living things do not spontaneously arise from non-living things. His experiment with pieces of meat and flies showed that animals are generated only by other living animals.

Reptiles

The name for Class **REPTILIA** means "creeping animals." All reptiles, great and small, are cold-blooded and must maintain their body temperature by absorbing heat from their environment. Most reptiles have a three-chambered heart and dry, scaly skin. Unlike amphibians, reptiles only have lungs, and they do not return to the water to reproduce. Lizards, turtles, and many snakes lay leathery eggs on land after internal fertilization.

Crocodiles and alligators are **CARNIVORES**, as are many snakes. Many of the lizards are **INSECTIVORES**. Turtles tend to be **OMNIVORES**, which means they will eat many different kinds of foods. An animal that eats just plants is an **HERBIVORE**.

FIGURE 13.9. ALLIGATOR MISSISSIPPIENSIS
American Alligator

FIGURE 13.10. BALD EAGLE
Haliaeetus leucocephalus

FIGURE 13.11. PHEASANT
Phasianus colchicus

FIGURE 13.12. MALLARD DUCK
Anas platyrhynchos

Birds

Birds are good *aviators*. *Aviation* refers to flying. An *aviary* is a large bird cage. The Latin word *"avis"* means "bird," and Class **AVES** is for the birds! Now that we have "aves" figured out, what do you suppose is the name of a person who studies birds? Would you believe it is "ornithologist"? An ornithologist is a person who studies birds. The root word in this case is from the Greek word for bird, *"ornithos."*

Members of Class Aves all have feathers, but they also have scales! Bird feet are scaly. Birds are **WARM-BLOODED**, which means that they can maintain a steady body temperature regardless of environmental temperatures (within limits). Most birds can fly.

The varied beaks and feet of birds are excellent examples of how shape is related to function. A bald eagle's talons are designed for grabbing prey (Figure 13.10), a pheasant's feet are good for walking (Figure 13.11), and a duck's webbed feet are perfect paddles (Figure 13.12). In these same birds we see a sharp, hooked beak for tearing meat, a stout, pointed beak for seeds, and a spoon-shaped beak for digging worms and waterweeds out of the mud.

The familiar robin's nest is evidence of the way birds reproduce by laying eggs on land. Unlike the eggs of reptiles, bird eggs have fragile shells, and the young of most birds require parental care.

Mammals

Like the birds, the animals in Class **MAMMALIA** are warm-blooded animals with a four-chambered heart. Unlike birds, or any other animals, mammals have hair and mammary glands (Figure 13.13). These mammary glands produce milk to feed the young that are born alive. Because of selective breeding, a modern cow's mammary glands produce enough milk to provide us with ice cream, cheeses, whipped cream, butter, whole and skim milk, in addition to feeding her calf.

Most mammals live inside their mothers before birth, developing within the **UTERUS**, or womb. While in the uterus, the young mammal is attached to the **PLACENTA**, a special organ visible in Figure 13.14. The placenta is a capillary-rich organ which allows the diffusion of food, oxygen, and wastes to and from the unborn and its mother. Although you, and other placental mammals, received food and oxygen from your mother while inside the uterus, the placenta ensured that your blood never mixed

FIGURE 13.13. MAMMALS
The mammary glands of an elephant, like those of many other mammals, are inside the udder. Mammary glands are the structural characteristic used to place animals into Class Mammalia.

with your mother's. An embryo can actually have a different blood type than his or her mother! Your belly button is the point at which you were attached to your placenta by your umbilical cord as your life began inside your mother.

Most mammals possess a placenta and belong to Subclass Eutheria (Figure 13.15). The platypus and the spiny anteater are a couple of egg-laying mammals, belonging to Subclass Protheria (Figure 13.16). The opossum (Didelphis virginiana) kangaroo, and koala have a subclass of their own, Metatheria, because they have a pouch for

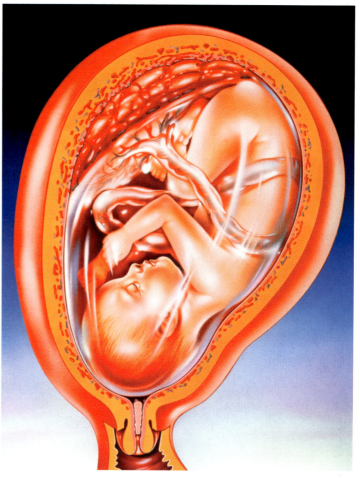

FIGURE 13.14. A PLACENTA
Artwork of a nine-month-old unborn human, Homo sapiens, a placental mammal. The placenta (red, at upper left) is attached to the lining of the uterus (orange) and acts, via the umbilical cord (pink coils), as an organ of respiration, nutrition and excretion for the baby.

FIGURE 13.15. EUTHERIA
The porcupine (Erethizon dorsatum) belongs to Subclass Eutheria because it has a placenta.

FIGURE 13.16. PROTHERIA
The platypus (Ornithorhynchus anatinus) is a mammal which reproduces by laying eggs, so it is in the Subclass Protheria.

FIGURE 13.17. METATHERIA
The koala (Phascolarctos cinereus) has a pouch for its young instead of a placenta, so it is a member of Subclass Metatheria.

their young (Figure 13.17). The opossum has no placenta and the tiny baby opossum must crawl into the mother's pouch to grow. These differences explain why there are subclasses in Class Mammalia.

Class Mammalia is divided into orders on the basis of teeth types and the shape of the legs, feet and hands. Human beings belong to the Order Primates along with monkeys and apes. Humans are classified in Family

FIGURE 13.18. ALOUATTA SENICULUS
Like <u>Homo sapiens</u>, the mantled howler belongs to the Order Primates.

Hominidae, Genus Homo, and species sapiens, so the scientific name of human beings is <u>Homo sapiens</u>. The Latin word "*sapiens*" means "the wise one," which is an appropriate name because only human beings, of all organisms, possess the ability to reason.

With <u>Homo sapiens</u>, you have completed your study of the six kingdoms into which all creatures, great and small, are organized. In the second half of this text, you will study the seven main systems which carry out the life functions for the human body (see Figure 13.19). In order to understand the systems of the body, you will first study the five nutrient groups and their importance for the human body. You will also learn about cellular respiration and photosynthesis, the processes that store and release energy to power the life functions in all the cells of the human body.

Worksheets:
13.1–13.3, 13.5–13.6

Diagram:
13.4

Microscope:
13.7

Test:
Midway Review

Research Paper:
Animal Classification

MUSCULOSKELETAL	DIGESTIVE	CIRCULATORY	RESPIRATORY	EXCRETORY	ENDOCRINE	NERVOUS
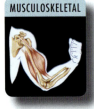		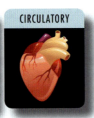	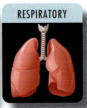	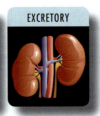	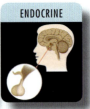	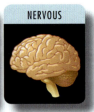

FIGURE 13.19. SYSTEMS OF THE HUMAN BODY
There are seven main systems in the human body.

The Christian Family

Man is unique among all creatures on earth, for man alone is created in the image of his Creator. While there are similarities between man and animals, the differences are of utmost importance not only in understanding our place in the universe, but also in understanding our relationship with our Creator God.

Animals lack that great gift given to man: free will. Free will is closely associated with the gift of reasoning, which animals posses only in a rudimentary way. Man alone is capable of understanding the consequences of his actions, the damage caused by sin, and the great good brought about by his obedience to his Father. Christian parenting includes training in the use of God's unique gifts to man, gifts that animals lack.

FIGURE 13.20

FIGURE 13.21

"Parenting" among fish and amphibians usually ends with the laying of eggs. Other animals care for their young only until offspring are physically capable of meeting their own needs. Human parents, on the other hand, are not only concerned with the physical well-being of their children, but also foster their emotional, intellectual, and spiritual growth.

In the *Catechism of the Catholic Church*, the home is referred to as the "first school of Christian life," in which children are safeguarded in love and learn to worship God. Moreover, human families are modeled after the Holy Trinity, and form the most basic community of all social life. It is in the Christian family that children learn how to use their God-given freedoms in a reasoned, moral way.

The human family's unique place in Creation is discussed in *Familiaris Consortio* (*On the Role of the Christian Family in the Modern World*), where it is noted that this "school of deeper humanity" not only cares for the young, but also for those who are sick and elderly, in a bond of service to one another amidst the sorrows and joys of our earthly life.

Most animals stay with their parents only until offspring have learned how to meet their own physical needs. In contrast, within the sheltering love of a human family, children learn to function not simply as physical beings meeting physical needs, but also as social and spiritual beings created for a purpose in a society, with souls made for the glories of Heaven.

NUTRITION

The eyes of all look hopefully to you;
    you give them their food in due season.
You open wide your hand and satisfy the
    desire of every living thing.

—Psalm 145:15–16

FIGURE 14.1.
There is a lot more to the topic of nutrition than just things you do or don't like to eat.

Nutrition

Living Chemistry

Nutrition! What do you think of when you hear the word "nutrition"? Carrots? Spinach? Liver? Or do you think of candy, cake, and ice cream? There is a lot more to the topic of nutrition than just things you do or don't like to eat.

There are five basic **NUTRIENT** groups: water, fats, proteins, carbohydrates, and vitamins and minerals. Most foods are a combination of these five groups.

Water

FIGURE 14.2. MODEL OF A WATER MOLECULE
Water, also called hydrogen oxide, is necessary for every form of life known to mankind.

Approximately 60% of Average Adam is water. Of course, that means that if you weigh 88 pounds—that is, a mass of 40 kg—then over 52 lbs or 24 kg of you is water! This water is not pure, but is filled with dissolved chemicals of all sorts.

Pure water is made of molecules with two hydrogen atoms fastened to one oxygen atom (Figure 14.2). There are many billions of molecules of water in one tiny drop!

The watery part of your blood, called plasma, must maintain a proper pH. That means there must be the correct number of atoms with positive charges as compared to those atoms with negative charges. Similarly, cells must maintain a proper balance of dissolved minerals in the cytoplasm and nucleoplasm. The concentration of minerals in a cell controls the flow of water into or out of a cell through the process of osmosis. In Chapter 21 we will investigate how your kidneys work like the filter on a swimming pool to maintain proper pH in your blood and mineral balance in your cells.

Humans can often survive up to a month without food, but only a few can last more than four days without water. Depending on your size, you should drink four to eight glasses every day for your body to function at its best.

Fats

The amount of energy in food is measured by how much heat it could produce when burned. The unit of measurement for heat is the calorie. Average Adam needs approximately 2,200 food calories per day, while the average high school girl needs about 200 calories less than Average Adam.

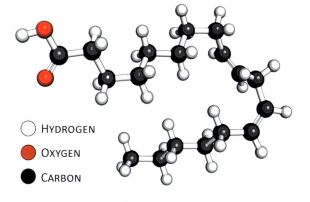

○ HYDROGEN
● OXYGEN
● CARBON

Fats and oils are special compounds used for the long-term storage of energy in a living system. When your body takes in too much chemical energy in the form of food, much of the excess will be saved in **FAT** molecules. These molecules are made of carbon (C), hydrogen (H) and oxygen (O) atoms, with many more hydrogen atoms than oxygen atoms.

FIGURE 14.3. One molecule of linoleic acid, an unsaturated omega-6 fatty acid. Linoleic acid is an essential fatty acid for humans.

Oils and fats are very similar chemicals. The only difference is that oils are liquids at room temperature, while fats are solids. Fats are part of your cell membranes. Oils help lubricate and soften the skin. In your teenage years, your body may get carried away with its oil production for a couple of years. Washing carefully and regularly will keep this excess oil from being a real problem. Without these oils your skin would quickly dry out and crack—like the bottom of a dried-up mud puddle!

You eat fats and oils every day. French fries, potato chips, and foods cooked in oil supply this nutrient in ample amounts. Bacon is mostly fat. Oil-and-vinegar salad dressing is another source of oil in modern diets.

Fats are also good insulators, as the example of the blue whale demonstrates. The blue whale lives most of its life in the cold waters near Antarctica. As a warm-blooded animal, the whale must maintain a higher body temperature than the temperature of the water in which it lives. The whale's fat, or blubber, works like a good coat, or the insulation in a house, to keep its body heat from escaping into the water. The blue whale, like most of its relatives, is an endangered species because it was hunted for the tons of blubber found on each whale. Whale oil was burned in lamps and stoves, a use which demonstrates the fact that fats and oils are high-energy compounds.

FIGURE 14.4. REDHEAD DUCK
Like whales, ducks have thick layers of fat under their skin. This allows them to swim in ice cold water.

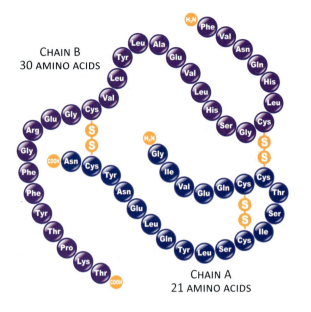

CHAIN B
30 AMINO ACIDS

CHAIN A
21 AMINO ACIDS

FIGURE 14.5. MOLECULE OF HUMAN INSULIN

Proteins are made of many smaller molecules called amino acids. Note that although the amino acids in the picture are drawn as round balls, each one is actually made of many atoms. A molecule of human insulin, pictured above, is one of the smallest and simplest of proteins.

Proteins

Have you ever seen a **PROTEIN**? You have if you have ever looked into a mirror! See that handsome face, that beautiful hair? Protein! Your muscles, skin, and hair are proteins. But what exactly are proteins?

Proteins are large molecules made of smaller molecules called **AMINO ACIDS** (Figure 14.5). There are 22 amino acids necessary for your body to work and grow.

A single protein molecule is made of hundreds, even thousands, of amino acids. Many different proteins may be made from the same 22 amino acids, just as millions of words can be made from just 26 different letters.

Your body can make some of the amino acids it needs, but the so-called "essential amino acids" can be obtained only through your diet. Meat, eggs, and milk are important in a balanced diet if you are to get the essential amino acids your body requires.

Proteins, built up from amino acids, are made of carbon, hydrogen, oxygen, and nitrogen (N). Some proteins also have sulfur (S) or phosphorus (P) in them, but nitrogen is always in every protein.

Hemoglobin is a protein in the blood that contains iron (Fe). Hemoglobin is the protein in your red blood cells that carries the oxygen to every cell in your body. If hemoglobin is to carry oxygen, your diet must provide the iron necessary for the "heme" protein. The chemical formula for hemoglobin gives an idea of how complex protein molecules are: $C_{3032}H_{4816}O_{872}N_{780}S_8Fe_4$. You don't have to know the formula, but you should know that nitrogen must be present if the molecule is a protein.

Some of the most important proteins in your body are enzymes. **ENZYMES** are proteins that help specific chemical reactions to occur. For instance, amylase is a digestive enzyme in your saliva which breaks down starch molecules. Lysozyme, an enzyme in your tears and saliva, breaks down bacterial cell walls. Your life would be over if your enzymes stopped working. A temperature of 106 °F (41.5 °C) or more can change the shape of enzymes so they can no longer perform their job. If your body temperature rises that high it is critical that your receive immediate medical treatment to lower your body temperature.

FIGURE 14.6. PROTEINS

Carbohydrates

A **CARBOHYDRATE** is any of the chemicals in the body made of carbon, oxygen, and hydrogen, with two hydrogen atoms for each oxygen atom. Thus, the name "carb - o - hydr - ate" comes from **carb**-on, **o**-xygen and **hydr**-ogen. Carbohydrates are different from water, which also have two hydrogen atoms for each oxygen atom, because they always include carbon. Unlike protein molecules, carbohydrate molecules do not include any nitrogen atoms. Finally, carbohydrates are unlike fats, which contain many more hydrogen atoms than oxygen atoms, because carbohydrates contain only two hydrogen atoms for each oxygen atom. Smaller carbohydrate molecules are sugars, while bigger ones are starches.

Sugars

For humans, the most important carbohydrate is the simple sugar glucose. Sometimes called blood sugar, **GLUCOSE** is the "gasoline" for the body's engine. Your body can change other carbohydrates, fats, and even proteins into glucose!

The white sugar used for tea or to make cookies is sucrose. Sucrose is a complex sugar that your body breaks into glucose so it can use its chemical energy to stay alive. Glucose is very important!

Looking at Figure 14.8, do you see the ring of carbon and oxygen atoms in the glucose molecule? In a molecule of glucose there is only one sugar ring. This indicates that glucose is a simple sugar, or **MONOSACCHARIDE**. Fructose (fruit sugar) is also a monosaccharide. Sucrose and lactose (milk sugar) are **DISACCHARIDES**, complex sugars. The name "disaccharide" indicates that there are two sugar rings in each molecule of sucrose or lactose. See Figure 14.9.

FIGURE 14.7. SUGARS
Mono- and disaccharides are found in many foods, including milk (lactose), fruit (fructose), honey (glucose), and table sugar (sucrose).

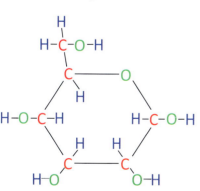

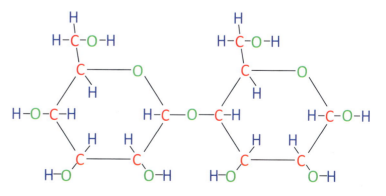

FIGURE 14.8. GLUCOSE
The structure of just one glucose molecule is represented above. $C_6H_{12}O_6$ is the chemical formula. Your cells oxidize glucose to get energy. Billions of glucose molecules were turned into carbon dioxide and water in your body just during the time it took to read this caption.

FIGURE 14.9. SUCROSE
A sucrose molecule is formed from two glucose molecules (minus two hydrogen atoms and one oxygen atom). Your body breaks down sucrose into glucose in the process of digestion. Since there are two sugar rings in a sucrose molecule, sucrose is a disaccharide, a complex sugar.

Starches

Like sugars, starches are carbohydrates. Starch molecules are made of many, many sugar rings fastened together in long chains. Since starch molecules are made of many sugar rings, starches are **POLYSACCHARIDES** (Figure 14.12).

Much of what you eat is starch. Potatoes, crackers, bread, cereal, spaghetti, rice, and noodles are mainly starch. Your body breaks down starch molecules into glucose in the process of digestion.

FIGURE 14.10. STARCHES
Starchy foods must be broken down into glucose before being used to run the engines of life in each cell.

When your body breaks down into glucose the many starches that you eat in your lunch, it cannot use it all right away. It must save the glucose so that it can use some of the glucose each instant from lunchtime until you eat again. To store the glucose, your body takes many of the glucose molecules and joins them into a giant polysaccharide called glycogen. **GLYCOGEN** is a starch made from many glucose molecules. You will learn more about how glycogen is stored in the liver in Chapter 22. Glycogen is how your body saves glucose-energy for a short time. If your body takes in too much energy regularly, then it makes fats to save the energy over a long period of time.

Wood and paper also contain starch. The starch in wood is called cellulose. Paper is made from the cellulose fibers in the wood. Your body cannot break down the cellulose in wood or paper the way it can break down the starches in wheat, rice, or potato products. As a result, wood and paper are not nutrients for humans (this includes junior high school students!). However, there are some animals, fungi, and bacteria that can use wood or paper as a nutrient source.

FIGURE 14.11. Cows, sheep, and other ruminants are able to digest the cellulose in grass and hay because they form a mutualistic relationship with cellulose-digesting bacteria that live in their gut. The cows and sheep provide food and shelter for the bacteria, and in return the bacteria break down the cellulose into a form their hosts can digest. Termites are able to eat wood because of a similar mutualistic relationship with bacteria.

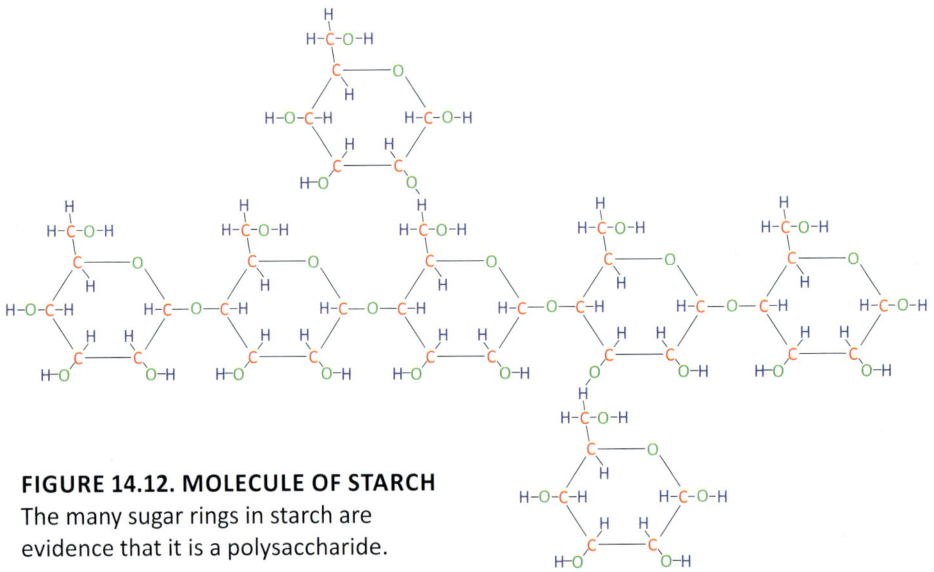

FIGURE 14.12. MOLECULE OF STARCH
The many sugar rings in starch are evidence that it is a polysaccharide.

Vitamins and Minerals

A **VITAMIN** is a complex organic molecule needed by your body in small amounts. For instance, some vitamins are co-enzymes, which means they help your enzymes. Figure 14.13 outlines the more common vitamins, their source, and what parts of your body they affect.

In terms of life science, a **MINERAL** is an inorganic compound or element necessary for an organism in small amounts. Some necessary minerals are listed in Figure 14.14. Diseases will result from a lack of these minerals just as they will if an organism lacks a vitamin.

VITAMIN	MAIN FOOD SOURCES	AFFECTS
A – carotene	carrots, milk	the eyes
B_1 – hiamine	cereals, green vegetables	the nerves
B_2 – riboflavin	cereals, eggs	the skin
B_3 – niacin	fish, meat, milk	digestion
C – ascorbic acid	oranges, lemons, limes	the gums and capillaries
D – calciferol	liver oil, milk	the bones
E – tocopherol	wheat germ	the nerves
K – vitamin K	spinach, lettuce	blood clotting

FIGURE 14.13. VITAMINS

MINERAL	MAIN FOOD SOURCES	AFFECTS
Calcium (Ca)	milk and milk products	bones and teeth
Chlorine (Cl)	table salt	digestion
Iodine (I)	fish, iodized salt	thyroid gland
Iron (Fe)	raisins, spinach, red meats	hemoglobin in red blood cells
Magnesium (Mg)	green vegetables	muscles and nerves
Phosphorus (P)	milk, green vegetables	bones & teeth
Potassium (K)	milk, meat, vegetables	muscle action
Sodium (Na)	table salt	heart beat
Sulfur (S)	green vegetables, fish, legumes	enzymes

FIGURE 14.14. NECESSARY MINERALS

Energy for Life

Nutrition requires more than just the chemicals needed to build a living body. Every living cell—archaean, bacterial, protistan, fungal, plant, and animal—must get energy to stay alive. Almost all cells use the process of **CELLULAR RESPIRATION** to release energy from the chemical bonds of food molecules.

Creatures can obtain the food molecules needed for cellular respiration in two different ways. Organisms that make their own food molecules, usually through the process of photosynthesis, are called **autotrophs**. The plants, as well as some bacteria and protists, are autotrophic. Note that

FIGURE 14.15. AUTOTROPHS AND HETEROTROPHS
Sunlight is used by autotrophs, like the green moss shown here, to make the food all the heterotrophs need. The Indian pipe has no chlorophyll and must grow on the remains of green plants.

even though they can make their own food molecules, autotrophic organisms must also carry out cellular respiration in order to convert the food molecules into energy.

Organisms which must take in food molecules that have been made by autotrophs are called **heterotrophs**. Animals, fungi, and some bacteria and protists are heterotrophic. Fungi, as well as many bacteria and protists, simply take in foods that are already digested. In animals, the food molecules needed for cellular respiration are obtained by ingestion of fats, proteins and carbohydrates. This is followed by digestion, in which the fats, proteins, and carbohydrates are broken down into glucose. Then absorption of the glucose into the cells occurs. Finally, energy is released from the glucose by the process of cellular respiration, which takes place in the "mighty" mitochondria of each living cell (see Chapter 5).

Cellular Respiration

As you have learned, glucose ($C_6H_{12}O_6$) is the food molecule your body uses for energy. Your body uses oxygen in order to break down glucose into carbon dioxide and water, the waste products of cellular respiration. When 12 oxygen atoms combine with the carbon, hydrogen, and oxygen atoms in one glucose molecule, the result is six molecules of carbon dioxide (CO_2), six molecules of water (H_2O), and a tiny burst of energy. This chemical process can be written in the form of an equation, as shown in Figure 14.16.

To store the energy released by cellular respiration, your body "ties it up" in the phosphate bonds of the molecule adenosine triphosphate (ATP). Later, when the energy is needed to power one of the life functions, your cells release it from the ATP molecules by breaking their phosphate bonds. You will learn more about ATP and cellular respiration in a high school biology course.

Photosynthesis

Photosynthesis is the opposite of cellular respiration. In respiration, a more complex molecule (glucose) is broken down to release the energy stored in its chemical bonds. In photosynthesis, light energy is used to take simpler chemicals (CO_2 and H_2O) and make a more complex compound with higher-energy bonds (glucose). The chemical equation for photosynthesis is shown in Figure 14.17.

The process of photosynthesis involves two main phases: the **light phase**, which requires sunlight, and the **dark phase**, which does not require sunlight. In the light phase, chlorophyll, the green pigment in plant cells, helps "capture" light energy. This light energy is used to split water molecules into hydrogen atoms and oxygen atoms.

In the dark phase of photosynthesis, hydrogen atoms are combined with six carbon dioxide molecules to make glucose. The glucose has more energy in its chemical bonds than the carbon dioxide and water did, so it can be used as food energy by living cells.

$$C_6H_{12}O_6 \ + \ 6\,O_2 \ \longrightarrow \ 6\,H_2O \ + \ 6\,CO_2 \ + \ energy$$

glucose + oxygen $\longrightarrow$ *water + carbon dioxide + energy*

FIGURE 14.16. CHEMICAL EQUATION FOR CELLULAR RESPIRATION

$$6\,CO_2 \ + \ 12\,H_2O \ \xrightarrow{\textit{light energy}} \ C_6H_{12}O_6 \ + \ 6\,O_2 \ + \ 6\,H_2O$$

carbon dioxide + water $\xrightarrow{\textit{light energy}}$ *glucose + oxygen + water*

FIGURE 14.17. CHEMICAL EQUATION FOR PHOTOSYNTHESIS

As you can tell from the chemical equation in Figure 14.17, photosynthesis produces oxygen and water as well as glucose. Plants release the oxygen and water through their stomata as waste products. They store the glucose they have produced inside their leaves, stems, roots, and seeds. This glucose is then used to power the plant's life functions, or if the plant is eaten by a heterotroph, it is used to power another creature's life functions! Autotrophs, such as plants, are at the base of all food chains, because they convert the energy from the sun into a form that living cells can use as energy. In other words, your body is actually powered by sunlight!

Worksheets:
14.1–14.8

Formal Lab:
14.9

CHEMOSYNTHESIS

You have learned that autotrophs make their own food, usually through photosynthesis, using the energy of the sun. However, in the pitch-black depths of the ocean floor live colonies of chemosynthetic bacteria, autotrophs that create their own food supply without the benefit of sunlight. How is this possible?

Many of these specialized bacteria are found next to volcanic hydrothermal vents, which spew hot minerals such as hydrogen sulfide from volcanoes beneath the ocean floor into the waters which surround the bacteria. Not through photosynthesis, but through a process called **CHEMOSYNTHESIS**, these chemosynthetic bacteria turn the hydrogen sulfide into the element sulfur, at the same time producing simple nutrients to sustain themselves and the creatures that feed upon them.

In other parts of the ocean depths, chemosynthetic bacteria live and thrive inside of tubeworms. The bacteria absorb hydrogen sulfide from the worms, and then chemosynthesize nutrients which benefit both the bacteria and their host tubeworm.

Just as the process of photosynthesis begins the food chains that feed most animals and people who dwell in the light, the process of chemosynthesis begins a food chain that feeds creatures who dwell in darkness.

FIGURE 14.18. Shrimp and crabs living near the summit of an active submarine volcano graze on the chemosynthetic bacteria which grow on the rocks at hydrothermal vents.

TESTING FOR NUTRIENTS

In order to do science, there has to be
something to observe. Science explains
a great deal about how things behave,
but nothing about why things exist in
the first place.

—Fr. Raymond de Souza

FIGURE 15.1. TEST FOR STARCH
Lugol's solution stains a sample blue-black when starch is present.

TESTING FOR NUTRIENTS

More Chemistry

Chemistry is the basis for many of the advances and discoveries in the life sciences. For instance, the fight against disease is very much a chemical war. Food chains begin with the chemistry of photosynthesis. Your very life depends on the chemical reaction of cellular respiration. The foods we eat are chemicals and our bodies are the test tubes and beakers in which we break down food chemicals and use the pieces for energy or as the building blocks of our bodies!

In this chapter we will learn about several chemical tests which scientists use to measure the amount of energy and type of nutrients in foods.

Calories

The **HEAT** given off is one way of measuring the energy content of foods. Fats have the most energy per gram. However, fats are hard for the body to use. Carbohydrates, more easily digested, are the main energy source for the body. Figure 15.2 is a chart comparing the amount of energy in different foods.

In laboratories where the calories in a food sample must be measured very accurately, a **CALORIMETER** is used. It is possible to determine the approximate calories in a food source by burning it under a test tube of water. For instance, if you want to know the number of calories in a peanut, you would first use a thermometer to record the centigrade temperature of the water. After the peanut has been burned underneath a test tube containing 10 grams (10 ml) of water, you would record the highest **TEMPERATURE** reached by the water. The energy released from the

FIGURE 15.2. CALORIC CONTENT OF FOODS
"Mg" and "I" are the chemical symbols for magnesium and iodine. See Figure 4.4 in Chapter 4 for a list of other minerals important for life.

Food Sample	Calories per 100g	Main Nutrient Group	Main Vitamin/ Mineral
Almonds	630	Fat	E
Apples	60	Carbohydrate	C
Beans, dried	330	Carbohydrate	B_1
Beef, lean	230	Protein	B_2
Bread	260	Carbohydrate	B_1
Butter	730	Fat	A
Cashew	600	Fat	B_2
Peanut	590	Fat	Mg
Tuna, in oil	200	Protein	I
Watermelon	30	Water	C

chemical bonds as the peanut oxidized (burned) can be calculated using the definition of a **CALORIE**:

$$1 \frac{cal}{g \times °C}$$

For example, if the temperature of the 10 g of water was originally 18.1 °C, then after the peanut was burned, the water's temperature was 18.7 °C. The total calories of heat released were **at least**:

$$\text{HEAT} = (\text{mass of } H_2O) \times (1\frac{cal}{g \times °C}) \times (\text{temp. change of } H_2O)$$

$$\text{HEAT} = (10 \text{ g}) \times (1\frac{cal}{g \times °C}) \times (0.6 °C)$$

The units g and °C cancel to give:

$$\text{HEAT} = 10 \times 1 \times 0.6 \text{ calories}$$

$$\boxed{\text{HEAT} = 6 \text{ cal}}$$

Why did I emphasize "**at least**"? Because some of the heat was probably released into the air and test tube instead of into the water.

Carbohydrates

Besides measuring the amount of energy in foods, scientists also use chemical tests to identify foods as belonging to one of the five basic nutrient groups: carbohydrates, fats, proteins, vitamins and minerals, and water. Being able to identify foods in this way allows scientists to make great advances in the study of life science.

For instance, in the chapter on nutrition, we said that sucrose (white sugar), is a carbohydrate, which means that it is made of carbon, oxygen, and hydrogen. Did you think it was strange that black carbon is one of the elements in white sugar? A simple test can be done to prove that white sugar, sucrose, is made of carbon, hydrogen, and oxygen.

If you were a chemist performing this test with the proper equipment, you would place a small amount of white table sugar into a small beaker and saturate it with concentrated sulfuric acid. Sulfuric acid has a very strong ability to take water out of substances, including sugar. ⚠️ It can also remove the water from your clothes and skin, which is why this experiment is not safe to perform at home!

After a few moments the beaker would get so hot that it would be hard to hold. This is because the reaction between sugar and sulfuric acid releases some of the energy in the sugar's chemical bonds. A definite temperature change is one indication that a chemical reaction is occurring. Some of the odor you would notice would be from burnt sugar and some would

FIGURE 15.3. CARBON
The amount of white sugar shown on the left produced the amount of carbon on the right. The hydrogen and oxygen that were bonded to the carbon have escaped as water.

be from sulfur compounds from the acid. In just a few more moments, water, made from the hydrogens and oxygens in the white sugar and the acid, would start to escape as steam. Once the hydrogen and oxygen have escaped, all that would be left in the beaker of sugar would be a large tube of carbon and the sulfuric acid. The carbon would be black and greatly expanded compared to the original sugar (Figure 15.3).

Starches

Starches (polysaccharides) are one of the two major groups of carbo-hydrates. The test which chemists use to determine whether starch is present in a food sample is quite simple.

Place a drop of **LUGOL'S SOLUTION**, which contains iodine, onto the sample being tested. Lugol's solution is brown and starch, if it is pure, is white. If the spot of iodine turns blue-black, then you know that starch is present in the food sample!

Look back at Figure 15.2. Do you think that peanuts will test positive for starch? Don't be too hasty in deciding! The chart only indicates the *main* nutrient group in peanuts. Most foods contain more than one nutrient group.

Simple Sugars

Monosaccharides are the sugars with only one sugar ring. Digestion turns much of the starch and some of the fat in your diet into glucose, a simple sugar. Fruits already contain fructose, another simple sugar, when you ingest them.

FIGURE 15.4. TEST FOR STARCH

FIGURE 15.5. TEST FOR SIMPLE SUGARS

Color After Heating	Amount of Simple Sugar
BLUE	none
GREEN	very little
YELLOW	fair amount
ORANGE RED TO BRICK RED	lots of simple sugar

FIGURE 15.6. SIMPLE SUGAR TEST
When a food is carefully and gently heated with Benedict's solution, a color change indicates the presence of simple sugars.

To test for simple sugar, put some of the food sample into a test tube and cover it with blue **BENEDICT'S SOLUTION**. Heat this mixture for approximately three minutes. Figure 15.6 will allow you to interpret your result.

What color will result when sucrose, table sugar, is tested? Think carefully before you answer; table sugar is a disaccharide!

Proteins

Proteins from milk, eggs, and meat are sources of amino acids in your diet. Proteins are digested into amino acids. Amino acids are used to build and repair cells and to make protoplasm.

⚠️ You should be familiar with the following tests for protein, but do not attempt to perform them at home. The first test involves sodium hydroxide solution and copper sulfate solution. A chemist would perform the test by placing equal amounts of water and a food sample into a test tube and shaking the test tube. He would then stir in an equal amount of 10% sodium hydroxide solution (NaOH) and add three drops of 3% copper sulfate solution ($CuSO_4$). If the mixture in the test tube turned a violet or pink-violet color, it would indicate the presence of proteoses and peptones from protein.

A second test requires just as much caution. A chemist would add the food sample to a small amount of concentrated nitric acid, boil it, pour off the acid, and rinse the sample with water. Then he would cover the sample with ammonium hydroxide (NH_4OH). An orange color would indicate that protein is present.

FIGURE 15.7. TEST FOR PROTEIN
Test tubes containing negative (left) and positive (right) tests for proteins using hydroxide solution and copper sulfate solution. The more purple the solution, the more protein is present.

Vitamins and Minerals

The body uses small amounts of vitamins and minerals for controlling chemical reactions (metabolic regulation). It is easy to test for the presence of several minerals. For instance, adding starch to a solution can be used to test for iodine. If iodine is present, the starch will turn blue-black.

Chlorine can be detected by adding a few drops of silver nitrate solution ($AgNO_3$) to the sample. A white solid, called a **PRECIPITATE**, forms when chlorine is present.

Fats

Fats and oils are mainly used by the body for long-term storage of energy and for insulation. They are also used to lubricate. Cholesterol, a fatty sterol, can be a problem in the heart and arteries of people with excess fat in their diet!

To determine whether there are fats in a food sample, simply rub the food sample on a piece of paper towel or napkin. Fats and oils will usually leave a **TRANSLUCENT** spot on the paper that will not evaporate overnight. Water, unlike fats and oils, will make a spot that quickly dries up.

Water

While water is the most abundant compound in the body, it is not a source of energy for the body. It provides no minerals or vitamins needed for bones and enzymes. Water is not used to get the amino acids needed for the growth and repair of skin, hair, and muscles. Rather, the water in your body is a **SOLVENT** in which the chemicals of life are dissolved and react with each other. Each dissolved chemical is a **SOLUTE**.

You can use blue cobalt chloride paper ($CoCl_2$) to test for the presence of water. Cobalt chloride paper is usually blue, but it turns white in the presence of liquid water or water vapor.

To determine how much of a food sample is water, use a triple beam balance (Figure 2.4 in Chapter 2) to determine the mass of a food sample. Allow the sample to dry out completely, and then use the balance again to determine the mass of what is left after drying.

The following sample problem will illustrate how to determine the percent of water in a food sample. A percent of anything is the amount of that thing divided by the total amount and then multiplied by 100.

FIGURE 15.8.
TEST FOR CHLORINE
When silver nitrate solution is added to chlorine, a white precipitate forms.

FIGURE 15.9.
TEST FOR FAT
Fat leaves a translucent spot on paper which will not evaporate overnight.

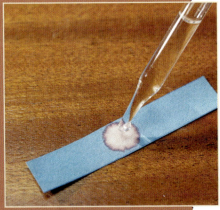

FIGURE 15.10.
TEST FOR WATER
Cobalt chloride ($CoCl_2$) paper turns white on contact with a drop of water.

If a piece of fresh, juicy watermelon has a mass of 10.0 g and after total drying has a mass of only 0.7 grams, then follow these steps to determine what percent of it was water:

1. Subtract the mass of the watermelon when dry (0.7 g) from its mass when it was fresh (10.0 g). This computation gives the mass of the water that was originally in the sample:

$$10.0 \, g - 0.7 \, g = 9.3 \, g$$

2. Divide the mass of the water by the total mass of the food sample when it was fresh:

$$9.3 \, g \, / \, 10.0 \, g = 0.93$$

3. Multiply by 100 to write the answer as a percent. Don't forget to use a percent sign (%).

$$0.93 \times 100 = 93 \, \%$$

So the piece of watermelon was 93% water! No wonder it is called "watermelon"!

$$\% \, THING \, = \, \frac{AMOUNT \, OF \, THE \, THING}{TOTAL \, AMOUNT} \times 100$$

FIGURE 15.11. WATERMELON
Watermelon is more than 92% water! The human body is approximately 60% water. All creatures need H_2O.

 Worksheets: 15.1–15.4

 Experiment: 15.5–15.6

Filtering

Sometimes nutrients from different food groups are mixed together. One way to separate substances from each other is by using a filtering apparatus. A filtering apparatus works because some nutrients are **SOLUBLE**, which means that they will dissolve in water, and some nutrients are not soluble and will not dissolve in water. For example, corn starch and powdered glucose are both white powders. If you have a mixture of them you can separate the mixture by adding water and filtering (see Figure 15.12). The starch would be the **RESIDUE** left in the filter paper. The glucose would be in the **FILTRATE**. Once you evaporate the water from the filtrate, you will have pure glucose.

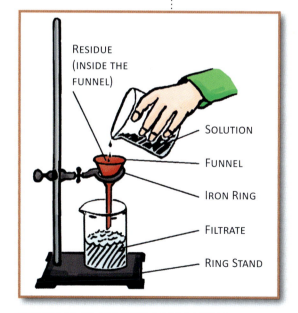

FIGURE 15.12. FILTERING APPARATUS
The ring stand is used to hold the iron ring, which holds the funnel.

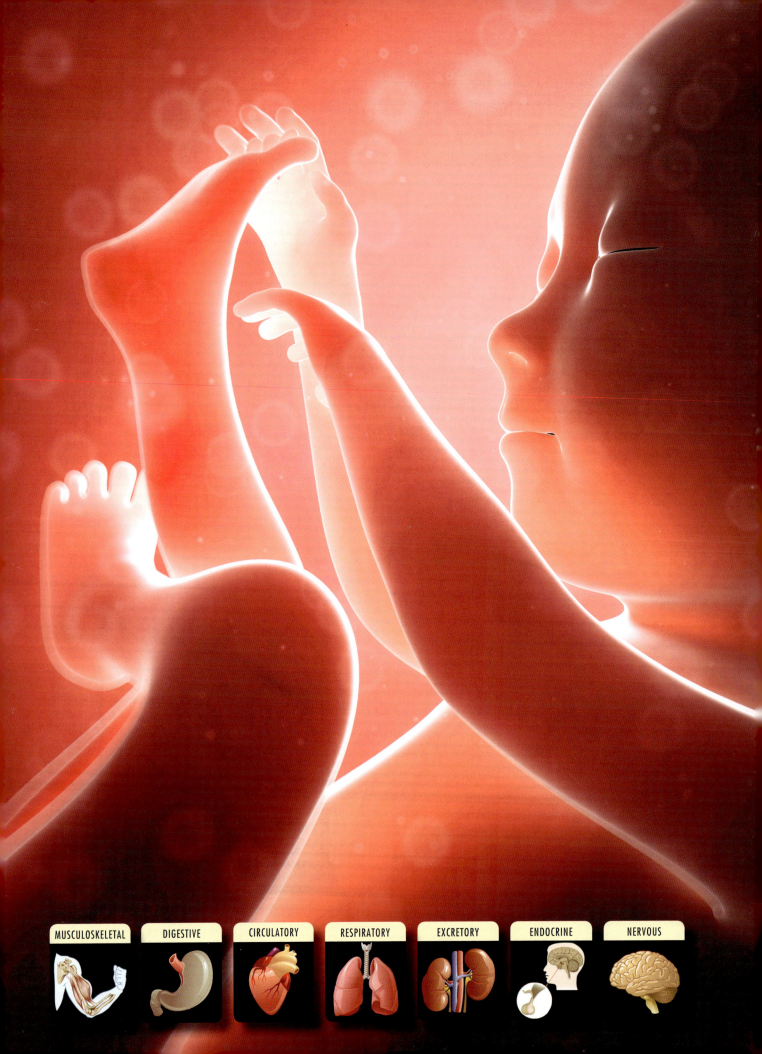

MUSCULOSKELETAL DIGESTIVE CIRCULATORY RESPIRATORY EXCRETORY ENDOCRINE NERVOUS

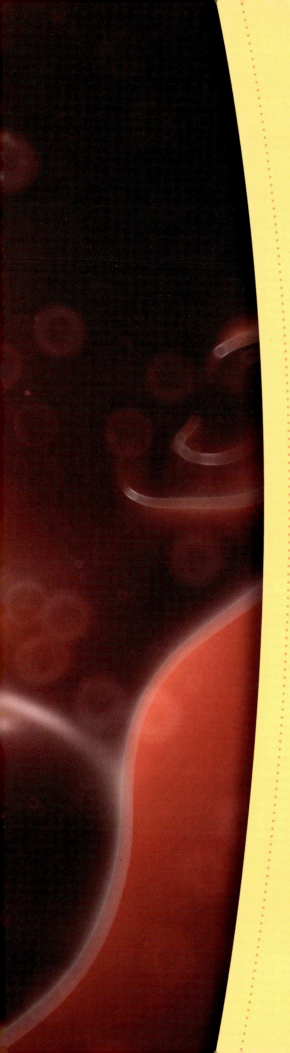

INTRODUCTION TO SYSTEMS

[Two months after fertilization], the little fellow will be just the size of my thumb. And it's because of that that all the mothers telling fairy tales to the children are speaking about the Tom Thumb story, because it's a true story. Therefore, each of us has been a Tom Thumb in the womb of the mother, and women have always known that there was a kind of underground country, a kind of vaulted shelter, with a kind of red light and curious noise in which very tiny humans were having a very curious and marvelous life. That is the story of Tom Thumb.

—Servant of God Jérôme Lejeune

FIGURE 16.1. ILLUSTRATION OF UNBORN CHILD IN THE WOMB

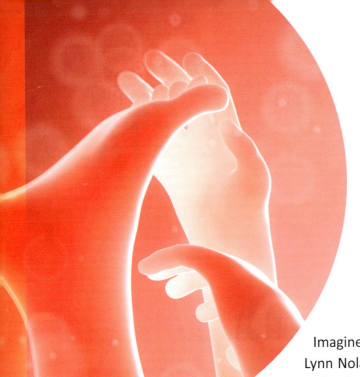

INTRODUCTION TO SYSTEMS

Imagine the tremendous forces that the hand and arm of Lynn Nolan Ryan underwent when he pitched a baseball at 162.3 km/hr on August 20 of 1974. In a split second, Ryan's hand went from zero to more than 100 mph and then stopped again!

Consider a man, Calvin Phillips, just 67 cm (2 ft 2 1/2 in) tall at 19 years of age! Calvin would just barely reach the abdomen of the typical junior high school boy or girl. On the other hand, Zeng Jinlian, a young Chinese girl, was 247 cm tall (8 ft 1 in) at 17 years of age!

The human body is amazing. It is amazing in what it can do, in the variety of shapes and sizes it comes in, and in the organization it displays. The human machine is a collection of parts and pieces that work together in a wonderful way to allow us to taste, see, move, feel, hear, think, grow, and remember. As we study "the plumbing" of the body, so to speak, it is important to realize that all of the parts of our bodies work together. Each part has its function that contributes to the life of the whole organism.

FIGURE 16.2. The human foot is made of many different kinds of tissue.

Cells to Systems

Every living thing is made of cells. Inside the cells are smaller organelles: the mitochondria, golgi bodies, and all the rest. A group of cells with the same shape and the same function forms a **TISSUE**. For instance, your epidermis, or skin, is a tissue made of many epidermal cells; your epidermis protects the rest of your tissues. The muscle tissue in your arm is made of skeletal muscle cells, which are all designed to contract and extend.

A group of tissues that work together to perform a single function is an **ORGAN**. Your stomach, an organ of the digestive system, consists of muscle, nerve, epithelial, glandular, and circulatory tissues. These tissues work together to contain and digest the food you eat.

A group of organs working together is called a **SYSTEM**. Together, your mouth, esophagus, stomach, small and large intestines, and an assortment of other organs form your digestive system. The systems carry out the life functions for an organism. In Figure 16.3 each system is matched with a life function.

SYSTEM	LIFE FUNCTION
Skeletal	Irritability
Muscular	Irritability
Digestive	Nutrition
Circulatory	Transport
Respiratory	Respiration
Excretory	Excretion
Endocrine	Synthesis
Nervous	Irritability
Reproductive	Reproduction

The life function of growth is carried out at the cellular level in all of the systems.

FIGURE 16.3.
LIFE FUNCTIONS AND SYSTEMS
The life functions may be matched up to the systems in the human body. Refer to Chapter 1 to refresh your memory about what each life function involves.

Regions of the Body

The body consists of four basic regions: the head, chest, abdomen, and limbs. See Figure 16.4.

The **head** is a collection of sensory organs and a mass of nerve tissue. The head includes the skull or cranial cavity.

The **chest cavity** is a hollow region that contains lungs and heart. The organs in the chest are protected by the ribs.

The **abdominal cavity** contains most of the digestive system. The chest and the abdomen together are called the torso.

The **limbs** are also called arms and legs.

FIGURE 16.4. REGIONS OF THE BODY
The chest and abdomen put together may be called the torso. The arms and legs are often called limbs.

Servant of God Jérôme Lejeune

Jérôme Lejeune (1926–1994) was a French doctor who discovered the genetic cause for Down syndrome. People with Down syndrome have mild to moderate intellectual disabilities and often look different from other people. Dr. Lejeune discovered that people have Down syndrome because they are born with an extra copy of one of their chromosomes. As you know, chromosomes are double strands of DNA and contain the information to operate the cell. Normally, human beings have 23 pairs of chromosomes in each cell. Down syndrome is caused by having an extra copy of chromosome number 21, so its official name is Trisomy 21.

Dr. Lejeune dedicated his whole life to searching for a cure for Down syndrome. Meanwhile, he also became involved in another battle. Some people were starting to say that since children with Down syndrome looked different and had handicaps, they were not worthy to live. Instead of caring for children with Down syndrome, these people said, their parents should have aborted them before they were born. Dr. Lejeune knew that an extra chromosome could not change a person's soul or make him less of a person, and he was not afraid to be a witness for the rights of unborn children.

FIGURE 16.5. SERVANT OF GOD JÉRÔME LEJEUNE

When Dr. Lejeune first discovered the cause for Down syndrome, he became very famous and received many awards. All that changed when he became involved in the pro-life movement. Although Dr. Lejeune always spoke and acted with charity, he was often treated with ridicule by his fellow scientists. Instead of supporting his attempts to find a cure for Down syndrome, the university where he worked kept him in a low-paying position, and there were even threats to his life. Dr. Lejeune refused to back down, and continued to defend the unborn for the rest of his life. Dr. Lejeune died of cancer in 1994, a few weeks after Pope John Paul II appointed him the first president of the Pontifical Academy for Life. In 2007 the cause for Jérôme Lejeune's canonization was opened.

FIGURE 16.6. CHILD WITH DOWN SYNDROME

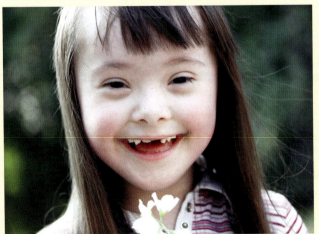

Did you know?

Jérôme Lejeune was homeschooled during high school. When Jérôme was fifteen, his father took his two sons out of the local school so that he could guide their education himself. During this time, Jérôme and his brother founded a theater company, became fluent in Latin and Greek, and constructed various contraptions and projects of their own.

Significant Events in a New Life

When your life began, you were a single cell smaller than the sharp point of a needle. Just nine months later, you were a complex organism of billions of cells all working together to cry and kick! During those nine months, your cells became organized into tissues, organs, and systems, and you tripled in size many times. Let's explore how these changes occurred.

Day 1

Your life began when the sperm cell from your father met and united with the egg cell from your mother. During fertilization, the two cells became a single cell. You are completely unique, not entirely like either of your parents or your ancestors. When conceived you were smaller than the period at the end of this sentence.

Week 1

You, the fertilized egg, journey through your mother's fallopian tubes to enter her uterus (sometimes called the womb). By the end of seven days, you sink into the spongy lining of the uterus and implant yourself to receive nourishment from tiny blood vessels. You are growing at a rapid rate and have grown from a single cell to a cluster of cells.

Week 2

Now you are firmly situated in the supplying goodness of your mother's womb. At about ten days you begin to send her signals that you are there. You begin to affect nearly all of your mom's body systems, even though you and the balloon-like sac of waters which protects you are still smaller than the seed of an apple.

Week 3

Your heart begins beating at three weeks. Your brain, backbone, spinal column, and nervous system are forming and the foundation for all your systems is carefully being established. Simple kidneys, a liver and the digestive system are taking shape. The rapid growth of your backbone is what causes your tiny body to "curve."

FIGURE 16.7. HUMAN LIFE
These illustrations show several of the stages in a human life. Beginning at the moment of conception, the life functions are in clear evidence. Overcoming disease and avoiding accidents or purposeful destruction, the new and unique person will mature through the rest of the stages of life and will reach old age.

Counter-clockwise from bottom: fertilized egg; 2-cell stage; 4-cell stage; 8-cell stage; embryo at 4 weeks; fetus at 6 weeks; fetus at 7 weeks; fetus at 8 weeks; newborn.

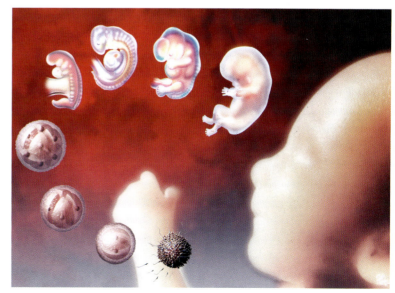

Week 4

By the end of four weeks, you are about the size of an apple seed, and ten thousand times larger than you were as a fertilized egg. On your twenty-fourth day you have no arms or legs, but just two days later, tiny buds appear for your arms, and then your legs bud only two days after that!

FIGURE 16.8.

Month 2

Your head is now almost half your total size. Brain waves can be detected and recorded at forty days. Facial features such as the nose, ears, lips, and tongue are forming. Near the end of this second month, your skeleton begins to change from cartilage to true bone. Your jaws also form, complete with milk-teeth buds in the gums. Your muscular and nervous systems are developing rapidly. Your body responds to touch, though your mom won't feel your movements until the fourth or fifth month. You, a miniature infant, have now developed and grown to an inch in length! By eight weeks, all your systems are formed, and until adulthood the changes in your body will be primarily in size.

Month 3

In your third month of life you grow to be more than two inches in length. You become more energetic and very graceful, like an astronaut floating and enjoying his gravity-free space capsule. By the tenth week, your fingers and toes are completely formed, complete with fingerprints and footprints which will never change except in size. Your entire body, except for non-facial portions of the head, is sensitive to touch. You can feel pain from the sixth week on. Finger and toenails appear, and the genitals show a clear differentiation and already contain primitive egg or sperm cells. Your vocal chords are completed, and you would cry if you could at this age.

Month 4

This month is marked by rapid growth as you grow to ten inches in length. At this point you can weigh half a pound or more. Your face takes on facial expressions similar to your parents, fine hair grows on your head, and eyebrows and eyelashes appear. Some babies even start sucking their thumbs at this age!

Months 5 and 6

Now you, the unborn baby, had a wonderful experience! You heard and recognized your mother's voice! You are now very coordinated, and sounds provoke energy reactions. Your lungs are well-developed and ready to perform. If you were born now, you could survive with adequate care.

Months 7-8-9

During your last three months before birth you triple in weight to more than seven pounds, and grow to be twenty inches long. You begin to find your "quarters" very cramped. Your skin begins to look smooth and polished as you develop a layer of fat beneath your skin. You also develop antibodies which will protect you from disease later in your life. Your heart is pumping three hundred gallons of blood a day! You are now ready to change your residence to continue the life which began nine months ago, as you move through childhood, adolescence, maturity, and old age.

Worksheets:
16.1–16.3, 16.5–16.6

Diagram:
16.4

Report:
16.7

Microscope:
16.8

Tony Melendez

Whether you're a talented baseball player or a quiet bookworm, unusually short or tall or somewhere in between, you are a precious gift, created by your loving Heavenly Father for a unique purpose in life, a purpose that He has not given to any other person.

Consider a baby, born without arms. What kind of future could this child possibly have? How could he function in school, use a computer, or do any sort of activity that required hands and arms? In the world's eyes, this baby might seem to have no future at all. But not in God's eyes, or in God's unfathomably wise plans.

This particular baby, Tony Melendez, grew into a young man who taught himself to play guitar with his feet! A gifted Catholic songwriter and musician, Tony was invited to play and sing for Pope John Paul II during the Holy Father's 1987 visit to Los Angeles, California. Inspired by this young man's use of his God-given talents and hope-filled singing, Pope John Paul sprang from his seat, climbed onto the platform where Tony sat, and embraced him, saying "My wish to you is to continue giving this hope to all people."

FIGURE 16.9. TONY MELENDEZ WITH POPE JOHN PAUL II

Since that time, Tony has performed at the Vatican, World Youth Day, and won numerous awards. Tony continues to inspire people the world over with his music, and through his participation in pro-life work and ministry to the disadvantaged.

The Skeletal and Muscular Systems

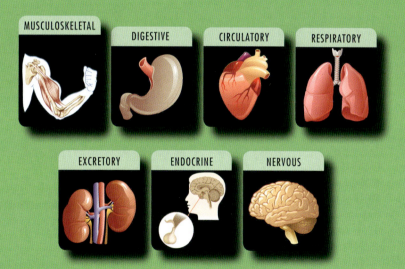

MUSCULOSKELETAL DIGESTIVE CIRCULATORY RESPIRATORY

EXCRETORY ENDOCRINE NERVOUS

FIGURE 17.1. ILLUSTRATION OF A SKATEBOARDER'S SKELETAL SYSTEM

THE SKELETAL AND MUSCULAR SYSTEMS

Make no bones about it! You need your skeleton for more than life science class!

The 206 bones of the human skeleton (Figure 17.8) are more than just supports on which to hang muscles and organs. Support is the most obvious function of our internal skeletal system, but there are four other important functions as well.

1. The skeleton protects vital organs. For example, the skull protects the brain.

2. The skeleton provides storage of minerals.

3. The moveable bones are levers to which the muscles are attached (Figure 17.2).

4. Many bones, such as the femur, ribs, sternum, and ilium, contain bone **MARROW** where red and white blood cells are manufactured.

While a bone is alive, it has a skin-like covering called the **PERIOSTEUM**. Marrow is found in the soft center of bones and is where your blood cells are made. Bones are hard and rigid because they contain calcium salts.

The skeletal system includes several kinds of connective tissue besides **BONE**. Cartilage is a rubber-like tissue that acts as a shock absorber between bones. **CARTILAGE** is also used for support in the ears and nose where some flexibility is required.

A **LIGAMENT** is a thin, tough, and fibrous connective tissue that connects bone to bone. A **TENDON**, also string-like, is the connective tissue that attaches a muscle to a bone, or one muscle to another. If you touch the underside of your knee while holding your

FIGURE 17.2.
BONES ARE LEVERS
The knee, elbow, and fingers have hinge joints so that the muscles can use the bones as levers.

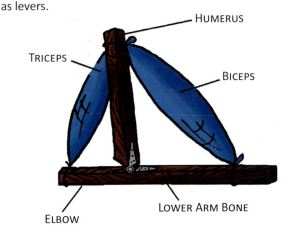

HUMERUS

TRICEPS

BICEPS

ELBOW

LOWER ARM BONE

154

Chapter 17

foot up, you can feel the two tendons which attach your thigh muscle to your shin bone.

Fat is a type of connective tissue which is not usually associated with bones, cartilage, ligaments, and tendons. Fat, deposited in **ADIPOSE CELLS**, provides insulation more than support (see Figure 17.3).

Joints

Figure 17.4 shows a hinge **JOINT** in the elbow. Similar joints are in the knees and fingers. A hinge joint, like the hinge on a door, allows movement along only one plane.

Your wrists, ankles, and backbone move by means of a gliding joint. The gliding joint allows a limited amount of twisting movement.

The hip and shoulder have a ball-and-socket joint. The stick shift in many standard cars is a ball and socket. The ball-and-socket joint allows more movement than the hinge joint and gliding joint.

A fourth type of joint is immovable, such as the solid joints in the skull. You can observe an immovable joint in Figures 17.4 and 17.5. In babies, the immovable joint in the skull is normally open so that the brain has room to grow. Later on, the joint grows together. The immovable joint in the skull of Elena, the girl in the X-ray, was already closed when she was three months old, so she had to have surgery to open it up (Figure 17.5).

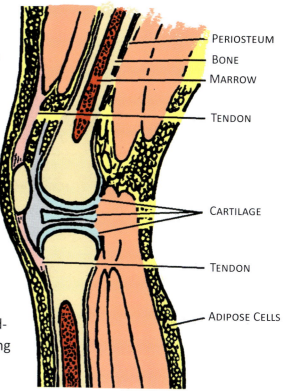

FIGURE 17.3. TISSUES IN A KNEE JOINT
Bones are complex organs made of many tissues. Bones are alive and blood vessels must bring in food and oxygen and remove wastes.

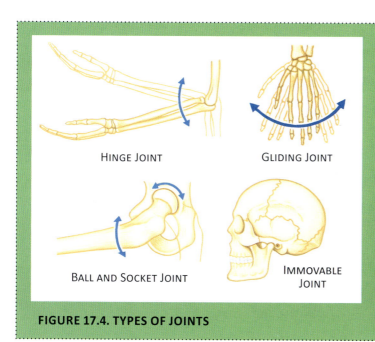

HINGE JOINT

GLIDING JOINT

BALL AND SOCKET JOINT

IMMOVABLE JOINT

FIGURE 17.4. TYPES OF JOINTS

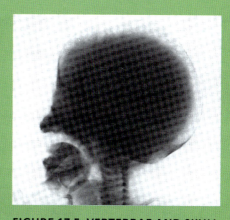

FIGURE 17.5. VERTEBRAE AND SKULL
This X-ray photograph of a three-month-old girl's neck and skull shows the vertebrae of the neck which protect the spinal cord. The skull protects the brain.

Worksheets:
17.1–17.4

Diagram:
17.5–17.6

Experiment:
17.7

Muscles

Here's a question you can sit on and think about for a while: what is the largest muscle in the body? There are over six hundred to choose from. You can "sit on" this question because the answer is the gluteus maximus or buttock muscle.

Muscles are important for their ability to contract. There are three different types of muscle tissue. If you picture a weight-lifter when you think of muscles, you are thinking of **SKELETAL MUSCLES**. This type of tissue has cells with more than one nucleus. Skeletal muscle cells can also be recognized by the **STRIATIONS** visible under a microscope.

The muscles attached to your skeleton are found in pairs. When one contracts, the opposing muscle must extend. For instance, when we "make a muscle," we tighten our biceps and relax our triceps, as shown in Figure 17.6. To extend our arm again, we relax our biceps and contract our triceps.

Skeletal muscles are sometimes called **VOLUNTARY** muscles, because you can usually decide whether you want to move them or not. The skeletal muscles of the body perform the life function of irritability by allowing you to respond to stimuli.

There are two other types of muscle tissue, found in the organs of other body systems. **SMOOTH MUSCLE** is found in the digestive system and in glands and blood vessels. Smooth muscle tissue does not have striations. Your body controls these muscles without your conscious effort. Smooth muscle, because it contracts and relaxes regularly, not just when you want it to, is called **INVOLUNTARY** muscle.

The third type of muscle tissue is **CARDIAC MUSCLE**, the muscle in your heart. By the time you were born, your cardiac muscle had already worked non-stop for over eight months! Cardiac muscle is striated like skeletal muscle, and it has one nucleus in each cell. Like smooth muscle, cardiac muscle is involuntary. Cardiac muscle cells branch off each other and can look like tiny letter H's under the microscope.

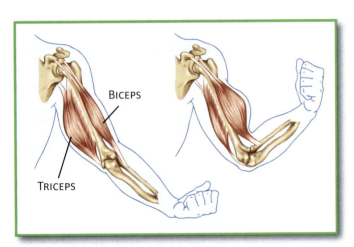

FIGURE 17.6. BICEPS AND TRICEPS
Your biceps and triceps are needed to raise and lower your arm.

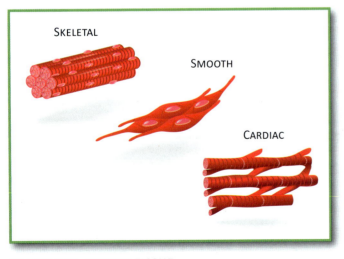

FIGURE 17.7. MUSCLE TISSUE
Skeletal muscle is the tissue that makes up the muscular system of the body. The other two kinds of muscle cells are in the organs of other systems of the body.

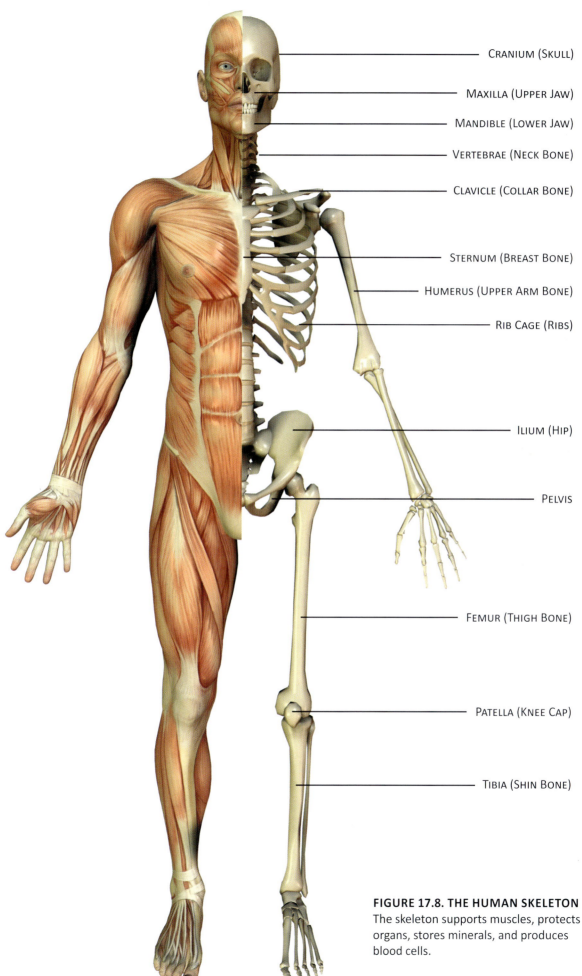

MUSCULAR AND SKELETAL SYSTEMS

CRANIUM (SKULL)

MAXILLA (UPPER JAW)

MANDIBLE (LOWER JAW)

VERTEBRAE (NECK BONE)

CLAVICLE (COLLAR BONE)

STERNUM (BREAST BONE)

HUMERUS (UPPER ARM BONE)

RIB CAGE (RIBS)

ILIUM (HIP)

PELVIS

FEMUR (THIGH BONE)

PATELLA (KNEE CAP)

TIBIA (SHIN BONE)

FIGURE 17.8. THE HUMAN SKELETON
The skeleton supports muscles, protects
organs, stores minerals, and produces
blood cells.

MUSCULOSKELETAL

DIGESTIVE

CIRCULATORY

RESPIRATORY

EXCRETORY

ENDOCRINE

NERVOUS

THE DIGESTIVE SYSTEM

And this is the true purpose of anatomy: to raise the observers from the astonishing craftsmanship of the body to the dignity of the soul, and then, by both these miracles, to the knowledge and love of their Creator.

—Bl. Nicolas Steno

FIGURE 18.1.
Mechanical digestion begins in the mouth.

The Digestive System

After the last chapter and all that talk about bones, I hope you can *stomach* a chapter about the digestive system! The organs that break down complex foods form a long tube right through the middle of your body! You need the products of digestion for energy (glucose), for growth and repair (amino acids), and for metabolic regulation (minerals).

Tongue

Digestion begins in the mouth. The **TONGUE** is a muscular organ covered with sensory bumps called **TASTE BUDS** (Figure 18.2). Foods that are poisonous often taste bad, so taste serves to prevent animals from eating these foods. Taste can also cause people to eat too much of certain foods!

Teeth

The **MECHANICAL DIGESTION** of food begins with the teeth. Mechanical digestion is simply making the food into smaller pieces of the same material. Cutting up a piece of meat is mechanical digestion!

Adults have thirty-two teeth, which come in four types. **INCISOR** teeth, used to bite off food, are flat and wide like chisels. Rabbits, squirrels, and beavers have very pronounced incisors. Horses have good incisors which they use to bite off grass. Cows must tear the grass since they have no incisors at all! (Figure 18.3.) Human beings have four incisors on the upper jaw and four on the bottom jaw (Figure 18.4).

On either side of your four top incisors and four bottom incisors should be a **CUSPID** tooth (Figure 18.4). Cuspids are for ripping meat. Cuspids, or canine teeth, are prominent in cats, dogs, and Count Dracula of horror movie fame. Although your four cuspids are not as sharp as those of many carnivores, you can feel the points with your finger.

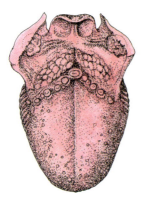

FIGURE 18.2. TONGUE
The taste buds on the tongue detect four sensations: sweet, salt, sour, and bitter. The tongue is also necessary for proper speech.

160

FIGURE 18.3. SKULL AND TEETH OF A COW
Depending on what an animal eats, some types of teeth may be extra large, extra small, or missing altogether.

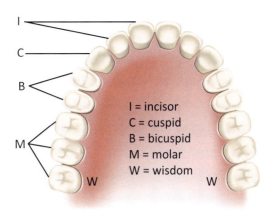

I = incisor
C = cuspid
B = bicuspid
M = molar
W = wisdom

FIGURE 18.4. HUMAN TEETH
Each kind of tooth has a special shape for a special function. There are 20 teeth in a set of baby teeth. A full set of adult teeth should have 32 teeth total (top and bottom together).

People with healthy teeth have eight **BICUSPID** teeth—two on the top and two on the bottom of each side (Figure 18.4). "*Cuspid*" means "point" and a cuspid tooth has one point. You already know that "*bi-*" means "two," so now you know what a bicuspid tooth is: a tooth with two points. Bicuspids are used to grind food.

A **MOLAR** tooth is large and quite flat. You can probably see four molars on each side of your mouth, two on the top and two on the bottom. Your last molars, called wisdom teeth, will come in during your late teens or early twenties (Figure 18.4). Molar teeth crush even hard foods into many tiny pieces. These tiny pieces have much more surface area than large pieces, which is important for chemical digestion. Chewing your food well aids digestion because it increases the surface area of the food.

Chemical Digestion

Surface area is needed for **CHEMICAL DIGESTION** so that your digestive enzymes can come into contact with every part of the food. Chemical digestion is different from mechanical digestion because in chemical digestion, foods are changed into different chemicals.

For example, the starch in a cracker is crunched up by your teeth. Since it is still starch, the cracker has only been mechanically digested at this point. The **SALIVA**, a liquid secreted by the salivary glands in the walls of the mouth, contains salivary **AMYLASE**. Amylase is one of the enzymes we discussed as examples of proteins in Chapter 14. The amylase changes the starch of the cracker into sugar. Big molecules of starch are broken into

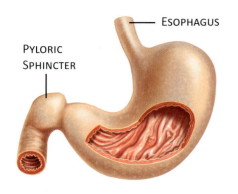

PYLORIC
SPHINCTER

ESOPHAGUS

COMPOUND	EFFECT
Water (H_2O)	a solvent to dissolve chemicals allowing reactions to occur
Hydrochloric Acid (HCl)	kills many microbes and provides the proper pH for pepsin to work
Pepsin	an enzyme that begins the chemical digestion of proteins

FIGURE 18.5. DIGESTION IN THE STOMACH

the smaller molecules of sugar. This is chemical digestion! The chemical digestion of starch begins in your mouth; fats and proteins must wait until later for their chemical digestion to begin.

After the tongue pushes the food mixed with saliva into the pharynx, the back of the throat, the food enters the **ESOPHAGUS**. This "food tube" is shaped like a soft hose. The food is pushed down the esophagus by waves of contractions called **PERISTALSIS** (Figure 18.7). You do not have to control peristalsis consciously because the esophagus is made of involuntary, smooth muscle tissue, lined with special epidermal cells. The small and large intestines also use peristalsis to move food through the digestive system.

Stomach

The **STOMACH**, shaped like a short, wide letter J, is also made of smooth muscle tissue. It churns your food without your thinking to tell it to. The inside of the stomach is folded into many wrinkles lined with glandular epithelial tissue. These special epidermal cells make gastric juice. The stomach digests food for about two to five hours. The exit of the stomach is controlled by the **PYLORIC SPHINCTER**, a doughnut-shaped valve (18.5).

A summary of chemical digestion in the stomach is shown in Figure 18.5. The lining of the stomach secretes gastric juice which contains the chemicals necessary for chemical digestion to continue. Note that the chemical digestion of proteins begins in the stomach, when the enzyme **PEPSIN** and hydrochloric acid (HCl) begin changing the proteins into amino acids (Figure 18.6).

HCl Acid

Pepsin

Pepsin +
HCl Acid

FIGURE 18.6. PEPSIN AND HYDROCHLORIC ACID
For pepsin to digest proteins, it needs to be converted into an active form by hydrochloric acid. In the experiment at left, the pieces of meat soaked in just HCl and just pepsin have been broken down only slightly. The meat in the test tube with both pepsin and HCl (right) has been entirely broken down.

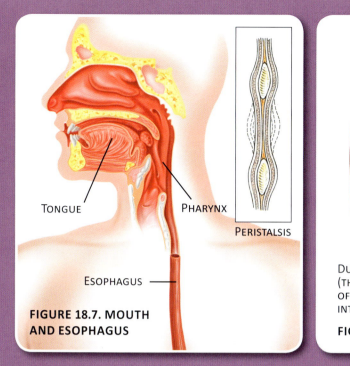

TONGUE

PHARYNX

PERISTALSIS

ESOPHAGUS

FIGURE 18.7. MOUTH AND ESOPHAGUS

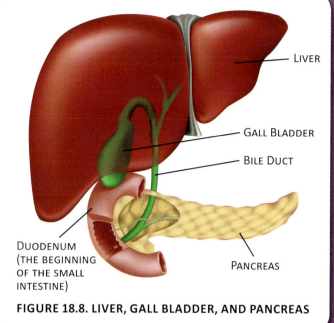

LIVER

GALL BLADDER

BILE DUCT

DUODENUM (THE BEGINNING OF THE SMALL INTESTINE)

PANCREAS

FIGURE 18.8. LIVER, GALL BLADDER, AND PANCREAS

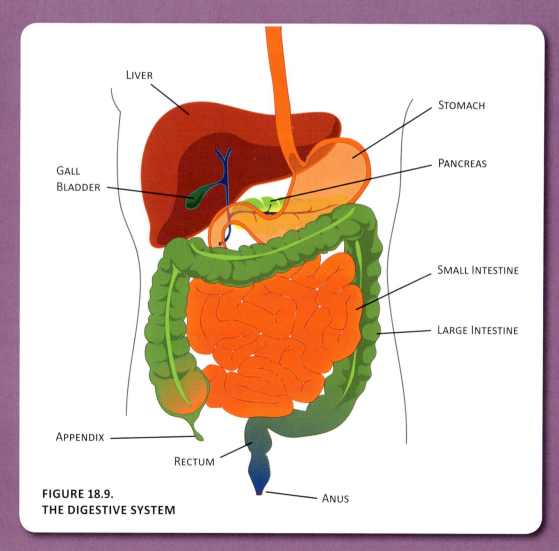

LIVER

STOMACH

PANCREAS

GALL BLADDER

SMALL INTESTINE

LARGE INTESTINE

APPENDIX

RECTUM

ANUS

FIGURE 18.9. THE DIGESTIVE SYSTEM

SOURCE	COMPOUND	EFFECT	FINAL PRODUCTS
From the liver:	Bile	an emulsifying agent that breaks fat up into tiny globules	
From the pancreas:	Amylase	an enzyme that converts starch into maltose and other sugars	
	Trypsin	an enzyme that acts on proteins	Amino acids
	Lipase	an enzyme that acts on lipids (fats)	Fatty acids and glycerol
From the small intestine:	Maltase	an enzyme that acts on maltose (a sugar)	Glucose
	Sucrase	an enzyme that acts on sucrose	Glucose

FIGURE 18.10. INTESTINAL DIGESTION

Small Intestine

When the pyloric sphincter opens, the partially digested food enters the **SMALL INTESTINE** to begin final digestion. Don't confuse "small" with short; the small intestine is approximately twenty-three feet long in Average Arnold and other adults! The small intestine, made of smooth muscle cells, is lined with glandular epithelial cells and villi (Figure 18.11). This special lining of the intestine makes intestinal juices. Digestion in the small intestine is summarized in Figure 18.10. As you can see from the chart, the chemical digestion of fat begins in the small intestine. Final digestion of carbohydrates, proteins, and fats is completed in the small intestine.

There are several digestive organs that the food never goes through. The **LIVER**, the largest organ in your body, is made of glandular tissue. It produces **BILE** (Figure 18.8). The bile is saved up in a small, balloon-shaped **GALL BLADDER**. The bile is squirted through the bile duct into the beginning of the small intestine as the food passes through. The **PANCREAS** makes pancreatic juice which enters the small intestine along with the bile (Figure 18.8).

Roughage, material that cannot be digested, is important in a diet to keep the smooth muscles of the intestinal wall in good condition. Vegetables and whole grains are good sources of roughage, also called dietary fiber.

Absorption

Once digestion is complete, the small intestine carries out absorption. A clean piece of the inside of the small intestine looks almost like velvet, soft and fuzzy. Under a microscope, tiny finger-like projections called villi become visible (Figure 18.11). They appear much like root hairs in shape and they serve the same function: to increase surface area for absorption. To do the same job without villi, the small intestine would have to be many kilometers long instead of eight to nine meters!

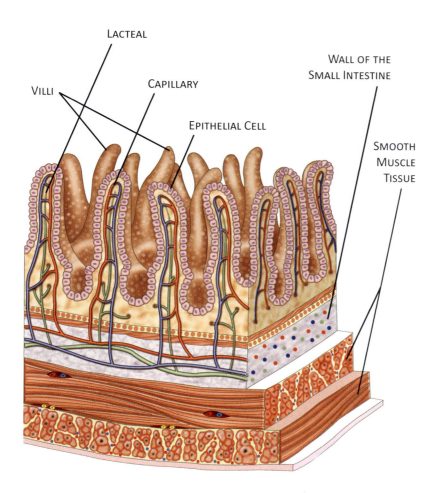

LACTEAL

VILLI

CAPILLARY

EPITHELIAL CELL

WALL OF THE
SMALL INTESTINE

SMOOTH
MUSCLE
TISSUE

FIGURE 18.11. WALL OF THE SMALL INTESTINE
The small intestine is lined with glandular epithelial cells, which make intestinal juices such as maltase and sucrase. The final products of digestion are absorbed through the villi: glucose and amino acids into the capillaries, fatty acids and glycerol into the lacteals.

Villi contain tiny blood vessels called capillaries, which absorb the glucose and amino acids as they pass through the thin walls of each **VILLUS**. Inside each villus there is also a **LACTEAL**, a small lymph vessel, that absorbs the fatty acids and glycerol. These end products of fat digestion are transported from the lacteals to the thoracic duct in the chest, where they are released into the blood.

Large Intestine

The **LARGE INTESTINE** is only about one-fifth the length of the small intestine, but it is much fatter (Figure 18.9). The function of the large intestine is to absorb and recycle much of the water in the fecal material. The fecal material is all of the contents of the large intestine.

There are mutualistic bacteria that use the organic molecules in the large intestine's contents as a food source. We learned that mutualism benefits both organisms. What do these intestinal bacteria do for you? They make vitamin B and vitamin K!

Bacteria, enzymes, and the final remains of undigested food form the stool inside the **RECTUM**. The stool is eliminated through the **ANUS**.

Worksheets:
18.1–18.2, 18.4–18.6

Diagram:
18.3

Formal Lab:
18.7

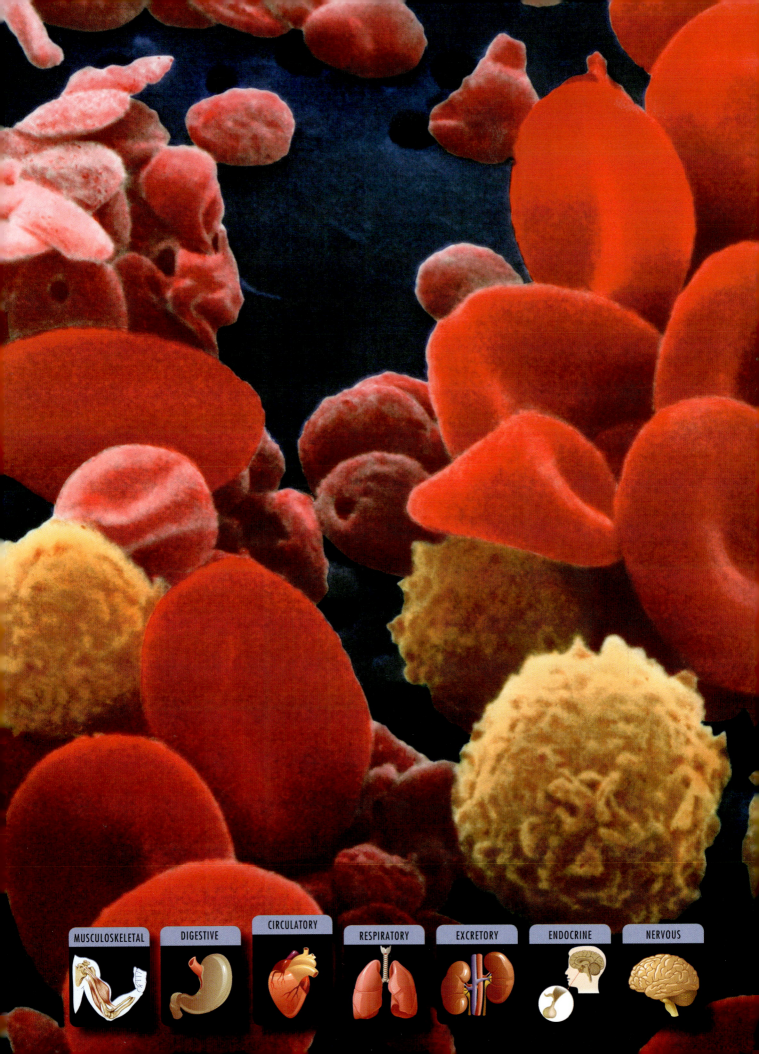

MUSCULOSKELETAL DIGESTIVE CIRCULATORY RESPIRATORY EXCRETORY ENDOCRINE NERVOUS

Chapter

19

THE CIRCULATORY SYSTEM

Pulchra sunt quae videntur,
pulchriora quae sciuntur,
longe pulcherrima quae ignorantur.

Lovely the things that are seen;
Lovelier, those that are understood;
Loveliest by far, the things unknown.

—Bl. Nicolas Steno

FIGURE 19.1. BLOOD CELLS AND PLATELETS
Colored scanning electron micrograph of human blood showing red blood cells, white blood cells, and platelets. Platelets are small cell fragments that play a major role in blood clotting.

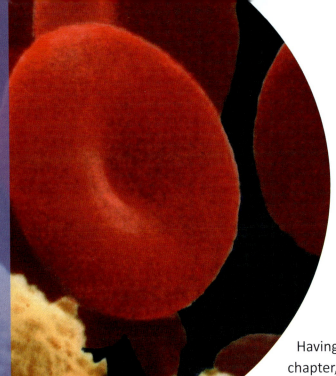

THE CIRCULATORY SYSTEM

Having spent some time *digesting* the material in the last chapter, let us now get straight to the *heart* of the circulatory system. The job of moving materials throughout every part of the human body is accomplished by the arteries, capillaries, veins, and heart.

The Heart

The **HEART** is the most important organ in the circulatory system. Average Adam's heart began its work more than eight months before Adam was born! The human heart begins beating about three weeks after conception and continues pumping day and night, year after year, until the person dies. In Average Arnold, Adam's dad, the heart contracts 70 to 72 times per minute and pumps approximately 7,000 liters of blood per day! It is rare for an individual to survive more than a few minutes if his heart stops beating.

The sinoatrial node is a small spot on the wall of the heart at the top of the right atrium. This spot generates an electrical "signal" which travels through the heart. When the cardiac muscle cells receive the signal, the cells contract and blood is squeezed out of the heart, into the arteries, and through the body. Since the sinoatrial node causes the rhythmic beat of the heart, it is often called the pacemaker.

Systemic Circulation

The path of the blood's journey through the body is amazing for its orderliness and complexity. The first European to figure out the circulation of the blood was William Harvey of England, who published a book on the subject in 1628. The Chinese had learned of the true

FIGURE 19.2.
A PIG HEART
Your heart is about the size of your fist. This pig heart is about the same size as a human heart. If you do not remember what cardiac muscle cells look like, turn back to Figure 17.7 in Chapter 17.

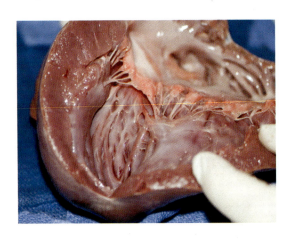

circulation of the blood nearly 700 years before Harvey's "discovery," but their knowledge was not known to Europeans.

Refer to Figures 19.3–4 to trace the path of the blood as you read about systemic and pulmonary circulation, the two types of circulation in the human body.

Systemic circulation begins in the left **ATRIUM**, where oxygen-rich blood moves through a one-way valve into the heart's left ventricle. The left **VENTRICLE**, the strongest chamber of the heart, pumps the bright red blood through another valve into the **AORTA**. The aorta is the largest of the arteries, and branches into many smaller arteries. Each **ARTERY** is a thick-walled, muscular blood vessel that carries blood away from the heart. Remember: the "a" in artery is for **away**. Arteries are thick-walled because they must withstand the blood pressure exerted by each muscular contraction of the powerful left ventricle.

The arteries finally branch into vessels so small that the blood cells must line up single file to get through. Each microscopic blood vessel is a **CAP-ILLARY**. William Harvey knew that the blood made a circle somehow, but

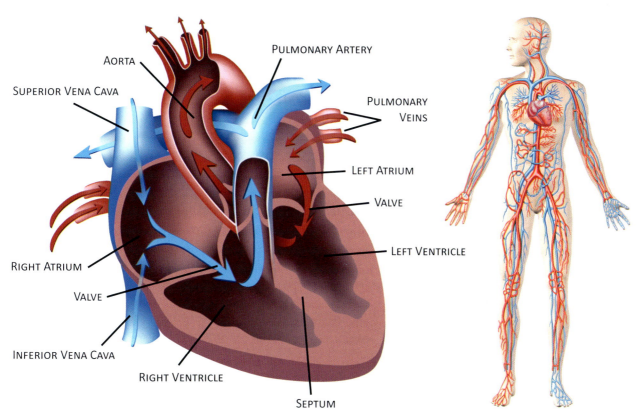

FIGURE 19.3. HUMAN CIRCULATORY SYSTEM
When determining the left or right side of a heart, you must think of the heart as your own. To remember that the atria are the upper chambers of the heart and the ventricles are the lower chambers, think of the V in "ventricle" as an arrow pointing down and the A in "atrium" as an arrow pointing up. The ventricles, which pump the blood to the lungs and the rest of the body, are larger and more powerful than the atria, which only pump the blood through a valve into the ventricles.

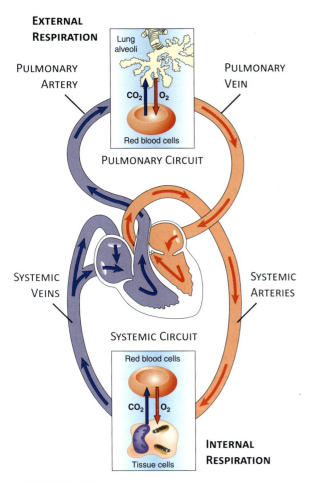

Lung alveoli

CO_2 O_2

Red blood cells

PULMONARY ARTERY

PULMONARY VEIN

PULMONARY CIRCUIT

SYSTEMIC VEINS

SYSTEMIC ARTERIES

SYSTEMIC CIRCUIT

Red blood cells

CO_2 O_2

Tissue cells

INTERNAL RESPIRATION

FIGURE 19.4.
The pulmonary vein is different from the systemic veins because it carries oxygen-rich, red blood. Similarly, the pulmonary artery is different from the systemic arteries because it carries oxygen-poor, "blue" blood.

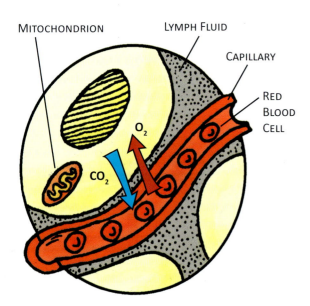

MITOCHONDRION

LYMPH FLUID

CAPILLARY

RED BLOOD CELL

O_2

CO_2

FIGURE 19.5. CELLULAR RESPIRATION
Oxygen and carbon dioxide are exchanged between the red blood cells and all the other cells of the body.

he never saw the capillaries because they are too small to see without a microscope. Our understanding of how the blood circulates through the body was not completed until 1660, when Marcello Malpighi of Italy correctly described the capillaries.

As the oxygen-rich blood from the arteries moves through the capillaries, the red blood cells give up their oxygen and glucose to the surrounding lymph fluid, which surrounds each cell. In exchange, carbon dioxide, a waste from respiration, is carried away from the cells (Figure 19.5).

A great number of capillaries are in the villi of the small intestine, where glucose diffuses into the blood to be carried to the cells in the rest of the body. Since every cell in the body requires oxygen and glucose, no part in the body is more than two or three cells from a capillary. It has been estimated that the millions, even billions, of capillaries in one adult's body have a combined surface area almost equal to that of one and a half regulation basketball courts!

After the blood in the capillaries has released its load of oxygen to the cells, the capillaries join together to form veins. Since the blood has traveled a long way from the heart by the time it passes through the capillaries, the blood pressure is much less in the veins than in the arteries. As a result, veins are thin-walled instead of thick-walled like the arteries, and each **VEIN** has valves to prevent the blood from flowing backwards. Remember: the "v" in veins is for **valves**.

The veins keep joining together until there are only two of them. One is the **SUPERIOR VENA CAVA**, which carries blood from the upper part of the body, and the other is the **INFERIOR VENA CAVA**, which carries blood from the lower part of the body. ("*Superior*" means "higher" and "*inferior*" means "lower" in Latin.) Both veins empty their oxygen-poor, "blue" blood into the right atrium. (Oxygen-poor blood is actually dark red, not blue.)

The blood has now made a full circle from the heart, out to all the systems of the body, and back again. However, the blood is now on the opposite side of the **SEPTUM**, the wall of muscle that divides the heart into two halves. **SYSTEMIC CIRCULATION**, the flow of blood through the systems of the body, is only half the story of circulation!

Pulmonary Circulation

The blood which enters the right atrium from the superior vena cava and the inferior vena cava is loaded with carbon dioxide from the cells in the rest of the body. Before the heart sends the blood out to the systems again, the blood must travel to the lungs to exchange the carbon dioxide for oxygen.

The right atrium squeezes the oxygen-poor blood through a valve into the right ventricle (see Figure 19.3). The right ventricle is smaller than the left ventricle because it only has to pump blood to the lungs and back instead of all through the body.

The right ventricle now pumps the blood through a valve into the **PULMONARY ARTERY**. The pulmonary artery branches into two arteries, one for each lung. Inside the lungs, the arteries branch into tiny capillaries which surround each of the air sacs which make up the lungs (Figure 19.6). Here at the air sacs, carbon dioxide diffuses out of the blood and oxygen diffuses in. The blood turns bright red.

The oxygen-rich "red" blood flows through the **PULMONARY VEINS** back to the left atrium. Once the blood reaches the left atrium of the heart, **PULMONARY CIRCULATION** is complete. The blood then starts over with systemic circulation.

Remember: arteries start with the letter "a" and they carry blood **away** from the heart. Veins start with the letter "v" and they have **valves**. The arteries and veins for pulmonary circulation are different from those in systemic circulation only in the kind of blood they carry (see caption to Figure 19.4).

Blood Tissue

The blood that flows through your veins and arteries is a special mixture of many chemicals and cells (see Figures 19.1 and 19.9).

1. Plasma is the liquid part of the blood. **PLASMA** dissolves many substances needed by the cells. Gases, enzymes, glucose, and salt are all transported in the plasma. Waste products being transported away from the cells are also dissolved in the plasma.

2. Red blood cells are tiny cells made in your bone marrow. A **RED BLOOD CELL** contains **HEMOGLOBIN**, the iron-containing protein needed to carry oxygen. Red blood cells are shaped like flexible, concave disks. This shape and their small size allows them to squeeze through tiny capillaries on their path through the body (Figure 19.8). A mature red

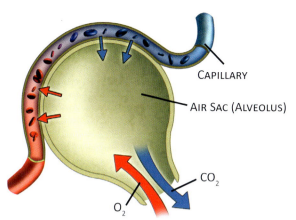

CAPILLARY

AIR SAC (ALVEOLUS)

CO_2

O_2

FIGURE 19.6.
EXTERNAL RESPIRATION
Every time the lungs fill with fresh air, oxygen diffuses out of the lungs' air sacs and into the capillaries, which carry it to the rest of the body. At the same time, carbon dioxide in the blood diffuses into the air sacs to be exhaled by the lungs.

Blessed Nicolas Steno

After reading about Catholic scientists such as Louis Pasteur and Jérôme Lejeune, you will probably be surprised to learn that some people believe devout faith in God cannot be combined with scientific reasoning. The story of Nicolas Steno is an example of how faith and reason work together "like two wings on which the human spirit rises to the contemplation of truth" (Pope John Paul II).

Nicolas Steno was born in Denmark in 1638, soon after the Protestant Reformation. As a young man he studied to be a doctor, but his scientific curiosity knew no bounds, and led him to make discoveries not only in anatomy, but also in geology, paleontology (the study of fossils), and crystallography (the study of crystals). Steno discovered many of the founding principles of the science of geology, and is known as the Father of Modern Geology. He also proved that the heart is made of muscle fiber, which was a groundbreaking discovery since most scientists at the time, including William Harvey, thought that the heart was made of a unique substance which allowed it to generate heat and produce emotions in addition to pumping blood.

Steno had been raised as a Lutheran, but in 1666 he settled in Catholic Italy, where he found the most support for his innovative ideas. A year later he converted to Catholicism after witnessing a Corpus Christi procession. In gratitude for the grace of conversion and out of love for the Blessed

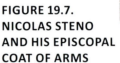

FIGURE 19.7. NICOLAS STENO AND HIS EPISCOPAL COAT OF ARMS

The blue cross is a symbol of faith in Christ's sacrificial love for man. The red heart is symbol of man's love for God, a love which Steno showed in his pursuit of truth through the natural sciences, in his dedication to evangelization, and in his care for the poor. Scientist that he was, Steno was careful to draw the left side of the heart larger than the right side.

Sacrament, Steno asked to become a priest, and was ordained in 1677, at the age of 39. Only two years later he was ordained a bishop and sent to northern Germany to re-evangelize those who had left the Church during the Protestant Reformation. He was especially known for his gentleness, his personal poverty, and his love for the poor. Whenever he had time, Steno continued his scientific research, focusing especially on the nature of the brain and nervous system. When Steno died in 1686, worn out by his missionary labors, he was mourned by both Catholics and Lutherans. Steno was beatified by Pope John Paul II in 1988; his feast is celebrated on December 5.

blood cell does not have a nucleus; this leaves more room in the cell for oxygen-carrying hemoglobin.

3. Red blood cells are the most numerous cells in the body. It is estimated that one-third of the 75 trillion cells in the human body are red blood cells. That is quite a few cells. How many? If Average Arnold lives to be 72 years old, there are more red blood cells in him now than there are seconds in 1000 of his lifetimes!

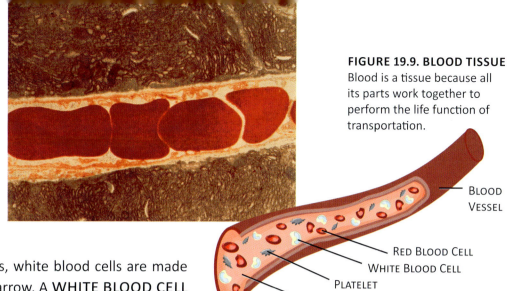

**FIGURE 19.8.
RED BLOOD CELLS**
A micrograph of red
blood cells squeezing
through a capillary.
Magnification: 750x

FIGURE 19.9. BLOOD TISSUE
Blood is a tissue because all
its parts work together to
perform the life function of
transportation.

BLOOD
VESSEL

RED BLOOD CELL
WHITE BLOOD CELL
PLATELET
PLASMA

4. Like red blood cells, white blood cells are made inside the bone marrow. A **WHITE BLOOD CELL** is a "soldier cell" that engulfs and destroys disease-causing microbes.

5. Platelets are cell fragments. Each colorless **PLATELET** helps in clotting the blood. The platelets, along with a protein called **FIBRINOGEN**, form the clot that stops a cut from bleeding.

Blood Types

Not everyone's blood is the same. There are four basic types of human blood, called types A, B, AB, and O. Each type of blood has a slightly different set of antibodies. (You will learn more about antibodies in Chapter 24.) When a patient needs a blood transfusion, the doctor must be careful to give him blood of the right blood type, or the antibodies in the patient's blood might mistake the new blood cells for invading germs. When incompatible blood types are mixed, antibodies cause the foreign blood cells to agglutinate, or clump, and the white blood cells rapidly attack and destroy the "invaders." People with type AB blood are called universal receivers because they can receive a blood transfusion from anyone. Type O people can donate blood to anyone, so they are called universal donors.

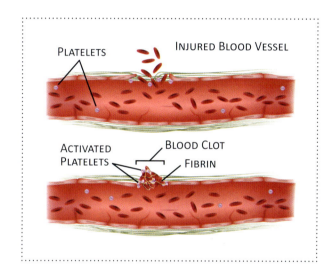

PLATELETS

INJURED BLOOD VESSEL

ACTIVATED
PLATELETS

BLOOD CLOT
FIBRIN

**FIGURE 19.10.
BLOOD CLOTTING**
Platelets are cell fragments
which help in clotting the
blood. The fibrinogen
dissolved in the blood
is converted into a solid
protein called fibrin when
forming a clot.

Summary

The main job of the circulatory system is the transportation of food, wastes, and chemicals throughout the body! White blood cells and antibodies in the blood help with an organism's immunity to disease.

The circulatory system is intertwined with every other system, especially the respiratory system. All the cells in the body, even the cardiac muscle cells of the heart, depend on the circulatory system to provide oxygen and glucose and to carry away carbon dioxide.

Worksheets:
19.1, 19.3–19.5

Diagram:
19.2

Microscope:
19.6

MUSCULOSKELETAL | DIGESTIVE | CIRCULATORY | RESPIRATORY | EXCRETORY | ENDOCRINE | NERVOUS

Chapter

20

THE RESPIRATORY SYSTEM

At the time when the Lord God made the earth and the heavens . . . the Lord God formed man out of the clay of the ground and blew into his nostrils the breath of life, and so man became a living being.

—Genesis 2:4–7

FIGURE 20.1. TAMAS CLEMENTIS, HUNGARIAN OPERA SINGER
Opera singers use their respiratory system to create beautiful music.

THE RESPIRATORY SYSTEM

I will admit that the opening lines of the last chapters don't exactly "take your breath away!" The respiratory system is truly breathtaking, though!

The function of the human respiratory system is to exchange gases. It also helps regulate body temperature.

Respiratory System

The **NOSTRILS** and mouth take in air. Both the nose and mouth help to moisten the air before it reaches the lungs. The nose is important for two other reasons as well. The hairs and the **MUCUS** lining of the nose

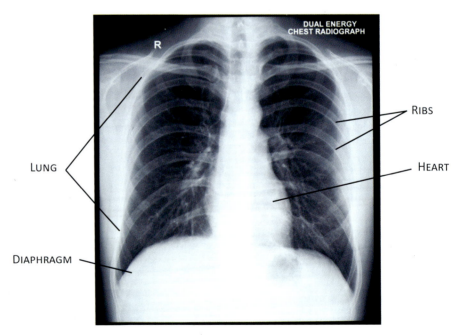

FIGURE 20.2. EXTERNAL RESPIRATION
The lungs, ribs, diaphragm, and heart are visible in this X-ray of the chest. When the diaphragm contracts, it moves downward and creates a vacuum in the chest cavity. Air rushes into the lungs to fill the vacuum.

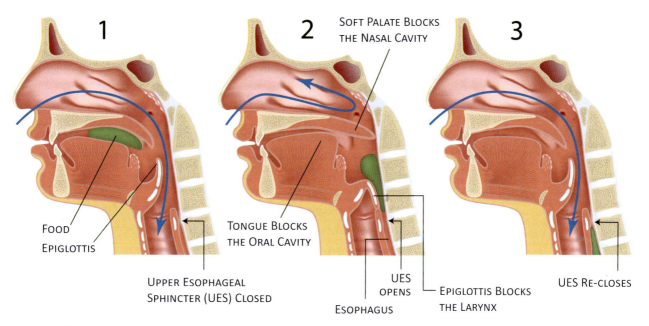

1

2 SOFT PALATE BLOCKS
THE NASAL CAVITY

3

FOOD
EPIGLOTTIS

TONGUE BLOCKS
THE ORAL CAVITY

UES
OPENS

ESOPHAGUS

EPIGLOTTIS BLOCKS
THE LARYNX

UES RE-CLOSES

UPPER ESOPHAGEAL
SPHINCTER (UES) CLOSED

FIGURE 20.3. FUNCTION OF THE EPIGLOTTIS
Thanks to your epiglottis, food goes into your stomach when you swallow, instead of into your lungs.

filter the air. The nasal passages also warm the air before it reaches the delicate inside of the lungs.

The air then moves into the **PHARYNX**, which is the space at the back of the nose and throat. The pharynx is connected to the esophagus and the wind pipe, or trachea.

The **TRACHEA**, the tube for air, is positioned in the neck in front of the esophagus, the tube for food. The inventor of the human machine put a special flap, called the **EPIGLOTTIS**, over the opening of the trachea to keep food out (Figure 20.3). If you have ever had food "go down the wrong pipe," you know that taking a breath and swallowing at the same time doesn't work. It makes you cough and choke until the piece of food comes up instead of going down into the lungs.

The trachea is held open by rings of cartilage. You can feel the cartilage rings in your own throat by placing your fingers just above the collar bone and sliding them up and down. The inside of the trachea is lined with ciliated epithelial tissue. These cells have mucus and cilia that trap dust and move it upward.

The lump in your throat, your voice box, is commonly called the Adam's apple, or if you prefer, the Harriet's apple! The proper name for the voice box is the **LARYNX**. Inside the larynx are the **VOCAL CORDS**, which are somewhat like two, tightly stretched rubber bands. The edges of the two vocal cords vibrate when air is forced past them (Figure 20.4). This creates sounds, which are formed into words by the tongue, teeth, and lips.

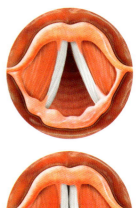

**FIGURE 20.4.
VOCAL CORDS**
The larynx houses the vocal cords, which are essential for speech. The vocal cords open (top) during breathing and close when one holds one's breath. When air is forced through partially closed vocal cords (bottom), the vocal cords vibrate and produce sound.

The trachea divides into two main branches, the bronchi, one for each lung. Inside the lungs, each **BRONCHUS** divides into many smaller **BRONCHIAL TUBES**, and these divide into tiny bronchioles (Figure 20.6). The bronchioles end in clusters of air sacs that look like microscopic bunches of grapes. Each air sac is called an **ALVEOLUS**. As you learned in Chapter 19, the air sacs are the place where the oxygen in the air diffuses into the blood. At the same time, carbon dioxide in the blood diffuses into the air sacs. See Figure 20.8.

Each lung contains an unbelievable number of air sacs. Their total surface area is estimated to be approximately 70 m^2. That means that if all the air sacs in one set of adult lungs were flattened out, they could cover the floors of approximately three average-sized living rooms!

The lungs are spongy because they contain so many alveoli, capillaries, and air. They are enclosed in a double layer of protective tissue, called the pleura. Under the lungs is the **DIAPHRAGM** (DYE-uh-fram), a smooth, dome-shaped muscle needed for breathing (Figure 20.2). Sometimes the diaphragm has spasms, which most people call **HICCUPS**.

Some animals, such as the bluegill, use gills for respiration instead of lungs. The amoeba and other protists respire—that is, exchange gases—through their cell membranes, and worms use their skin for respiration. Can you figure out why God gave humans lungs instead of designing them to respire through their skin like worms? Humans are larger than worms and thus have less surface area in comparison with their body mass. The surface area of Average Arnold's body is only 2 m^2, which is a lot less than the 70 m^2 which he needs for respiration. If people used their skin for respiration as worms do, we would each need the skin on thirty-five people to be able to breathe! And since moist membranes are needed for respiration, we would also have to stay slimy with mucus.

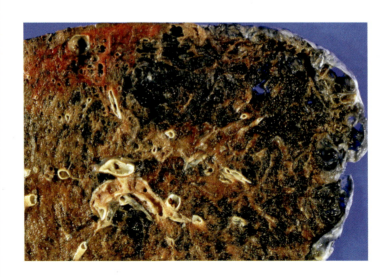

**FIGURE 20.5.
PULMONARY EMPHYSEMA**
Sectioned lung affected by a smoking-induced emphysema. In this disorder the air sacs in the lungs become enlarged and damaged reducing the surface area for the exchange of oxygen and carbon dioxide. Severe emphysema causes breathlessness which may be made worse by infections. There is no specific treatment available and the patient may become dependent on oxygen therapy.

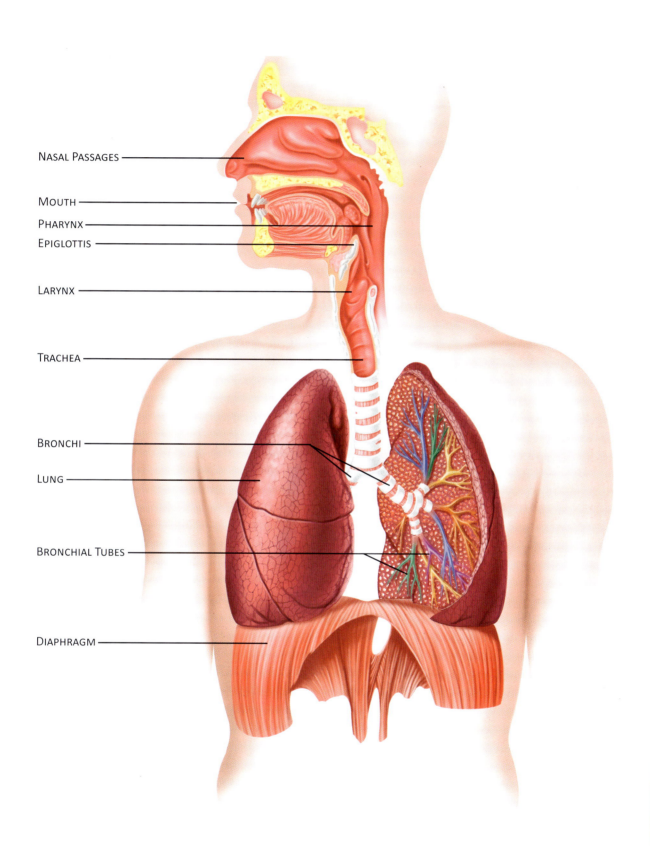

NASAL PASSAGES

MOUTH

PHARYNX

EPIGLOTTIS

LARYNX

TRACHEA

BRONCHI

LUNG

BRONCHIAL TUBES

DIAPHRAGM

FIGURE 20.6. THE RESPIRATORY SYSTEM
Moist membranes close to a supply of oxygen are needed for respiration.

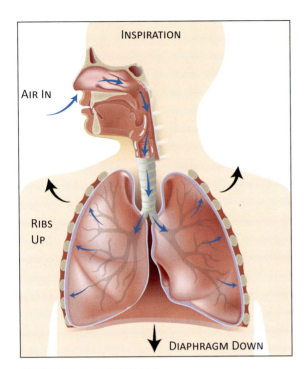
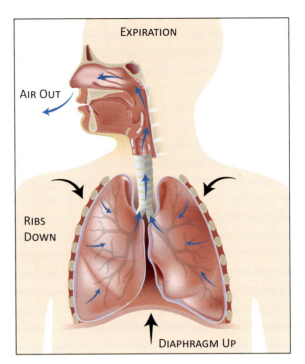

FIGURE 20.7. BREATHING
Inspiration occurs when the rib muscles and diaphragm contract, making the chest cavity larger. Air forces its way into the lungs. Expiration requires a relaxation of the rib muscles and diaphragm.

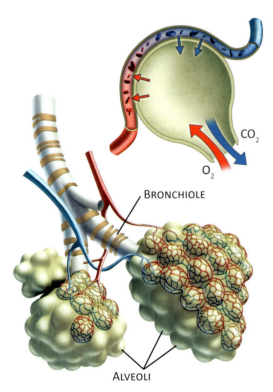

FIGURE 20.8.
The alveoli are microscopic air sacs filled with air and surrounded by capillaries.

External Respiration

We actually do not breathe in. Your body has no means of "pulling" air inside itself! To **INHALE**, the muscles between the ribs contract, lifting the rib cage. The diaphragm contracts at the same time, which makes it move lower. These motions cause the chest cavity to get larger (Figure 20.7). Because of the air pressure outside of the body, air rushes into the lungs to fill up the empty space. The process of breathing in is **INSPIRATION**.

To **EXHALE**, the rib muscles and diaphragm relax. The ribs drop downward and the chest cavity gets smaller. The air is forced out of the lungs. The process of breathing out is **EXPIRATION**. Recall that "*ex*", as in "exit," means "out."

While in the lungs, the air is changed in three important ways. First, **oxygen** moves from the alveoli into the capillaries by diffusion, because there is a much higher concentration of oxygen in the alveoli than in the capillaries. The hemoglobin in the blood grabs the oxygen molecules and carries it to the other cells in the body.

Second, **water vapor** evaporates from the moist surfaces of the alveoli into the air.

Third, **carbon dioxide**, a waste product of cellular respiration, moves out of the capillaries and into the alveoli (Figure 20.8). This movement happens by diffusion, because the carbon dioxide is more concentrated in the capillaries than in the alveoli.

Breathing is partly, but not completely voluntary. When you hold your breath, your cells still use up oxygen and make carbon dioxide waste. As more and more carbon dioxide moves from the cells into the blood, nerves in the walls of the arteries send messages to your brain. Your brain then sends messages to your diaphragm and rib muscles to contract, and you breathe in, whether you are ready or not.

Cellular respiration, the rest of the breath taking story of respiration, occurs in every cell, all the way from those in the air sac wall to those in the little toe.

Cellular Respiration

The exchange of gases—oxygen and carbon dioxide—in the cells is very similar to the exchange of gases in the lungs. Each gas diffuses from where there is a higher concentration to where there is lower concentration.

At each cell, oxygen is released by the hemoglobin in the red blood cells and diffuses out of the capillary and through the lymph fluid into the cell. Inside the mighty mitochondria of the cell, the oxygen is used for the **OXIDATION** of glucose. The energy released is stored in ATP molecules and used to carry out the life functions in each cell.

The oxidation of glucose releases carbon dioxide as a waste product. The carbon dioxide which has built up in the cell diffuses through the lymph fluid and into the capillary. The circulatory system transports the carbon dioxide waste to the lungs, which eliminate it from the body.

The excretion of wastes is the topic for the next chapter, but notice that we have already discussed part of that topic! The excretion of carbon dioxide is an example of how closely connected all the body systems are, since it involves the circulatory, respiratory, and excretory systems!

Do you remember learning about diffusion in Chapter 5? When there is a much greater concentration of a substance in one area, molecules in the substance naturally move away from each other and go toward the lower concentration. This movement from higher to lower concentration, without the use of energy, is called diffusion.

FIGURE 20.9. DIFFUSION
Diffusion of the molecules from a tea bag illustrates how molecules move from higher to lower concentration.

Worksheets:
20.1, 20.3–20.6

Diagram:
20.2

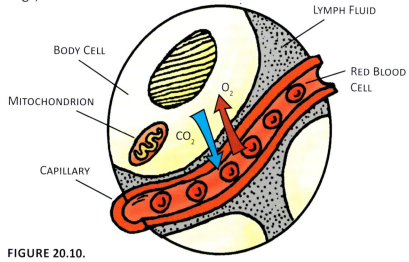

FIGURE 20.10.
CELLULAR RESPIRATION
Oxygen and carbon dioxide are exchanged between the red blood cells and all the other cells of the body.

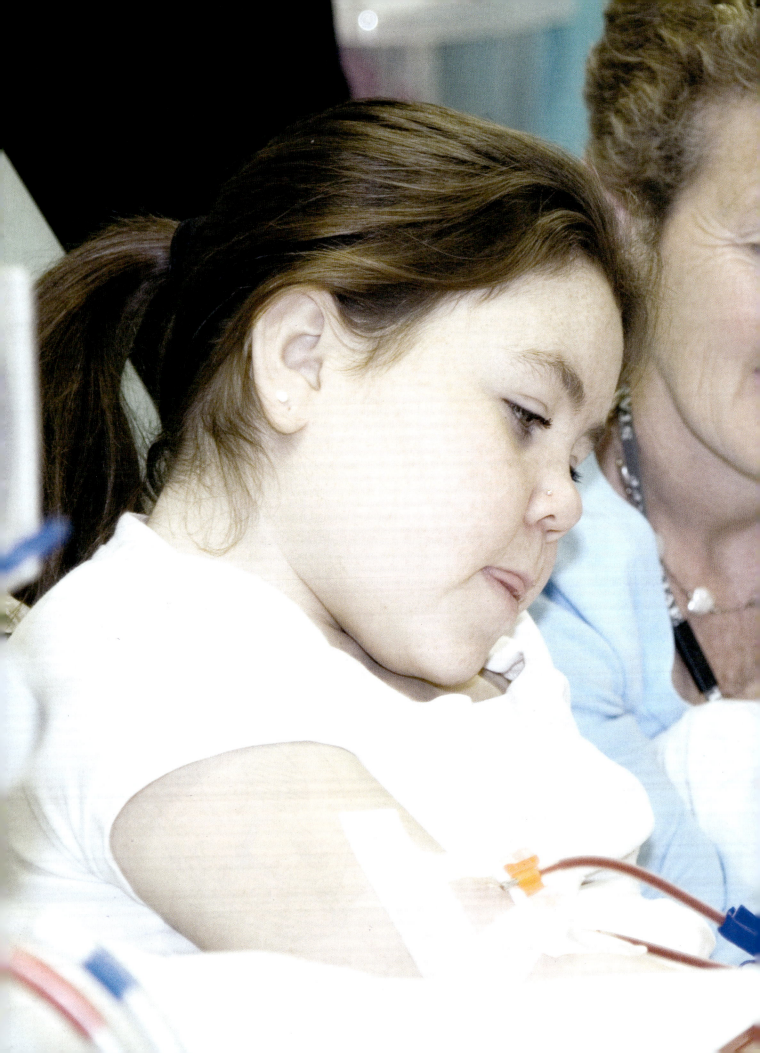

THE EXCRETORY SYSTEM

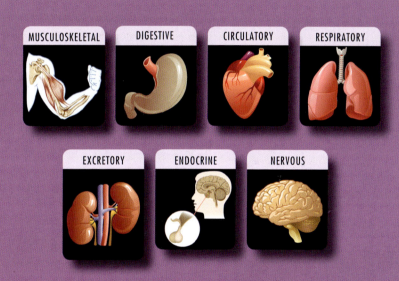

MUSCULOSKELETAL   DIGESTIVE   CIRCULATORY   RESPIRATORY

EXCRETORY   ENDOCRINE   NERVOUS

FIGURE 21.1. YOUNG PATIENT DOING SCHOOL WORK WHILE IN A DIALYSIS TREATMENT UNIT
Kidney dialysis, or hemodialysis, is required when the kidneys are unable to filter waste products from the blood. The patient's blood flows out of the body through a tube into a dialysis machine. This acts as an artificial kidney, removing waste products and excess fluid from the blood. The cleaned blood is then returned to the patient through a second tube. The procedure takes several hours and needs to be repeated several times a week.

THE EXCRETORY SYSTEM

It appears that the opening line of the last several chapters has been a *waste*, so for this chapter, we'll *eliminate* it!

The function of the human excretory system is to eliminate wastes from the body. Just as our rivers, lakes, and fields can become polluted by the build-up of wastes, your cells will become polluted and die if wastes are not constantly removed from them. The body has several different ways of excreting the wastes produced in your cells.

Lungs

The excretion of **carbon dioxide** and **water vapor** was already discussed in the previous chapter on the respiratory system. As you learned, carbon dioxide and water vapor diffuse from the blood into the alveoli (air sacs) of the lungs. Each time a person exhales, these wastes are eliminated through the **mouth** and **nostrils**. If CO_2 cannot be removed from the body, the organism dies of asphyxiation.

Large Intestine

In the chapter on the digestive system we learned that the large intestine reabsorbs water from the **solid wastes** left over from digestion. The **STOOL** is formed in the rectum and eliminated through the **anus**.

Liver

The largest organ in the body, the liver, is actually a waste treatment center. Its importance is indicated by the fact that nearly one-third of the blood goes through the liver with each contraction of the heart. The liver turns waste chemicals in the body into a form that other organs can excrete.

The liver converts ammonia in the blood into **UREA**. Ammonia (NH_3) is a toxic waste produced when the human body uses certain amino acids.

FIGURE 21.2.
LIVER AND SPLEEN
The liver is the largest organ in the body. The spleen helps the liver to remove worn-out red blood cells from the bloodstream. See Figure 18.8 in Chapter 18.

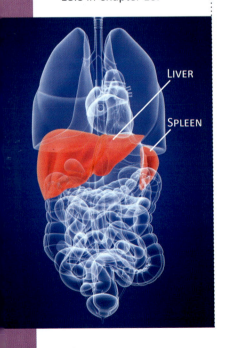

LIVER

SPLEEN

Urea is a colorless nitrogen compound that the kidneys can filter from the blood.

The spleen helps the liver to remove worn-out red blood cells from the bloodstream (Figure 21.2). The liver then recycles the worn-out red blood cells. The parts and pieces that are no longer usable, called **bile pigments**, are sent through the **bile duct** into the small intestine.

As you have learned, the liver also assists the process of digestion by producing bile for emulsifying fats. In Chapter 22 you will learn how the liver acts as a short-term storage center for glucose.

Kidneys

The circulatory system transports wastes from the cells and the liver to the kidneys situated in the lower back. The two, 10-cm-long kidneys act like the filter on a swimming pool, filtering out waste materials and allowing the purified liquid to pass through.

The kidneys are complex organs needed for the excretion of nitrogenous wastes (urea) and water. A person cannot live if both his kidneys fail, unless he uses an artificial kidney. When a person's kidneys fail to work properly, he may undergo DIALYSIS at a medical center. The dialysis machine is an

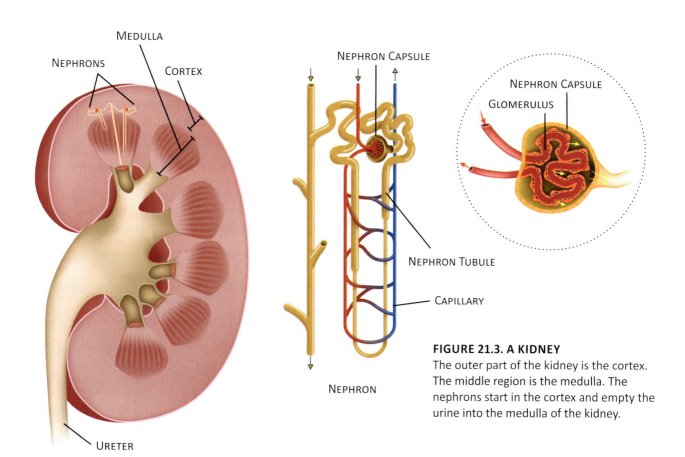

MEDULLA
NEPHRONS
CORTEX
URETER

NEPHRON CAPSULE
NEPHRON TUBULE
CAPILLARY
NEPHRON

NEPHRON CAPSULE
GLOMERULUS

FIGURE 21.3. A KIDNEY
The outer part of the kidney is the cortex. The middle region is the medulla. The nephrons start in the cortex and empty the urine into the medulla of the kidney.

artificial kidney that allows the diffusion of nitrogenous wastes from the blood through semipermeable membranes (Figure 21.1).

In the cortex of a healthy human kidney, urea and other wastes are filtered from the blood in approximately one million **NEPHRONS**. The end of each nephron, called the nephron capsule, holds a knot of capillaries called the **GLOMERULUS**. Inside the nephron capsule, **water, nitrogenous wastes,** and **salts** in the blood are absorbed from the capillaries and into the nephron capsule by diffusion. Once these wastes are removed, the blood in the capillaries is much thicker, so some of the water is actively put back into the capillaries by the **NEPHRON TUBULES**.

The nephron tubules lead from the nephron capsules, where the wastes are diffused out of the blood, to the medulla of the kidney, where the wastes are collected. These wastes, called **URINE**, are then passed through the two **URETERS** to the **URINARY BLADDER**. The bladder empties through the one **URETHRA**. Use the "a" in the word "urethra" to remember you have **a** urethra but **two** ureters (Figure 21.4). Urine exits through the **urethra**.

A summary of the excretory action carried out in the **URINARY TRACT** is included in Figure 21.5.

The urine is an excellent indicator of a body's condition in terms of health. An excess or deficiency of glucose or vitamins can be detected by testing the urine. Alcohol and drug abusers can be detected by urine tests, hopefully before they cause accidents that harm innocent people. A woman can determine if she is carrying an unborn child by means of another urine test.

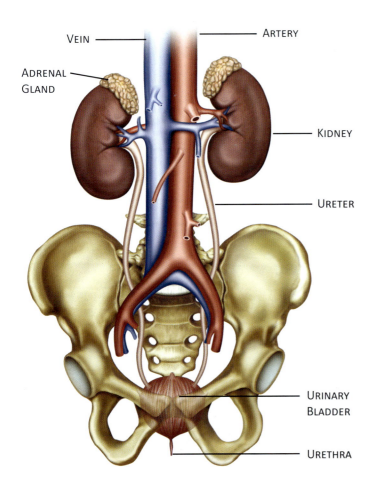

VEIN

ARTERY

ADRENAL GLAND

KIDNEY

URETER

URINARY BLADDER

URETHRA

FIGURE 21.4. URINARY TRACT
The urinary tract includes all the organs of the excretory system that produce and transport urine. Urine is formed in the kidneys from urea and other wastes.

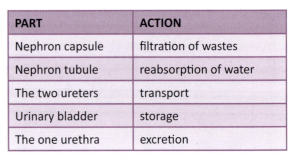

PART	ACTION
Nephron capsule	filtration of wastes
Nephron tubule	reabsorption of water
The two ureters	transport
Urinary bladder	storage
The one urethra	excretion

FIGURE 21.5. URINARY TRACT SUMMARY

186

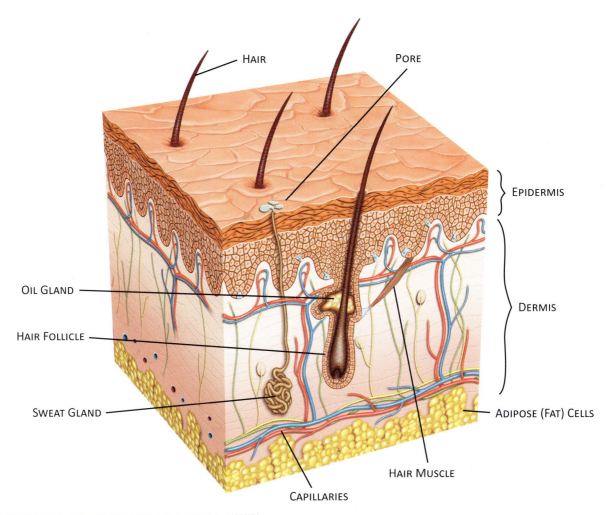

FIGURE 21.6. CROSS-SECTION OF HUMAN SKIN
The skin is a complex organ in the excretory system. Salts and nitrogenous wastes, dissolved in water, are excreted through the pores that lead to the sweat glands. Heat also escapes through the skin.

Skin

Skin allows the human body to excrete excess **heat, water, salts** and **nitrogenous wastes** not excreted in the urine. The outermost layer of skin, the EPIDERMIS, is composed of closely packed cells. This dense layer of cells protects the tissue underneath. The epidermis has many pores that open into the DERMIS, the layer of skin where the SWEAT GLANDS are located. Capillaries are found all through the dermis, especially around each sweat gland. Water, salts, and nitrogenous wastes are taken from the blood by the sweat glands and then excreted onto the surface of the skin through **pores** (Figure 21.6). Regular washing of the skin is important to keep these pores open.

Excess heat is eliminated by the skin when the capillaries open up wide to bring more blood near the surface of the body. The heat which the blood carries from the organs escapes through the skin. This is what makes people look flushed when they are too hot. The evaporation of sweat from the skin also lowers the body's temperature.

Worksheets:
21.1–21.2, 21.4–21.5

Diagram:
21.3, 21.6

Microscope:
21.7

MUSCULOSKELETAL

DIGESTIVE

CIRCULATORY

RESPIRATORY

EXCRETORY

ENDOCRINE

NERVOUS

Chapter 22

THE ENDOCRINE SYSTEM

Science itself does not address the question whether we should use the power at our disposal for good or for evil. The guidelines of what we ought to do are furnished in the moral law of God. It is no longer enough that we pray that God may be with us on our side. We must learn to pray that we may be on God's side.

—Wernher von Braun

FIGURE 22.1. TOM THUMB AND P.T. BARNUM
General Tom Thumb (1838–1883) was a popular dwarf performer in the Barnum & Bailey Circus. Tom Thumb's real name was Charles Sherwood Stratton.

THE ENDOCRINE SYSTEM

If you get the *message* in this chapter you should be able to keep your blood pressure under *control.*

The human **ENDOCRINE SYSTEM** is a group of ductless glands that produce chemical messengers. Glands are organs which synthesize, or make, chemicals for the body. A duct is a tube. The salivary glands make saliva and empty it into the mouth through salivary ducts. The liver synthesizes bile, stores it in the gall bladder, and releases it into the small intestine through the bile duct.

Unlike the liver and the salivary glands, endocrine glands do not have ducts. The chemicals are produced in special glandular cells and are secreted directly into the blood. Within a matter of seconds, these chemical messengers, called **HORMONES**, can cause great changes in breathing, heart rate, and capillary size. Of course, hormones can also act slowly over many years.

The function of the endocrine system and its hormones is to coordinate and control body growth and metabolism. That's a mouthful! The meaning of "coordinate and control body growth and metabolism" is best explained by several examples.

Imagine how awkward a baby would be if his left leg grew to adult size first, then the left arm, and then, years later, his right arm and leg. Or imagine if a tiger's body matured first and then its head and brain—you would have a very playful several hundred pounds of muscle, sinew, and claws! The reason these things do not happen in healthy individuals is that the endocrine glands help **coordinate growth** so the body grows and changes in an orderly fashion.

Now imagine what happens when you run a race. What do your muscles need to race to the finish line? Energy! In order to produce enough energy, your cellular respiration rate must keep up with your "race pace."

FIGURE 22.2.
A 100-meters dash in
Kamloops, Canada

This requires more glucose, which must be released more quickly from temporary storage in the liver. The glands in your endocrine system speed these processes up during your race, and then slow them down again when you stop running. This is what we mean when we say that the endocrine glands help **control metabolism**.

Pituitary Gland

The "master gland" that controls many of the other endocrine glands is located at the base of the brain. It is the **PITUITARY GLAND**, which is fastened to the hypothalamus of the brain (Figure 22.3). Many of the hormones of the pituitary gland are made in the hypothalamus.

One important hormone which the pituitary gland synthesizes (makes) and secretes (releases) is ACTH. ACTH is a nickname for a pituitary hormone that tells the adrenal glands to secrete their hormones. The **A** in **A**CTH is for *Adrenal*.

TSH is another hormone produced by the pituitary gland. TSH controls the thyroid gland, and its name means "**T**hyroid **S**timulating **H**ormone."

Do you see why the pituitary gland is nicknamed the "master gland"? Through ACTH, TSH, and other hormones, the pituitary gland controls many of the other glands in the endocrine system.

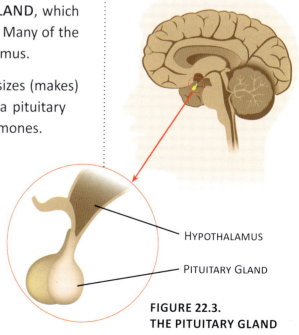

HYPOTHALAMUS

PITUITARY GLAND

**FIGURE 22.3.
THE PITUITARY GLAND**

FIGURE 22.4. Sandy Allen (right), with her mother Jackie (left) and her 12-year-old brother Michael (center), at home in Niagara Falls in 1980. Her abnormal height was due to a tumor in her pituitary gland. She was 231 cm tall (7 ft, 7 in).

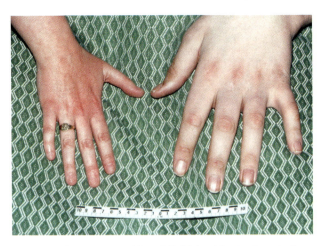

FIGURE 22.5. A normal hand (left) beside the hand of a person with acromegaly (right). Acromegaly is caused by excessive production of growth hormone. The condition can be controlled today with drugs.

Besides controlling other glands, the pituitary gland also secretes **GROWTH HORMONE**. In some adults, an overactive pituitary gland causes acromegaly, a disorder leading to changed features and enlargement of the hands and feet (Figure 22.5).

In a child, if the pituitary gland does not produce enough growth hormone, the child will not grow properly. He or she will be a dwarf. Pauline Musters, a girl from the Netherlands, was the shortest dwarf recorded. Pauline was 59 cm tall when she died at age 19. Today, injections of growth hormone can often compensate for an underactive pituitary gland and allow a child to reach a more normal height.

An overactive pituitary in childhood causes giantism (Figure 22.4). The tallest giant recorded was an American boy, Robert Wadlow of Illinois (see Figure 2.5 in Chapter 2). One of history's most famous giants was Charlemagne, emperor of the Holy Roman Empire.

Thyroid Gland

The **THYROID GLAND** is shaped like a bow tie. It is located just where a bow tie would be, below the larynx on the front of the trachea. This gland makes **THYROXIN**, an iodine-containing hormone which controls the rate of metabolism. Do you remember what metabolism is? Metabolism is the sum of all life activities. Thyroxin is necessary in proper amounts for normal physical and mental development.

Since thyroxin contains iodine, the thyroid gland can't make enough thyroxin if a person's diet lacks iodine. The body reacts as if the thyroid

FIGURE 22.6. A false chimney in Harvington Hall. The smoke-blackened bricks of this fireplace disguise the fact that the chimney is actually a secret passage into the attic.

St. Nicholas Owen

St. Nicholas Owen (1550–1606) was a dwarf, a skilled craftsman, a Jesuit lay brother, and a martyr during the persecution of English Catholics under Elizabeth I and James I.

Under the name of "Little John," Owen traveled from house to house, disguised as an itinerant carpenter. At night, after praying for God's assistance and receiving Holy Communion when possible, Owen dug underground passages, constructed false walls, and transformed staircases, sewage drains, and chimneys into places of safety—called "priest holes"—for priests and other Catholics being hunted by government agents. Over one hundred examples of Owen's work are known to date, but many may never be discovered, such was his ingenuity and skill. Owen is also believed to have masterminded the famous escape of Fr. John Gerard from the Tower of London in 1597.

In 1606, Owen was arrested after four days of hiding in one of his own priest holes. Owen and a companion gave themselves up in an attempt to draw attention away from two priests who

FIGURE 22.7. A secret panel concealing a priest hole in Harvington Hall, an English manor house. Harvington Hall contains a number of priest holes, several of them constructed by St. Nicholas Owen.

were hiding in the same house. Although Owen was cruelly tortured, he refused to betray his fellow Catholics by revealing their names or the locations of the priest holes he had constructed. Owen died under torture and was canonized in 1970 as one of the Forty Martyrs of England and Wales. Fr. Gerard wrote of him, "I verily think no man can be said to have done more good of all those who labored in the English vineyard."

gland is not big enough, so the lack of iodine causes a greatly enlarged thyroid gland in the neck called **SIMPLE GOITER** (Figure 22.8). In children, an underactive thyroid gland causes cretinism; their development is not normal.

FIGURE 22.8.
WOMAN WITH GOITER

Parathyroid Glands

Embedded inside the back of the thyroid gland are the parathyroid glands. The name of the hormone secreted by the parathyroid gland is easy to remember: parathormone. Its name is a combination of the words **parath**yroid and **hormone**. Parathormone controls the body's use of calcium and phosphate compounds. You already know that the calcium is needed for bones and teeth. The phosphates are needed for the nerves.

Thymus Glands

The thymus glands in the center of the chest help develop a child's immune system. In adults, it stimulates immune system activity.

Pancreas

Inside the pancreas are small spots of tissue different from the surrounding tissue. To a researcher looking through a microscope, these spots appear like islands in the sea of pancreatic cells. These spots of tissue, called the **ISLANDS OF LANGERHANS**, are an important part of the endocrine system. I'll bet you can figure out the name of the scientist who discovered them! Another name for the Islands of Langerhans could be the "sugar

St. Giuseppe Moscati

St. Giuseppe Moscati (1880–1927) was an Italian doctor who dedicated his life to caring for the sick. He would often treat poor patients without charge, and would even send them home with money for the medicine he prescribed. He assisted at Holy Mass every day, and encouraged his patients to receive the sacraments before undergoing surgery. St. Giuseppe Moscati trained many medical students at the local university, teaching them to care for their patients with love and respect. A brilliant physician, St. Giuseppe was one of the first doctors to use CPR to stimulate the heart, and also pioneered the use of insulin to treat diabetes. St. Giuseppe Moscati was canonized in 1987.

FIGURE 22.9.
ST. GIUSEPPE MOSCATI

islands," because they make glucagon and insulin, the hormones that control the glucose levels in the body.

As you know, glucose is the chemical food which your cells use to produce energy through the process of cellular respiration. When you eat a candy bar or enjoy a good meal, large amounts of glucose are absorbed into your bloodstream. As you learned in Chapter 14, the extra glucose that you do not need right away is temporarily stored in your liver in the form of glycogen. Then, when more glucose is needed, the liver breaks down the glycogen into glucose and releases it into the bloodstream. **GLUCAGON**, produced by the pancreas, is the hormone that controls the release of glucose from its temporary storage in the liver. The pancreas also produces **INSULIN**, which allows the absorption of the glucose into the cells.

Since glucose is the source of energy for each living cell, insulin is needed for life itself. When the pancreas does not work properly or is damaged so that the Islands of Langerhans cannot make insulin, **DIABETES** results. Daily injections of insulin can allow a diabetic to live for many years. Today, experimental computer chips are being put under the skin of some diabetics. The computer chips release insulin into the blood automatically when needed. If this new arrangement is discovered to work, it would allow diabetics to live without daily injections.

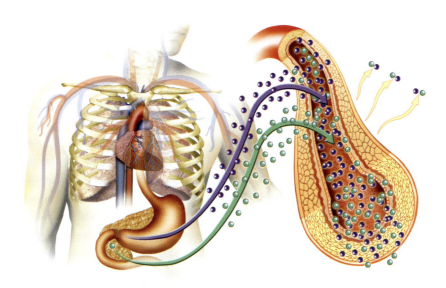

FIGURE 22.10. INSULIN REGULATES THE ABSORPTION OF GLUCOSE
When glucose (purple) is digested by the stomach and absorbed into the bloodstream, the pancreas in healthy individuals responds by releasing insulin (green) into the bloodstream. Insulin is the hormone which causes cells to absorb glucose for the purpose of cellular respiration. If a person's pancreas no longer produces insulin (type 1 diabetes), the person's cells will not be able to absorb the glucose in the bloodstream, and the person will be unable to produce the energy for life.

FIGURE 22.11. When you get in "a fight or a fright," adrenalin from the adrenal glands increases your heart rate and respiratory rate.

Worksheets:
22.1–22.5

Research:
22.6

Adrenal Glands

On top of the kidneys are the **ADRENAL GLANDS**, sometimes called the glands of combat (see Figure 22.11). The hormone made by the outer part of the adrenal glands, called the cortex, is **CORTISOL**. Cortisol regulates sugar metabolism and reduces inflammation and allergic reactions.

It is the **ADRENALIN** from the center of the gland, the adrenal medulla, that gives the adrenal glands their nickname: glands of combat. Another name for the hormone adrenalin is epinephrine.

Adrenalin is dumped into the bloodstream whenever you get into a fight or a fright. The adrenalin causes the heart to beat faster. That moves the blood faster so the cells get oxygen and glucose at a more rapid pace. To get more oxygen you must also breathe more rapidly and adrenalin speeds up the respiratory rate. It also causes an increase of glucose in the blood. Once all that happens you are ready to rough it or run!

Sex Glands

The gonads are the endocrine glands particular to each sex. In a male, the testes, located in the scrotum, produce the hormone testosterone. The testosterone causes the beard and other secondary male characteristics to develop. In a female, the ovaries in the lower abdomen secrete estrogen, which causes the secondary female characteristics to develop. The gonads help to change a child's body into an adult body. As you will learn in Chapter 24, the gonads also produce the sperm and egg cells needed for the conception of a new human person.

Summary

The major glands in the human endocrine system are illustrated in Figure 22.12. The complex job of getting billions of cells to grow and change in an orderly fashion is done by the endocrine system. Without it your body would be a wreck.

Modern medicine has helped some victims of endocrine disorders through injections of hormones or dietary improvements. There is still plenty to be learned about how the human body, with all its systems, works together in a healthy individual. Life scientists are needed who will study and learn and eventually discover the still unknown secrets of the endocrine system.

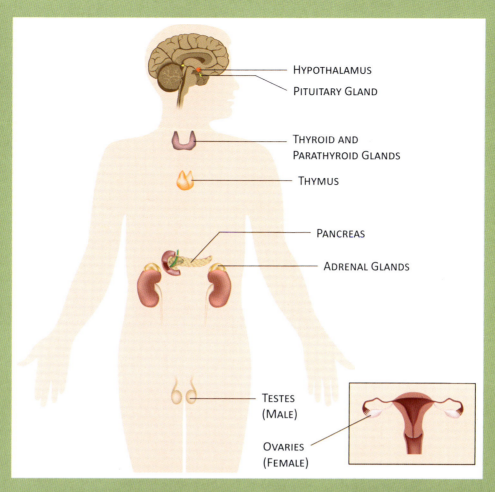

GLAND (OTHER NAMES)	LOCATION	HORMONE AND EFFECT
Pituitary (Master gland)	Center, base of the brain. This gland is attached to the hypothalamus of the brain. Some of its hormones are made there.	Controls the other glands. Produces ACTH for the adrenal gland and TSH for the thyroid. Produces growth hormone.
Thyroid (Bow tie gland)	In the neck below the larynx	Iodine-containing thyroxin controls metabolism.
Parathyroid	On the thyroid gland	Parathormone controls Ca for bones, P for nerves.
Thymus	In the chest	Immune system development and stimulus
Islands of Langerhans ("Sugar islands")	In the pancreas	Insulin for absorption of glucose. Glucagon controls release of glucose from the liver.
Adrenal (Combat glands)	On top of each of the kidneys	Adrenaline increases heartbeat and rate of breathing. Cortisol for sugar metabolism and reduced inflammation.
Testes (male gonads) Ovaries (female gonads)	In the scrotum Inside the lower abdomen	Testosterone causes secondary male characteristics. Estrogen causes secondary female characteristics.

FIGURE 22.12. THE ENDOCRINE SYSTEM
The hormones produced by the ductless glands are the chemical messengers which coordinate the systems of the body so that they work together.

MUSCULOSKELETAL

DIGESTIVE

CIRCULATORY

RESPIRATORY

EXCRETORY

ENDOCRINE

NERVOUS

THE NERVOUS SYSTEM

Nature is a book whose history, whose evolution, whose "writing" and meaning, we "read" according to the different approaches of the sciences, while all the time presupposing the foundational presence of the Author who has wished to reveal Himself therein.

—Benedict XVI

FIGURE 23.1. BRAILLE
People who are blind can read by using the Braille system of writing, in which different combinations of bumps represent letters and sounds.

THE NERVOUS SYSTEM

PARTS OF THE NERVOUS SYSTEM

If the opening lines of the past chapters got on your *nerves*, then I know you won't *mind* that this is the last chapter in which you will *see* or *hear* one of them.

The nervous system consists of all the cells of the body that can detect, send, or store information for later transmission. The functions of the nervous system are many. The functions of the nervous system and the special organs and cells which carry them out are summarized in Figure 23.2.

FUNCTION	PART
Controlling involuntary actions	The medulla, part of the brain
Controlling balance	The cerebellum, part of the brain
Data input	The five sense organs
Reflex actions	The spinal cord in the backbone
Transmission of messages	The outer nerve cells and spinal cord
Memory	The cerebrum, part of the brain
Controlling voluntary actions	The cerebrum, part of the brain
Thinking	The cerebrum, part of the brain

FIGURE 23.2. FUNCTIONS OF THE NERVOUS SYSTEM

Neurons

The basic unit of the nervous system is the **NEURON**. Neurons are similar to the wires and circuits in a radio or television because neurons carry electrical messages. Unlike electrical wires, however, neurons will transmit an electrical **IMPULSE** in one direction only (Figure 23.3).

There are three main types of neurons. **SENSORY NEURONS** are the nerve cells that receive data from the organism's environment. Sensory neurons transmit a signal to the spinal cord or brain. The sensory neurons are especially concentrated in the sense organs: the eyes, ears, nose, tongue, and skin. Each of these sense organs has its own sensory neurons with special parts called **RECEPTORS**. Receptors come in different shapes for receiving different types of information.

ASSOCIATIVE NEURONS are the nerve cells that connect the sensory neurons to the motor neurons. They are "associated" with both the input of information and the sending out of commands to body parts. Associative neurons are concentrated in the spinal cord and brain. These neurons are the nerve cells that form ideas.

MOTOR NEURONS are the nerve cells that carry impulses to the body's "motors," the muscles and glands (Figure 23.3). Since muscles and glands can cause an effect they are termed **EFFECTORS**. Paralysis occurs when motor neurons are cut or stop working properly. Motor neurons can be found all through the body.

How do neurons receive and transmit messages? Most neurons don't actually touch each other. Instead they have branch-like parts called **DENDRITES** that come very close to, but don't touch, other nerve cells.

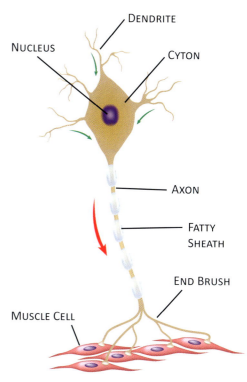

FIGURE 23.3. A MOTOR NEURON

One end of a motor neuron receives an impulse from an associative neuron. The other end transmits the message to a muscle. Although neurons are microscopic in diameter, their axons can be as long as 1.5 m!

Luigi Galvani

Luigi Galvani (1737–1798) was a Catholic doctor, professor, and scientist. In 1780, he was dissecting a frog and noticed that the muscles twitched when he touched the nerves with a spark of electricity from his steel scalpel.

This accidental observation revealed the connection between electricity and muscle movement, and led to our modern understanding of the nervous system.

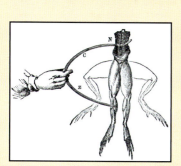

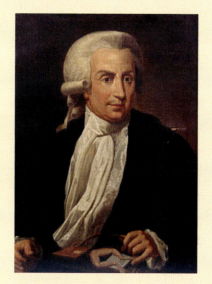

FIGURE 23.4. LUIGI GALVANI

Galvani is best known for his scientific discoveries, but those who knew him admired him more for his dedication to God, his patients, and his students. As a doctor he treated everyone who needed his help, whether or not they could pay him. He taught at the University of Bologna for many years, and never ended his lectures without "exhorting his pupils to a renewal of their faith by leading them always back to the idea of the eternal Providence which develops, preserves and causes life to flow among so many different kinds of things."

Galvani received many honors for his scientific discoveries, but the honor he valued most was his membership in the Third Order of St. Francis. At his request, Galvani was buried in the simple brown habit of the Franciscan Order.

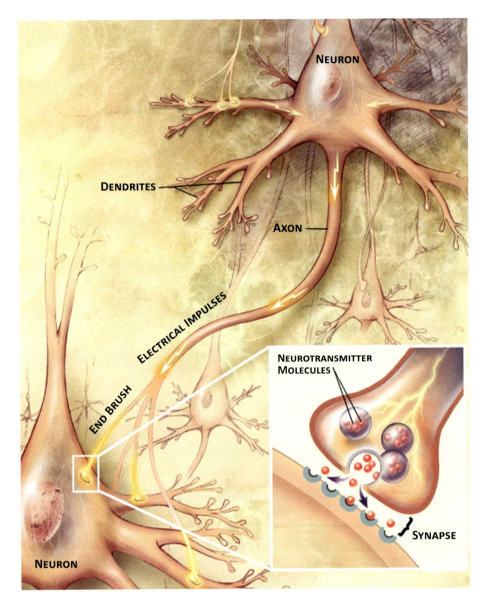

FIGURE 23.5. NEUROTRANSMITTERS CROSSING A SYNAPSE
Neurons receive electrical impulses through their dendrites and transmit the electrical impulse to another cell through their axons. The tiny space between the neuron's axon and the receiving cell is called the synapse. The electrical message is carried across the synapse by chemicals called neurotransmitters. When the neurotransmitter reaches the other cell, it is converted back into an electrical impulse to continue its journey.

When electrical nerve impulses are received by a dendrite, they travel to the cell body, or **CYTON**, then along the **AXON**. The axon is the long, thin part of a nerve cell which is covered with a fatty sheath, like a wire covered with plastic insulation (Figure 23.3). At the far end of the axon is the end brush, where the message is distributed to another cell.

At the end brush, the electrical nerve impulse is changed into a chemical message. The nerve chemical, a **NEUROTRANSMITTER**, moves across the **SYNAPSE**, which is the tiny space between the end brush and the other cell (Figure 23.5). When the neurotransmitter reaches the other cell, it initiates an electrical impulse to transport the message through that cell. Pain killer drugs, like aspirin, work because they stop the neurotransmitter from crossing the synapse.

The Brain

The brain and spinal cord are the center of all nervous activity in the body. Together they are called the **central nervous system**. The brain, a great mass of nerve cells, has three main regions which are protected by the skull.

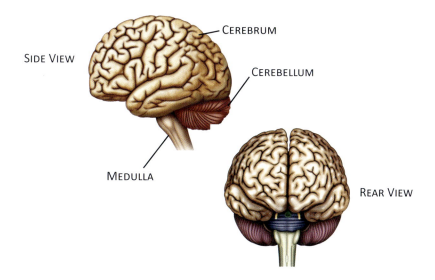

SIDE VIEW

CEREBRUM

CEREBELLUM

MEDULLA

REAR VIEW

FIGURE 23.6. THE BRAIN
Each part of the brain has specific functions. The largest part, the cerebrum, has special areas that control speech, sight, voluntary movement, thinking, and memory.

The **CEREBRUM** is the largest part of the brain. The outer part of the cerebrum consists mostly of grayish cytons, or cell bodies, while the inner part is white due to the fatty sheaths of the axons. The brain is divided into left and right hemispheres. It is covered with winding bumps called **CONVOLUTIONS** (Figure 23.6). The cerebrum controls thinking and problem solving as well as sight, speech, and voluntary movement.

The **CEREBELLUM** in the lower rear of the cranial cavity controls coordination and balance (Figure 23.6). The Latin word "*bellum*" means "war" or "contest." To win a fight or contest the combatant's coordination and balance must be very good. Use the old word "*bellum*" in cerebellum to associate this part of the brain with the coordination and balance needed by a warrior.

The **MEDULLA** oblongata is sometimes called the brain stem (Figure 23.6). The medulla is the control center for the smooth, involuntary muscles of the human digestive system. The medulla also controls the heart beat for the circulatory system and the breathing rate in the respiratory system.

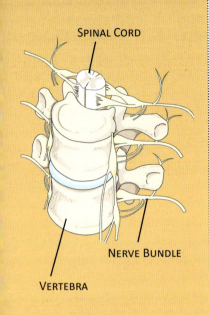

SPINAL CORD

NERVE BUNDLE

VERTEBRA

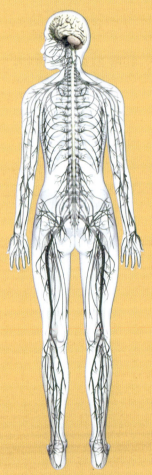

**FIGURE 23.7.
THE NERVOUS SYSTEM**
The brain and spinal cord
form the central nervous
system. The side nerves
that branch out from the
spinal cord are called
the peripheral nervous
system. The spinal cord
is protected by the
vertebrae of the spinal
column, or back bone.

The Spinal Cord

The spinal cord is a long bundle of associative neurons and the axons of many sensory and motor neurons. The spinal cord is protected by the bony vertebrae in the spinal column. Many reflex actions take place through impulses sent from the spinal cord. The spinal cord is the brain's connection to the torso and limbs.

There are thirty-one pairs of nerve bundles that go out through spaces between the vertebrae to all the muscles and glands in the body (Figure 23.7). These side bundles also include the axons of sensory neurons bringing data into the central nervous system. All of these side nerves together are the **peripheral nervous system**.

THE FIVE SENSES

It is impossible for anyone with all of their senses to imagine the thoughts and frustrations of someone whose eyes, ears, or both don't function properly! The example of individuals such as Helen Keller, who became both blind and deaf when she was very young, can help people appreciate their senses. The senses are the means by which the brain gets its data.

The Eyes

The eyes contain the sensory neurons that detect light energy. There are two types of neurons that detect light energy. ROD CELLS are neurons designed for black-and-white vision in dim light. CONE CELLS are neurons for color vision. Think of the "c" in "cone" to remember that cone cells are for *color* vision. Both rod and cone cells cover the back of the inside of each eye (Figure 23.8). This tissue of rod and cone cells is called the RETINA. The information from the rod and cone cells in the retina is transmitted to the brain by the OPTIC NERVE.

Figure 23.8 shows the **sclera**, a protective outer layer of tissue. The sclera is also called the "white" of the eye. Light that is reflected off the objects around you enters your eyeball through an opening called the **pupil**. The pupil is the black circle in the center of your eye, and is surrounded by the IRIS, a colored ring of muscle that adjusts the size of the pupil to allow more or less light to enter the eye.

The transparent CORNEA is located directly in front of the pupil, and the **lens** is located directly behind the pupil. The cornea and lens work together to focus the light onto the retina (Figure 23.9). The space between the cornea and the lens is filled with a watery fluid called **aqueous humor**. The rest of the eyeball is filled with a thicker, jellylike fluid called **vitreous humor**.

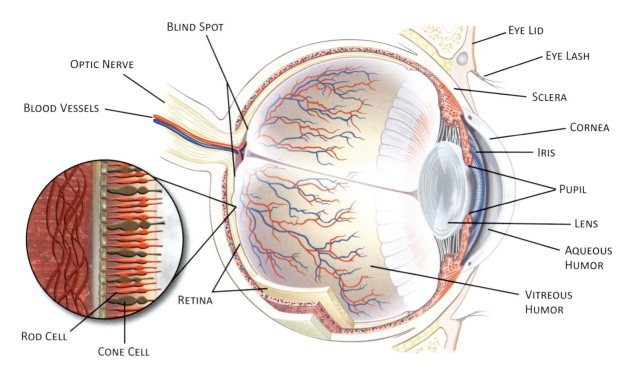

BLIND SPOT

OPTIC NERVE

BLOOD VESSELS

EYE LID

EYE LASH

SCLERA

CORNEA

IRIS

PUPIL

LENS

AQUEOUS HUMOR

VITREOUS HUMOR

RETINA

ROD CELL

CONE CELL

FIGURE 23.8. EYE CROSS-SECTION
Like an expensive camera, the human eye has an automatic focus and light control (iris), a lens, and a photosensitive surface (retina). The eyelid is a "lens cover" to protect the delicate cornea. You blink once every two to ten seconds to lubricate the eye.

The retina of each eye has a tiny "blind spot" at the place where it is connected to the optic nerve (Figure 23.9). This is because there are no rod or cone cells on this spot. To "see" your blind spot, close one eye and stare at a distant object. Hold a pencil, with the eraser end up, about 15 cm in front of your open eye. Slowly move the pencil back and forth, up and down. Keep staring straight ahead and you will see the end of the pencil disappear at a certain point. At that point, the light rays from the end of the pencil are falling on your blind spot where there are no rod or cone cells.

Why did you have to close one eye to see your blind spot? When both your eyes are open, the brain puts the impulses received from both optic nerves together to make one image. Each eye fills in the blind spot from the other eye.

Two eyes are also needed for depth perception. Anyone with an eye patch or only one eye should be extremely cautious when driving a car or engaging in other activities that require good depth perception.

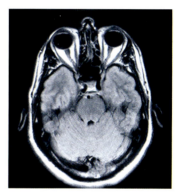

FIGURE 23.9. OPTIC NERVES
This MRI image of the head shows the nose and eyes at the top and the ears on either side. The optic nerves are the gray bands which extend from the bottom center of the eyes down to the brain. The gray bands on either side of each optic nerve are muscles which move the eyeballs.

FIGURE 23.10. When light from an object enters the eye, the lens focuses it onto the light-sensitive retina. The retina then transmits the image to the brain through the optic nerve. The image on the retina is flipped because the light rays travel in straight lines and cross over inside the eye. The brain is used to this, and interprets the image as right side up.

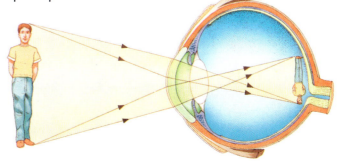

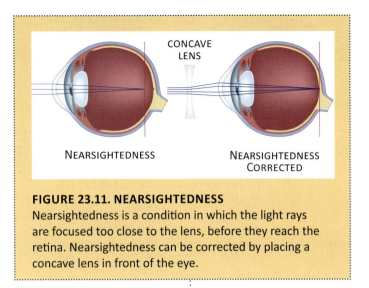

FIGURE 23.11. NEARSIGHTEDNESS
Nearsightedness is a condition in which the light rays are focused too close to the lens, before they reach the retina. Nearsightedness can be corrected by placing a concave lens in front of the eye.

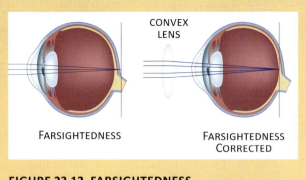

FIGURE 23.12. FARSIGHTEDNESS
Farsightedness is a condition in which the light rays are focused too far from the lens. Farsightedness can be corrected placing a convex lens in front of the eye.

For a person to see, the lens, the retina, the optic nerve, and the part of the brain that handles the optic impulses must all work properly. Blindness results when the sense of sight is destroyed by damage to the eye.

People who are nearsighted have eyes in which the light is focused before it gets to their eye's retina. By the time the light reaches the retina it is out of focus. This can happen if the lens of the eye is too thick or if the eye is oblong in shape. **NEARSIGHTEDNESS** can be corrected by placing a concave lens in front of the eye to bend the light rays apart before they pass through the cornea and pupil into the eye (Figure 23.11).

FARSIGHTEDNESS is the opposite problem. The light reaches the retina before it comes into focus. A convex lens can bend the light rays closer together and the eye's own convex lens can focus the light on the retina for clear vision (Figure 23.12).

The Ears

Most people consider sight their most important sense. The ability to hear is a close second. To hear a car horn beep a warning, to hear your mother call, "Time for supper!", and to hear your favorite song may seem like trite, everyday events, but who would want to lose his sense of hearing? The delicate pair of instruments that allow a person to hear are both intricate and interesting (Figure 23.13).

The outer ear includes the ear lobe, ear canal, and eardrum. The ear lobe, or pinna, is supported by cartilage which allows it to bend without breaking. Sound waves in the air are gathered by the ear lobe and directed towards the eardrum by the ear canal. Just as the vocal cords in the larynx vibrate to produce sounds, so the sound waves in the air cause the ear drum to vibrate.

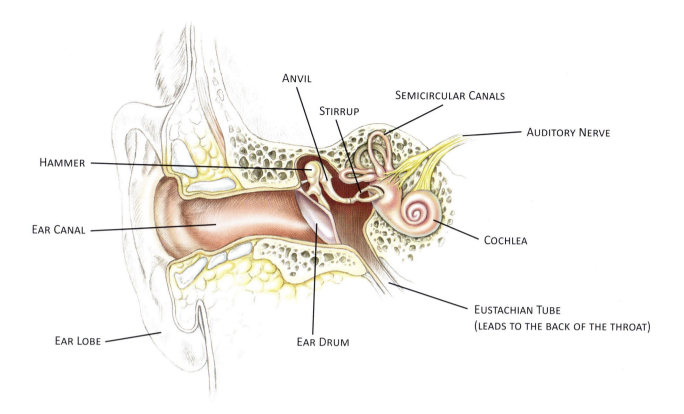

HAMMER

EAR CANAL

EAR LOBE

ANVIL

STIRRUP

SEMICIRCULAR CANALS

AUDITORY NERVE

COCHLEA

EUSTACHIAN TUBE
(LEADS TO THE BACK OF THE THROAT)

EAR DRUM

FIGURE 23.13. THE EAR
The name "cochlea" comes from the Latin word for snail. It is inside the snail-shaped cochlea that sound vibrations are changed into nerve impulses.

The middle ear contains three tiny bones which were named for their shapes: the hammer, the anvil, and the stirrup. The stirrup is the smallest of the body's 206 bones. Together, the hammer, anvil, and stirrup transfer the vibrations of the eardrum to the liquid inside the cochlea.

The snail-shaped **COCHLEA** is located in the inner ear. When the liquid inside the cochlea vibrates, it causes nerve endings inside the cochlea to "fire." The nerve endings send electrical impulses along the **AUDITORY NERVE** to the brain, and you hear!

The ear is also necessary for the body to keep its balance. The **SEMICIR-CULAR CANALS** are three loops in the inner ear that also contain fluid and nerve endings. When your head moves, the fluid in the semicircular canals moves as well and nerve impulses are sent to the cerebellum. Then the cerebellum sends messages to the muscles that must adjust so that your body stays balanced. By spinning around rapidly several times and then stopping, you can set the fluid inside the canals in motion. Even though you've stopped, the fluid is still moving and the nerves are still sending their messages. The brain thinks your body is still spinning and you experience dizziness.

The **EUSTACHIAN TUBE** is a tube that connects the middle ear to the pharynx. When your ears "pop" as you travel up a hill in a car, it is a sign that the air pressure has changed. To release the pressure, you need to get some of the air behind the eardrum out. If you swallow with your mouth open, the extra air behind the eardrum will go through the eustachian tube and your ears will feel normal again. If you rapidly go down

Hands that "Hear" and "See"

Have you ever celebrated St. Juan Diego's feast day with a treat-filled piñata? Perhaps you were handed a stout stick, blindfolded, turned in circles for a moment, and then invited to strike. Dizzy and unseeing, how could you possibly know the piñata's location—or did you? Without the sense of sight, were you able to compensate for the loss in other ways?

Perhaps you listened carefully to friends' laughter or other sounds to determine which way to turn. Did you make a few gentle, exploratory "pokes" into the air to see if you might make contact? If you did these things, you used your senses of hearing and touch to help "cover" for the loss of vision.

Our Lord designed our senses to complement one another, but also to help compensate one for another. That is, when one sense is lost, it isn't unusual for another to help make up for the loss. For instance, those who cannot hear often use sign language, a system of signs which relies on the sense of sight or touch, to communicate with their family and friends (Figure 23.15). Similarly, those who are blind can read using the braille system of writing, thanks to Louis Braille, who invented a way of writing with bumps. (By the way, did you know that Louis Braille was a devout Catholic?)

The inspirational Helen Keller, who as a small child lost both her vision and her sense of hearing, was adept at using touch to learn about and communicate with the world around her. At first, Keller communicated primarily through sign language and braille.

FIGURE 23.14. Helen Keller (left) with her teacher Anne Sullivan (right). Helen Keller could understand spoken language by placing her fingers on the speaker's lips.

However, Keller's ultra-keen sense of touch eventually allowed her, by placing her fingers on the speaker's lips, to understand spoken language through her sense of touch! In time, Keller also learned to speak. Although she had lost two of her five senses, this remarkable woman went on to graduate from Radcliffe College, becoming a noted author and public speaker admired around the world.

FIGURE 23.15. SIGN LANGUAGE Boy signing the word "swing" in American Sign Language

the other side of the mountain, you must swallow again to force air back through the eustachian tube into the space behind the eardrum.

The inability to hear is called deafness. Many people who are deaf are also mute. Their muteness, the inability to speak, is very often a result of not being able to hear others or themselves speaking. This is because you learn to speak by listening to others speak.

The Nose

The sense of smell is located in the nose. The sensitive ends of the **OLFACTORY NERVE** detect odors in the air (Figure 23.16). Without the sense of smell, the flavor of foods is greatly reduced. The pleasant odor of most foods is required to make the food have its characteristic taste.

The Tongue

We discussed the sense of taste when we investigated digestion. The tongue detects sweetness, saltiness, sourness, and bitterness. Acids cause the sour taste. Salt ions cause the salty taste. Many different organic compounds, including sugar, cause the sensation of sweetness. The bitter taste is caused by organic compounds called alkaloids. If the bitter taste is too strong, you reject the food. This is a protective function, since many poisons are alkaloids!

The Skin

The sense of touch is located in the skin. Figure 23.17 illustrates the five different kinds of sensory receptors in the skin: touch, pressure, pain, heat, and cold.

Touch receptors are closer to the surface than pressure receptors. Touch and pressure receptors allow the human hand, which is strong enough to wield a sledge hammer, to pick up a baby without hurting it.

There are also pain, heat, and cold receptors in the skin. These special sensory nerve endings send important data to the central nervous system that allows the body to protect itself from damage.

In learning about the skin, we've "covered" the entire body and its sense organs!

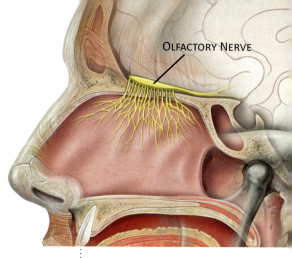

OLFACTORY NERVE

FIGURE 23.16. Your sense of smell depends on the olfactory nerve in your nasal cavity.

 Worksheets: 23.1–23.2, 23.4–23.8

 Diagram: 23.3

 Formal Lab: 23.9

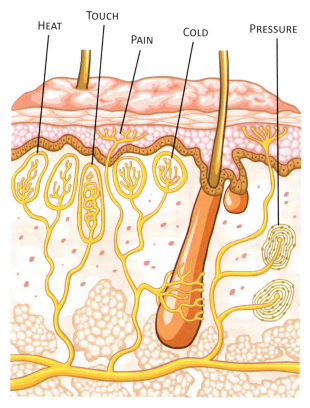

HEAT TOUCH PAIN COLD PRESSURE

FIGURE 23.17. TOUCH
There are five kinds of nerve endings in the skin. Note that the pressure sensors are deeper in the skin than the endings for pain, heat, cold, and touch.

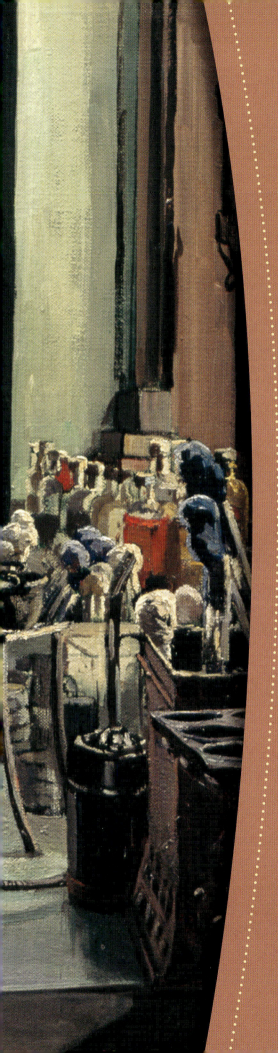

Chapter

24

DISEASE: THE FIGHT FOR LIFE

Great crowds came to Him, having with them the lame, the blind, the deformed, the mute, and many others. They placed them at His feet, and He cured them.

—Matthew 15:30

FIGURE 24.1. SIR ALEXANDER FLEMING, THE DISCOVERER OF PENICILLIN
A portrait of Alexander Fleming at work in his laboratory.

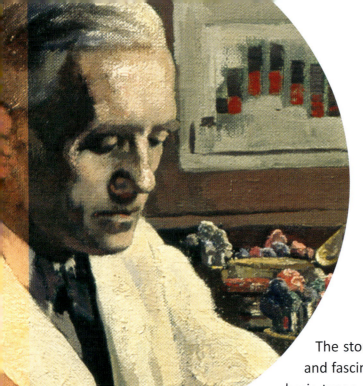

DISEASE: THE FIGHT FOR LIFE

The story of the human fight against **DISEASE** is complex and fascinating. In this chapter, you will learn about the two basic types of diseases: noninfectious diseases and infectious diseases. You will study the different ways your body defends itself against disease organisms, and you will be introduced to some of the great doctors and scientists in the history of medicine. Finally, you will learn about some of the major diseases and the organisms that cause them.

NONINFECTIOUS DISEASES

A **NONINFECTIOUS** disease is any disease that is not able to be "caught" by contact with the person who has it or with things they have touched. There are four basic types of noninfectious diseases.

Deficiency Diseases

Deficiency diseases are caused by a lack of certain nutrients in the diet. When a person's diet lacks a part of one of the nutrient groups, his body cannot carry out all the life functions successfully. Figure 24.2 shows the effects of a diet lacking in protein.

Deficiency diseases are not contagious and often can be cured simply by improving the diet. A glass of milk once a day can prevent the malnutrition shown in Figure 24.2. Today, most deficiency diseases occur in developing countries where the people suffer from poverty and famine.

SCURVY was one of the very first deficiency diseases which scientists discovered how to cure. Scurvy, a disease caused by a deficiency of vitamin C, became a major problem during the age of exploration when sailors spent months at sea without fresh fruits and vegetables. The sailors would become weak, their legs would swell, their teeth would fall out, and they would eventually die. James Lind, a Scottish doctor, knew that

FIGURE 24.2. DEFICIENCY DISEASE This child's diet lacks protein. As a result, the abdomen is distended and the muscles are underdeveloped.

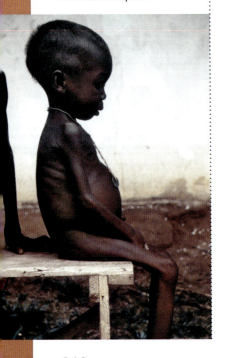

DISEASE	SYMPTOMS	CAUSE	CURE
Iron-deficiency anemia	tired, pale	lack of iron (Fe) causes a shortage of hemoglobin for red blood cells	eat leafy greens and liver
Beriberi	nerve problems	lack of vitamin B_1 causes a malfunction of the nerves	eat grains and milk
Goiter	large swelling on the throat	deficiency of iodine (I) causes the thyroid gland to grow extra large	use iodized salt, eat fish
Night blindness	inability to see at night	deficiency of vitamin A, carotene, impairs the eyes	eat carrots
Rickets	soft teeth and bones	lack of vitamin D, calciferol, causes the bones and teeth to lose calcium	eat fish oil and egg yolks; drink milk fortified with vitamin D
Scurvy	weakness, abnormal bleeding, gum disease	deficiency of vitamin C causes breakdown of capillaries and affects bone formation	eat oranges, use lemons and limes

FIGURE 24.3. DEFICIENCY DISEASES

many Dutch captains used citrus fruits as a regular part of the diet on their ships. Lind tried hard to convince the British navy to do the same. In 1795, the year after Lind died, England's warships all carried lemon juice for each sailor and scurvy began to disappear. (Seventy years later, British ships substituted lime juice for lemon juice, and British sailors became known as "limeys"!)

It was many years before scientists could explain why lemon juice prevented scurvy. In 1932, Charles Glen King finally isolated vitamin C from lemons and showed that scurvy is caused by a deficiency of this vitamin. Today, scurvy is almost eliminated in developed countries, and when it does occur, it can easily be cured by eating oranges and lemons.

Figure 24.3 lists some human deficiency diseases and the nutrient that is missing. Many people supplement their daily intake of food with a multiple vitamin pill.

Environmental Diseases

Some diseases are caused by a person's behavior or by the environment in which he lives. For instance, in Pennsylvania there are a number of cases of black lung disease resulting from working in coal mines. Another environmental disease is skin cancer, which may be caused by over-exposure to strong sunlight.

Environmental diseases can also result when people are exposed to toxic chemicals. It is important to use safety clothing and equipment when painting or using other chemicals. Improper disposal of toxic materials can contaminate the environment and put many people at risk.

ACROMEGALY	overactive pituitary in adults
ALLERGIES	overactive immune system
BLINDNESS	a malfunction of the eyes or the optic nerves
CRETINISM	underactive thyroid in a child
DEAFNESS	a malfunction of the ears or auditory nerves
DIABETES	underactive Islands of Langerhans—not enough insulin
DWARFISM	underactive pituitary in childhood
GIANTISM	overactive pituitary in childhood
NEAR- OR FAR-SIGHTEDNESS	incorrectly shaped eyes or the lens does not function properly

FIGURE 24.4. FUNCTIONAL DISORDERS

FIGURE 24.5. SICKLE CELLS
In sickle cell anemia, many of the red blood cells are shaped incorrectly and do not carry oxygen as they should.

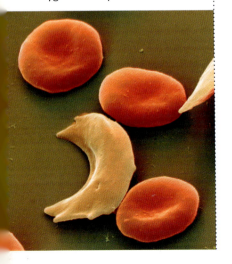

Environmental diseases can be caused by a person's behavior. Lung cancer is often caused by smoking, and drinking alcohol can cause diseases of the liver.

Functional Disorders

Functional disorders are caused by the malfunction of an organ or system. You have learned about many of them already in your study of the systems of the body. Like other noninfectious diseases, functional disorders are not contagious. For example, you cannot "catch" an **ALLERGY** from someone else (although you may inherit it from your parents). The chart in Figure 24.4 lists diseases that cannot always be cured, but are not a threat to others.

Genetic Diseases

A fourth type of noninfectious disease is genetic disease. This type of disease cannot be contracted from someone who has it but it can be inherited from one's parents.

Color blindness is a genetic disease that boys inherit more often than girls. People who are color blind are not able to see the difference between all colors.

HEMOPHILIA, bleeder's disease, is a genetic disease in which the blood does not clot properly.

Because genetic diseases are passed on in families, some genetic diseases are especially common in particular racial or ethnic groups. For instance, sickle cell anemia tends to be more common among people of African descent. In sickle cell anemia, the DNA instructions for the shape of the red blood cell are missing. The red blood cells should be round disks, but instead they are sickle-shaped and do not carry oxygen correctly (Figure 24.5). People with sickle cell anemia often feel weak and lack energy because their cells do not get enough oxygen.

Not all genetic diseases are inherited from a person's parents. Sometimes a chromosome in the nucleus of an egg or sperm cell is lost or damaged during fertilization. As a result, the instructions needed for the body to perform its life functions are also damaged. In Chapter 16 you learned about Down syndrome, a genetic disease caused by having an extra copy of chromosome number 21.

Changes in the DNA can also occur later in life in people who use drugs, drink alcohol, or smoke cigarettes. High exposure to X-rays and other

Hippocrates

Hippocrates, born in Greece about the year 460 B.C., is credited with being the "Father of Modern Medicine." Prior to his time, disease was thought to result from the whims of the gods, but Hippocrates' careful observations led him to believe that many illnesses were caused by living habits, diet, and environmental factors.

FIGURE 24.6. HIPPOCRATES

Imagine the difference that could be made in the health of literally billions of people across the centuries, if Christ reigned in every heart! Self-inflicted diseases would disappear, because people would recognize their bodies as temples of the Holy Spirit; conditions in Third World countries would improve dramatically as Christian leaders and citizens reached out to their brothers and sisters in the Lord.

Hippocrates was on the right track! Many serious (and often deadly) illnesses are self-inflicted to some degree or another: lung cancer by smoking; sexually transmitted diseases by immoral behavior; and Type 2 Diabetes by years of over-indulgence in a poor diet.

In Third World countries, diseases that stem from environmental factors—contaminated water supplies, famine, and lack of basic medical care such as vaccines and antibiotics—result in millions of deaths each year.

And there is more. In pre-Christian Greece, immoral behavior was rampant. But Hippocrates set a higher standard for physicians. He composed an oath to which all new physicians swore, promising to keep their patients from harm. Further, the oath-taker swore not to administer drugs intended to kill the patient, nor to cause the abortion of an unborn child. He promised instead to "guard my life and my art" with "purity and holiness."

Perhaps modern medicine could learn from an ancient Greek physician.

FIGURE 24.7. A DOCTOR INJECTS A CHILD IN NORTHERN INDIA WITH A VACCINE AGAINST MEASLES

FIGURE 24.8. MALNOURISHED CHILDREN IN GUATEMALA

Love and Responsibility

"Deep within yourself, listen to your conscience which calls you to be pure. . . . a home is not warmed by the fire of pleasure which burns quickly like a pile of withered grass. Passing encounters are only a caricature of love; they injure hearts and mock God's plan."

—Pope John Paul II

To animals, who have neither rational nor immortal souls, Creator God gave the ability to reproduce after their own kind.

But to Man, who does possess a rational, immortal soul, Creator God gave even greater gifts to accompany reproductive ability: free will, guided by an ability to reason; and the gift of partnering with God in creating new life. Unlike animals, these new lives have the capacity to live forever in Heavenly glory!

Yet, there are also earthly blessings that come to those who follow God's good plans for new life. Couples who practice chastity and abstinence

FIGURE 24.9.

benefit not only spiritually, but also emotionally, for each honors the dignity of the other. In fact, studies show that those who live in purity enjoy happier relationships and far more lasting marriages than those who don't.

Further, the physical damage caused by sexually transmitted diseases (STDs) is also avoided by those who remain pure. Fifty years ago, there were only two recognized STDs; now there are more than twenty-five, four of which are incurable. In other words, many of those infected will have to live out their entire lives with these diseases—and some will die from them. (Alarmingly, half of the new STD infections diagnosed every year are in young people between the ages of fifteen and twenty-four.)

With the blessings of holy purity and right use of free will, undamaged by emotional and physical suffering caused by impure relationships, couples joyfully enter into Holy Matrimony, welcoming children created in pure love. With what wisdom our Father God planned this sacred approach to procreation!

"[God] has assigned as a duty to every man the dignity of every woman."

—Pope John Paul II

FIGURE 24.10.

energy sources can also cause genetic changes. These genetic diseases are also environmental diseases.

INFECTIOUS DISEASES

An **INFECTIOUS** disease is one that can be contracted, or "caught," from another person. Infectious diseases are spread in several ways:

1. **Droplets**—when sneezing without covering the mouth millions of droplets are ejected into the air. Of course, if you cover your mouth and sneeze but then do not wash your hands, you will spread the germs causing the disease onto everything you touch.

2. **Food**—contaminated food and food waste that is not properly handled will allow the growth of disease-causing microbes.

3. **Contact**—a variety of diseases are spread by **DIRECT CONTACT**, in which the diseased person touches someone else. Some are spread by **INDIRECT CONTACT**; for instance, the germs might be on the clothing used by the diseased person.

4. **Cuts**—some diseases only infect you if your skin is cut or you have a **PUNCTURE** wound.

5. **Vectors**—when plants or animals carry a disease but do not die from it, they can then transmit the disease-causing organisms to a new **HOST**. The plant or animal which carries the disease is called a **VECTOR**, and must be controlled in order to control the disease.

Because diseases can be spread by vectors, pests that many people consider to be harmless actually can pose life-threatening risks. Fleas, ticks, chiggers, mosquitoes, and ants, especially prevalent in the spring and summer months, are known disease vectors.

Disease Defenses

There is a tremendous life-and-death battle going on right now in your body. Millions of casualties are being transported to central locations in your lymph system for processing. This fight for life is raging inside of you twenty-four hours a day. Your body would succumb to one of the billions of disease organisms with which you come in contact each day if it did not have an active defense against disease!

Your body has three lines of defense against disease organisms. Your epidermis, or skin, and the mucous membranes in the nose and throat, is your first line of defense. The epidermis, when clean and uncut, prevents entry of **PATHOGENS**.

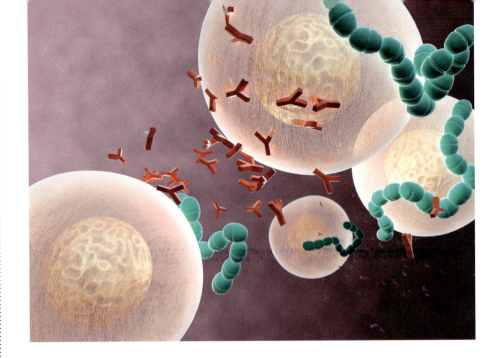

If the pathogens enter your body with your food, through the lungs, or through a cut, your second line of defense must take quick action to kill the invaders. The hydrochloric acid in gastric juice kills many of the microbes on ingested materials. In the rest of the body, an amoeboid army of white blood cells, called **PHAGOCYTES**, moves out of the capillaries to engulf and destroy the invaders.

The germs that survive face a third line of defense, **ANTIBODIES**. Antibodies are proteins that stop the effect of the germs or help your phagocytes to capture them. There are four main functions of antibodies:

1. **Neutralization** cancels the effect of poisons made by the pathogens (disease organisms). Neutralizing antibodies are called **antitoxins**, because "*anti*" means "against" and "*toxin*" means "poison." Your body makes antitoxins to protect you from the chemical warfare of germs.

2. **Lysis** dissolves the cell membranes of germs. Perhaps you have heard of Lysol, a disinfectant whose name has the same root as "lysis."

3. **Opsonization** weakens pathogens so that the phagocytes have the advantage and can win the battle against the germ cells.

4. **Agglutination** causes the microbes to clump together, making it easier for the white blood cells to engulf them.

IMMUNITY is the ability of an organism to resist disease. **Natural immunity** is built into the chromosomes that were inherited when the person's life began at fertilization. **Acquired immunity** is gained during a person's lifetime when contact with a disease organism activates the antibodies in the person's bloodstream. If the person survives the disease, he comes away from the battle with a long-term ability to resist that disease. This is called an **active acquired immunity**.

Active immunity can also be gained by being injected with a **VACCINE**. A vaccine contains germs or toxins (poisons) that have been weakened so it is easy for your body to destroy them. In the process of defeating the germs, your body gains active immunity. The next time you contact that pathogen, your body is ready and can resist the disease.

If a person is at high risk of infection and there is not enough time for him to develop active immunity through a vaccine, certain antibodies can be injected into his body to help him fight off the disease. This creates **passive acquired immunity** which lasts only a short time.

The Fight for Life

The fight for life against pathogens involves more than vaccines. One of the greatest advances in fighting infections came in 1865, when Joseph Lister of England used an **ANTISEPTIC** to cleanse his medical tools and hands before treating the next patient. Until that time, no one had realized that the doctors themselves were causing many of the lethal infections in their own patients by using poor hygiene and sanitation. You may recognize Lister's name in a mouthwash on the market today—Listerine—that is advertised to kill the microbes causing bad breath.

Just seventeen years after Lister's discovery, Robert Koch discovered the bacterium Mycobacterium tuberculosis and proved that it causes tuberculosis. This was one of the first germs proven to cause a specific disease. The work of isolating the disease-causing bacterium and proving that it causes the disease in question is done by rules now known as Koch's Postulates. These rules are used every day in medical labs around the world as scientists continue to fight disease (Figure 24.12).

In 1928 another step forward in the effort to save lives was made when Alexander Fleming discovered penicillin (see Chapter 8). Penicillin was the first **ANTIBIOTIC**, and it is still prescribed today to control many infectious diseases. Many antibiotics—for example, streptomycin and erythromycin—come from fungi, which is why their names contain the root word "*mycota*."

In 1935, sulfanilamide, a chemical made in a laboratory from red dye, was discovered by Gerhard Domagk to kill bacteria. Since then many other drugs have been manufactured to help in the fight against disease.

KOCH'S POSTULATES

1. The bacterium must be present in every case of the disease.

2. The bacterium must be grown in a pure culture.

3. Bacteria from the pure culture must cause the disease in a healthy organism.

4. The bacterium must be reisolated, cultured, and identified as identical to the original.

FIGURE 24.12. KOCH'S POSTULATES
Following these rules keeps scientists from identifying the wrong bacterium as the cause of a disease.

TYPES OF INFECTIOUS DISEASES

Viral Diseases

Smallpox

Smallpox is a deadly disease caused by a virus so small that more than half a million of them could fit on the head of a straight pin. In 1796, before scientists even knew what a virus was, Edward Jenner, an English doctor, discovered a vaccine for smallpox. This was the first vaccine ever invented.

FIGURE 24.13. Edward Jenner performing the first vaccination on James Phipps.

Jenner had noticed over several years that the milk maids who got cow pox, a relatively mild disease, did not contract smallpox, a disease similar to cow pox, but much more deadly. Jenner scratched the arm of a boy named James Phipps and put some of the pus from the cow pox into the scratch. James got cow pox, then got better. Now came the dangerous part. Jenner infected young Phipps with smallpox. Because James Phipps had first acquired immunity to cow pox, the smallpox disease could not get started in his body!

At first Jenner's tremendous discovery was rejected by the Royal Society in England. Cartoons appeared in the newspapers showing people with cow's heads after Dr. Jenner vaccinated them. But the vaccine's success in preventing smallpox soon convinced people, and millions have been saved by vaccines since that special day in 1796.

Rabies

Rabies, or hydrophobia, is a gruesome viral disease spread by warm-blooded animal vectors. Before 1885, a person bitten by a rabid animal would suffer a terribly painful illness that usually ended in death. In 1885, Louis Pasteur, the scientist who invented the process of pasteurization and discovered a vaccine for anthrax (see Chapter 6), was working on a rabies vaccine. Meanwhile, Joseph Meister, a young French boy, had been bitten and was almost sure to die of rabies. When Joseph Meister was brought to him, Pasteur had a difficult decision to make. He was not a doctor, so should he risk using an unproven vaccine that could itself kill the boy if Pasteur's deductions were incorrect? Or should he wait, and if the boy got rabies, see young Meister die of hydrophobia? Pasteur made his decision and began the fourteen vaccinations for rabies. Joseph survived!

FIGURE 24.14. A rabid dog's bite can be fatal. Your pets should be regularly vaccinated against rabies.

Yellow Fever

Although Jenner and Pasteur developed vaccines for smallpox and rabies, they did not know that the diseases were caused by viruses. Yellow fever was the first human disease proven to be caused by a virus. An often-fatal disease, yellow fever is spread by the bite of the female <u>Aedes sp.</u> mosquito. The yellow fever virus and its vector was identified in 1900 by Walter Reed, an American doctor. To control yellow fever, a chemical called DDT was used to control the mosquito population and thousands of lives were saved. Max Theiler developed a vaccine for yellow fever in 1937.

Polio

Polio is a viral disease which particularly affects young children. The polio virus attacks the motor neurons in the brain and spinal cord, causing severe disability and paralysis and often death. Without knowing everything about polio, Dr. Jonas Salk was able to make a polio vaccine in 1953. The first mass vaccination was done by Salk on nearly 2 million school children in 1954. In 1961 Dr. Albert Sabin made a polio vaccine that could be swallowed instead of injected. You or some of your family and friends would surely have been crippled by polio before reaching your present age if these vaccines had never been developed.

AIDS

We explained earlier that your body has three lines of defense to fight off diseases. This natural system of defense is called your immune system. Acquired immunodeficiency syndrome (**AIDS**), is a relatively new viral disease which causes the body's immune system to stop working correctly. AIDS is communicated by direct contact with infected body fluids or contaminated needles. Public health officials must be sure that the emergency blood supply is free of the AIDS virus. Currently there is no complete cure for AIDS, which kills its victim in two to three years after symptoms appear if left untreated.

Other Viral Diseases

Other viral diseases include colds, chicken pox, the flu, measles, warts, and the mumps. Some cancers are also caused by viral particles.

Bacterial Diseases

DPT

DPT is a vaccination required before entering school in order to prevent three diseases caused by members of Kingdom Bacteria. The "D" stands for diphtheria, which is caused by a bacillus bacterium and is spread by droplets. Diphtheria begins with a sore throat and fever, which are followed by severe breathing difficulties. An antitoxin for diphtheria was first developed in 1890 by Emil von Behring of Germany.

FIGURE 24.15. POLIO
Victims of polio who survive are often severely crippled. Thanks to routine vaccinations for polio, there has not been a case of naturally occurring polio in the United States since 1979.

The "P" in DPT stands for pertussis. This bacterial disease gets its common name, whooping cough, from the high-pitched gasps for air which a child makes as he struggles to breathe during a fit of coughing.

TETANUS, also called lockjaw, is caused by an anaerobic bacillus, which means that it is able to live without oxygen gas. Cuts often have the tetanus bacillus on them, but the oxygen in the air prevents it from growing. If you step on a rusty nail or get some other puncture wound, you are at risk for tetanus because such wounds can deposit bacteria deep in the wound where there is no oxygen. Tetanus, a potentially fatal disease, causes stiffness and severe muscle spasms in the jaw, neck, and abdomen.

Typhoid Fever

Typhoid fever, caused by the bacterium Salmonella typhi, is characterized by a high fever, headache, and diarrhea. There was an outbreak of typhoid in New York State during the summer of 1989. Health officials think it may have been contaminated orange juice that caused the outbreak. Typhoid may be spread by animal vectors, unwashed hands, poor sanitation, or contaminated food.

Lyme Disease

The deer tick (Ixodes dammini) is the disease vector that carries Lyme disease. The deer ticks contain a spirilli bacterium, Borrelia burgdorferi, which they can transmit to wildlife, pets, and humans. This bacterial disease can trigger persistent fever, chills and headaches for weeks, and if left untreated may lead to death. The bacteria are named after Dr. Willy Burgdorfer of the United States because he identified them in the bodies of deer ticks in 1982.

Other bacterial diseases include scarlet fever, caused by Streptococcus pyogenes, and tuberculosis, caused by Mycobacterium tuberculosis.

FIGURE 24.16. VECTORS
Deer ticks, Ixodes dammini, are disease vectors that transmit Lyme disease to humans.

Protistan Diseases

Malaria

Bacteria are not the only living organisms that cause disease. Malaria is caused by the protist Plasmodium falciparum.

For those who live in temperate and arctic climates, **MALARIA** has never been a major problem. Malaria occurs most often near humid swamps in tropical areas, so people originally believed that swamp air was the cause of the alternating chills and fevers of malaria. The very name "malaria" means "bad air"!

Malaria is not caused by bad air, but it is spread by something in the air! The female <u>Anopheles sp</u>. mosquito is the vector that transmits the disease-causing protist from an infected person to another person. Former use of DDT and the drainage of swamps have helped reduce the vector population, but malaria is still a major problem in tropical regions. Quinine, a chemical from the bark of a tree, is used to treat people with malaria.

Sleeping Sickness

African sleeping sickness, a fatal disease of the nervous system, is another tropical disease caused by a protist. For this disease, the tsetse (TSEH-tsee) fly is the vector that spreads the pathogen, <u>Trypanosoma brucei</u>. Life scientists have not yet been successful in developing a vaccine for African sleeping sickness. Perhaps someday you will discover a vaccine for this disease!

Amoebic Dysentery

Amoebic dysentery is a common complaint in areas that lack proper sanitation. Amoebic dysentery is caused by one of the amoeboid protists, <u>Entamoeba histolytica</u>. Amoebic dysentery is not usually fatal, but it causes severe nausea and diarrhea. This disease is spread mainly through water contaminated by sewage. The importance of the decay bacteria in helping to purify water at sewage treatment plants should be more appreciated!

Fungal Diseases

Thrush

Did you know that fungi can cause diseases? Thrush, or candidiasis, is caused by a yeast infection of <u>Candida albicans</u>. Thrush affects the tongue and is usually not serious if treated.

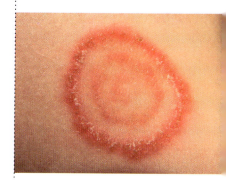

FIGURE 24.17. RINGWORM
Despite its name, ringworm is caused by a fungus, not a worm.

Ringworm

Ringworm is a fungal disease that causes a circular spot that spreads outward and heals from the center. This pattern gives the disease its name. Ringworm is very common, and can be prevented by not sharing sports clothes, towels, and equipment. Several genera and many species of fungi can cause ringworm, which is not serious if treated.

Athlete's Foot

Athlete's foot is caused when one of several fungi grows in the skin of the foot. The itching that results demands attention even if you don't remember the name of one of the fungi that cause it: <u>Trichophytron mentagrophytes</u>. Athlete's foot gets its name because it is usually contracted by walking barefoot through a communal shower or locker room.

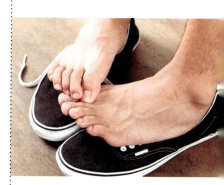

FIGURE 24.18. ATHLETE'S FOOT
A growth of the fungus <u>Trichophytron mentagrophytes</u> on a person's feet results in uncomfortable itching.

Flatworm and Nematode Diseases

Tapeworms

The flatworm <u>Diphyllobothrium latum</u> has a name that seems long. However, the tapeworm's name is not long at all in comparison with the tapeworm itself! <u>Diphyllobothrium latum</u> can grow up to ten meters long inside a human intestine! You learned about the beef tapeworm in Chapter 12. Tapeworms are usually contracted by eating meat that has been improperly cooked or prepared in unsanitary conditions. An infection by a tapeworm does not always result in noticeable symptoms, although it can cause discomfort and loss of appetite. Very rarely, an infection by pork tapeworm, <u>Taenia solium</u>, can result in severe neurological problems.

Hookworm and Pork Worm

Nematodes are another type of animal that can cause disease in humans. Hookworm, which bores through the sole of the foot, and pork worm, which infests pork, are two nematodes which were discussed in Chapter 12.

Prevention of nematode infestations is best accomplished by proper sewage treatment, the wearing of shoes, and personal hygiene after using the toilet. The largest parasitic nematodes in humans, <u>Ascaris lumbricoides</u>, can release 200,000 eggs per day! Not getting infected in the first place is the best method of nematode control.

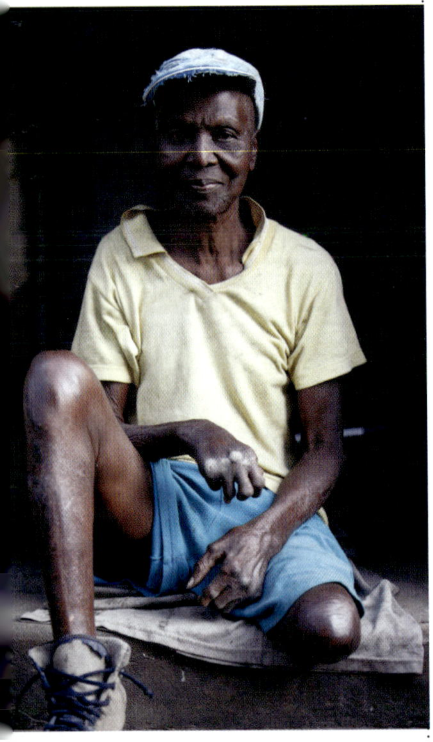

Plant Diseases

Most plants do not cause disease in the sense that we have been discussing disease here. Ingesting certain plants can certainly make a person sick or even kill them. Poison ivy, poison oak, and poison sumac can all cause a rash, but normally are not life-threatening. In the case of an individual who has an allergic reaction, immediate help should be sought.

Summary

You are the battlefield in a constant war! Hopefully, this chapter has helped you understand how you can assist your body in the fight for life. Many diseases can be prevented by an awareness of their causes and by good habits of nutrition and hygiene. Many other diseases can be prevented, arrested, or completely cured by vaccines, antiseptics, drugs, and antibiotics. Some diseases are still not understood, and the world needs a life scientist who will find the cause and the cure.

Worksheets:
24.1–24.10

Research Paper:
Fight against Disease

FIGURE 24.19.
MUCH TO BE DONE
This leper from Africa cannot regain his fingers and leg but with medication he can rejoin his family. Hansen's disease, or leprosy, an ancient and feared infectious disease, can be contained.

REDEMPTIVE SUFFERING

Who would choose a bed of rocks over a feather bed, or prefer an icy shower to soaking in a hot tub? Because it is our natural inclination to avoid physical suffering of any kind, it is hard to imagine that suffering might be transformed into a great good!

Yet, redemptive suffering—"turning what was meant for evil into good"—is modeled in Jesus Christ, who willingly endured agonizing torture and death on the Cross in exchange for the redemption of mankind. Thus, the greatest evil imaginable—the brutal murder of the Son of God—became the greatest good of all time.

While disease and suffering are not to be desired, when they come to us unbidden, we can turn them to good by offering them in union with the Cross, on behalf of others. Have you broken a leg? Offer it up to Our Lord on behalf of someone who has no legs. Have you caught the flu, and feel as if you're at death's door? Offer it up for someone whose soul is "dying" of mortal sin. By joining your sufferings to His, you have the astounding privilege of becoming a co-redeemer with Christ.

FIGURE 24.20.
BL. PIER GIORGIO FRASSATI

"You ask me whether I am in good spirits. How could I not be, so long as my trust in God gives me strength. We must always be cheerful. Sadness should be banished from all Christian souls. For suffering is a far different thing from sadness, which is the worst disease of all. . . . But the purpose for which we have been created shows us the path along which we should go, perhaps strewn with many thorns, but not a sad path. Even in the midst of intense suffering it is one of joy."

—Bl. Pier Giorgio Frassati,
who died of polio at age 24

ANIMAL BEHAVIOR AND REPRODUCTION

Men go abroad to wonder at the heights
of mountains, at the huge waves of the
sea, at the long courses of the rivers, at
the vast compass of the ocean, at the
circular motions of the stars, and they pass
by themselves without wondering.

—Saint Augustine

FIGURE 25.1. WEAVER BIRD BUILDING A NEST
Weaver birds, native to Africa, build intricate nests out of grass and leaf fibers.
Weaver birds build their nests by instinct, and do not have to go to school to
learn how. Each species of weaver bird builds its own type of nest, some with
long, tube-like entrances, some with false entrances to deceive predators, and
some in apartment-like clusters along with other birds.

ANIMAL BEHAVIOR AND REPRODUCTION

BEHAVIOR

Much of the behavior exhibited by animals is built into their neurons before they are born. The simplest responses don't even require the brain.

This is reflected in the expression, "to run around like a chicken with its head cut off." Standing, scratching, and many other movements are actions that some animals can carry out even if their brain has been destroyed. This is because these relatively simple responses are centered in the spinal cord.

Human beings also respond to certain situations automatically, with the brain only learning about the action after it has happened. Pulling your finger away from a hot pot of potatoes is an example of these quick responses, or reflexes. The human knee jerk response, which occurs when the doctor strikes your knee just below the knee cap, is another example of a reflex.

**FIGURE 25.2.
A SIMPLE REFLEX ARC**
The stimulus (hot coal) causes an impulse which triggers an immediate response from the associative neurons in the spinal cord, without involving the brain. A reflex arc is a pathway in the nervous system which saves time when an organism must respond to a stimulus right away.

Reflexes

Most simple reflexes are designed to protect the organism. When a boy in bare feet steps on a hot coal near a campfire, the pain receptors in his skin send a message along the sensory neuron to the spinal cord. The associative neurons in the spinal cord send out an impulse on a motor neuron that tells the muscles to move

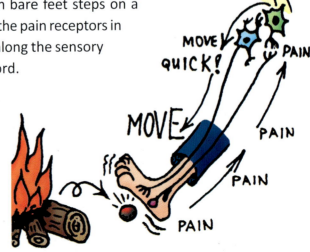

228

the foot, and do it fast! The associative neurons also send impulses up the spinal cord so that the brain knows what has happened.

All this action takes place in just a fraction of a second. In our example, the hot coal was the **STIMULUS** that initiated the reflex arc. Quickly pulling away the foot is the **RESPONSE**. This simple, quick response which does not require the brain is an **UNCONDITIONED REFLEX** (Figure 25.2).

A **CONDITIONED REFLEX** is also a quick response to a stimulus, but this reflex involves the brain. People practice a musical instrument or a sport so that they build up a series of conditioned reflexes that allow quick responses to certain stimuli. Have you ever played the game "Simon Says"? In this game, a player loses if he or she becomes conditioned to imitate the leader's actions instead of following the leader's instructions.

Our first understanding of reflexes came from experiments with dogs done by Ivan Pavlov, a Russian scientist. Saliva is normally secreted when food touches the tongue. This is a simple reflex which dogs and humans share. But Pavlov's dogs heard a bell each time they ate. After a short time, Pavlov could get the dogs to salivate just by ringing the bell! This is an example of a conditioned reflex.

Instincts

Many complex behaviors in animals are exhibited not because the animal has learned that the action is beneficial, but because of an inborn inclination towards that action. The knowledge of how and when to perform these complex actions is built into the animal's neurons and does not depend on experience. For instance, when a young robin builds its nest for the first time, it builds the same kind of nest that other robins build. Even if the bird in question has never seen another robin build a nest, it still builds the same kind of nest! This sort of built-in behavior is called an **INSTINCT**. Unlike simple reflexes, instincts are complex behaviors made up of a series of actions and directed towards a particular end result. Instincts are what cause some birds to migrate and some animals to hibernate.

Learning

LEARNING is a complex behavior in which a past experience causes an organism to adjust its responses to a situation. For instance, fertile chicken eggs normally hatch in twenty-one days. A hen's instinct is to sit on the eggs in her nest to keep them at 39 °C (just over 101 °F) for that time period. If the eggs are removed, the hen will often keep sitting on the

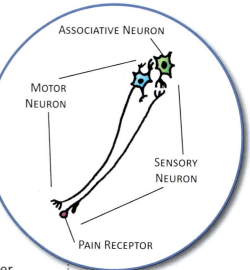

FIGURE 25.3. PARTS OF A SIMPLE REFLEX ARC
A simple reflex arc involves sensory, associative, and motor neurons.

FIGURE 25.4. BUILDING UP A SERIES OF CONDITIONED REFLEXES

nest. Her instincts cause her to keep the empty nest warm even though her actions are no longer appropriate. If the hen's eggs are often removed from her nest, however, she may in time learn to stop sitting on the nest when the eggs have been removed.

Animals can learn to control instincts but it is in humans that learning is most important.

Learning takes many forms. It always involves basing future responses on past experiences. That is why learning is so important to a young person. The experiences and information learned in school will determine later responses to real-life situations.

One way of learning is through experimentation. For instance, science experiments give an alert student the opportunity to experience science in action. There is no better way to learn science! We can also learn through others by listening to and observing their experiences. Books allow us to learn from the stored-up wisdom of many ages by reading and studying.

It is important to realize that not all learning requires experimentation. For instance, to learn about drug addiction you do not have to experience it. Many who start taking drugs just to see what it's like don't stop until an overdose, AIDS, or a drug-related accident stops them dead! In cases like this, it is much better to learn from the experiences of others.

Reasoning

The highest type of thought-related behavior is **REASONING**. Homo sapiens—that is, you and I—use reasoning to solve totally new problems. In order to reason, one must have learned and remembered many previous experiences. In addition, the brain must then correlate, that is, put together, experiences. It must project possible outcomes and devise a solution to the problem at hand. It seems *reasonable* to say that pupils who study well today will be better able to solve the problems of life tomorrow, through the process of reasoning.

SEXUAL REPRODUCTION

Some animals—starfish and planaria, for example (see Chapter 12)—are able to reproduce asexually through regeneration. Hydra, one of the cnidarians (Figure 11.3 in Chapter 11), reproduces asexually by budding. However most animals, including the three listed above, reproduce sexually at some time in their life cycle. You should recall from Chapter 11 that sexual reproduction requires the joining of two cells to form a new combination of DNA. Because of sexual reproduction you are similar in many ways to both of your parents, but you are not identical to either parent.

Conjugation

A simple form of sexual reproduction is called **CONJUGATION**. In conjugation, only some of the nuclear material in a cell is exchanged with another cell. The product is the zygote, a single cell with a unique set of DNA. In Chapter 8 we classified one group of fungi, the zygomycetes, in its own phylum just because they carry out conjugation and form zygotes. In Chapter 9, we learned that the green algae spirogyra reproduces by conjugation (see Figure 9.7).

Now you must think back to Chapter 7 and remember what a paramecium looks like! What special feature does the paramecium have that

FIGURE 25.6. Sexual reproduction results in offspring which are similar to their parents, but not identical.

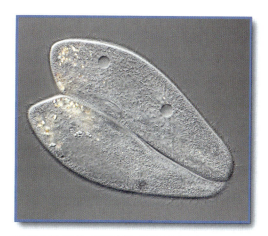

FIGURE 25.7. SEXUAL REPRODUCTION IN PARAMECIA

the amoeba and euglena do not? If necessary look back at Figure 7.14 in Chapter 7. A paramecium has two nuclei! The paramecium's macronucleus controls cell activities, as in other cells. The micronucleus is used by the paramecium to reproduce sexually by conjugation. To reproduce, two paramecia line up side by side and exchange their micronuclei. A new combination of DNA is then made possible.

Fertilization

A more complex form of sexual reproduction takes place through fertilization. Fertilization occurs when a smaller, motile **SPERM** cell fuses with a larger, nonmotile **EGG** cell. The egg is larger because it contains stored food for the new organism. In Chapter 22, it was explained that the male gonads are called the testes. The **TESTES** are the organs that produce sperm cells. **OVARIES** are the female gonads, which contain and release egg cells. In plants the sperm cells are inside the pollen grains on the anther. The egg cells are in the ovules inside the ovary.

The sperm and egg cells are called gametes, and are different from other cells because they have only half the usual number of chromosomes. Every species, great and small, has a definite number of chromosomes in each cell, and half that number in its gametes. For instance, a human muscle cell, nerve cell, or skin cell contains 46 chromosomes in its nucleus, while a human gamete contains only 23 chromosomes.

When fertilization occurs, the male and female gametes join together to form a single cell, the zygote. The zygote receives 23 chromosomes from the sperm cell and 23 chromosomes from the egg cell, so it ends up with a total of 46 chromosomes, the normal number for human beings. This is why gametes contain only half the normal number of chromosomes.

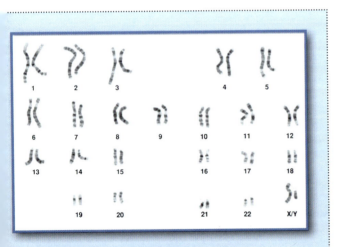

FIGURE 25.8. A HUMAN MALE KARYOTYPE
Light micrographs showing the complete set (karyotype) of normal human male chromosomes. Humans have 46 chromosomes in most cells, consisting of 23 pairs made up of one from each parent. The XY chromosome pair is shown in the bottom right. The Y chromosome shows that this person is male. Females have an XX chromosome pair instead.

Reproduction and Parenthood

Some animals, as we discussed in Chapter 12, have both testes and ovaries. The earthworm and hydra, for example, are hermaphroditic. Normally, hermaphroditic animals cannot or do not fertilize themselves. The gonads mature at different times or are located so that the organism must fertilize another member of its own species. In many flowers, the pollen and ovules mature at different times, thus preventing self fertilization.

In most fish and amphibians, fertilization takes place externally in the water. Reptiles and birds lay eggs that were fertilized inside the female's body. In most mammals, fertilization takes place in the mother's fallopian tubes, which connect the ovaries to the uterus.

Once the human egg is fertilized, only food and time are required for the new person to grow and change through the continuum of life. The most amazing growth occurs before birth. The zygote becomes an

THE MYTH OF OVERPOPULATION

Perhaps you have heard a version of this myth: as the world's population continues to grow, overcrowding creates miserable living conditions, pollution, and starvation. Yet, did you know that almost half of the world's people live in countries where birth rates have dropped below the level needed to maintain the same population? With shrinking populations, these countries may disappear, unless foreign immigrants are welcomed.

But what about overcrowding? In Sudan, one of the poorest countries in the world, there are about 13 people per square kilometer. In contrast, modern Monaco has a population density of about 17,000 per square kilometer; yet, this prosperous country boasts one of the highest standards of living in the world.

And starvation? As one might expect, no one is starving in "crowded" Monaco, but starvation is rampant in Sudan. Why is that? Monaco has a stable government, while Sudan has been ruled for decades by brutal dictators. These corrupt rulers have deliberately created conditions to cause the starvation of rival African tribes.

Still, where millions of people live in crowded cities, aren't air and water pollution serious problems?

FIGURE 25.9.

Not necessarily. In fact, pollution is related far more to the mismanagement of corrupt governments and poverty than it is to population. Modern, developed nations enjoy clean water and air, while their counterparts in underdeveloped, politically oppressed, poor countries do not. It is not population that determines these conditions. Rather, when free, educated people are allowed to use their God-given intellects and abilities, they develop the infrastructure that results in clean air and water.

Further, volunteers from these modern societies often assist in Third World countries, helping their citizens rise above poverty and advance as well. Perhaps you know Catholic priests, sisters, or lay volunteers who are engaged in this type of work.

In other words, creative people—children—are a blessing to society!

"Children are our most valuable resource."

—President Herbert Hoover

embryo, then a fetus, newborn, infant, toddler, child, adult and senior citizen. Chapter 16 outlines some of the significant events in the growth of a new person. Our understanding of how life begins was firmly established by Dr. Albert Liley, the "father of fetology." Dr. Liley even performed the first blood transfusion on an unborn baby.

In humans, when a man and a woman have sexual intercourse there is the possibility of a new life beginning. That new life requires care, nurture, and attention if it is to grow and flourish.

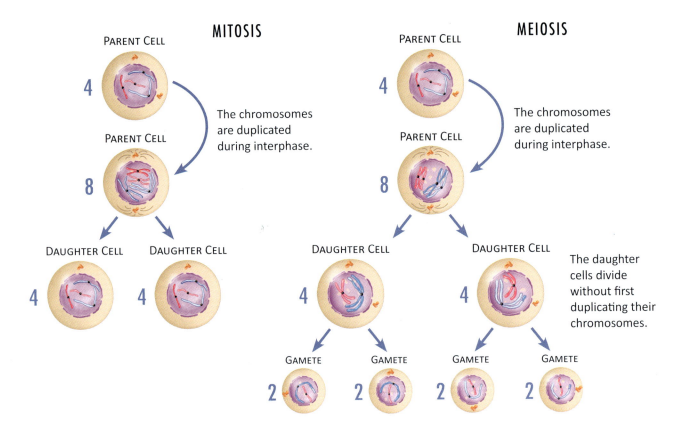

FIGURE 25.10. COMPARING MITOSIS AND MEIOSIS
Mitosis and meiosis both begin with a single cell, but mitosis results in two cells with the normal number of chromosomes, and meiosis results in four cells with half the normal number of chromosomes. The normal number of chromosomes for the cells shown above is four: two copies of the red chromosome and two copies of the blue chromosome. Note that the numbers to the left of each cell represent the number of chromosomes in the cell.

Meiosis

Do you remember learning about mitosis? Mitosis is the process of cell division in all parts of the body except in the gonads. Before reading further, turn back to page 98 to review the different steps in the process of mitosis.

Inside the testes and the ovaries a special kind of cell division, **MEIOSIS**, produces egg and sperm cells. Meiosis is the process by which cells are produced with only half the usual number of chromosomes. This is necessary so that the embryo will contain the normal number of chromosomes when the egg and sperm cells unite in sexual reproduction.

Mitosis and meiosis both begin with a single cell, but mitosis results in two cells and meiosis results in four cells. In meiosis, the cell undergoes cell division twice, but skips interphase the second time so that the chromosomes are only duplicated once. The result is four cells called gametes, each possessing only half the normal number of chromosomes.

Study Figure 25.10 to compare mitosis and meiosis. The numbers to the left of each cell represent the number of chromosomes in the cell. In Figure 25.10, the cells contain only two types of chromosomes: red and blue.

Inheritance

As already stated, sexual reproduction makes each offspring similar to its parents, but also allows for variation in a species. In the 1800s, **GENETICS**, the study of how traits are passed on from one generation to the next, was discovered to follow mathematical rules.

Gregor Mendel, a Roman Catholic monk, is considered the "father of modern genetics." Mendel the monk lived in a monastery; Mendel the scientist spent years carefully noting down the traits of pea plants in the monastery garden. Mendel's laws of heredity are accepted today as correct.

You just learned that every human cell except the gametes contains two complete sets of 23 chromosomes, one set from each parent. A single chromosome is made out of thousands of **GENES**, which are "pieces" of coded information. Each gene carries the instructions for a different characteristic, such as freckles, dimples, blood type, or hair color.

Since you received a complete set of 23 chromosomes from each of your parents, your cells contain two copies of every type of gene. Both copies of the gene contain instructions for the same characteristic, but the instructions are often slightly different. For instance, depending on the eye color of your parents, one of your genes for eye color might code for brown eyes, while the other gene codes for blue eyes.

Luckily, this does not result in striped or polka-dotted eyes! Even though you have two genes for eye color, your cells know exactly which gene to obey, because the gene for brown eyes is **DOMINANT** and the gene for blue eyes is **RECESSIVE**. Dominant genes always win out over recessive genes, so if one of your parents has brown eyes, you will almost certainly have brown eyes, too.

Why do I say "almost certainly"? Because even if your mother has brown eyes, she could still be carrying a gene for blue eyes. The gene for blue eyes is recessive, so it would not effect your mother's eye color. But your mother's gene for blue eyes could give *you* blue eyes if it is combined with another gene for blue eyes from your father. In fact, a blue-eyed baby could be born to two brown-eyed parents, so long as each of them carries a recessive gene for blue eyes. The Punnett square on the next page is a tool for understanding this.

FIGURE 25.11. MULTI-RACIAL FAMILY
The principles of genetics are beautifully illustrated in this photo of a multi-racial family. Can you figure out why none of the children has brown hair, even though one of the parents has brown hair? That's right! The gene for black hair is dominant.

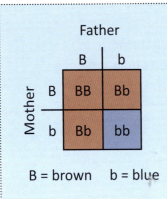

Father

	B	b
B	BB	Bb
b	Bb	bb

Mother

B = brown   b = blue

The letters at the top and left side of the Punnett square represent the genes for eye color which the mother and father inherited from their own parents. The mother and the father can each pass on one of their two genes to their child.

The letters in the colored boxes represent the possible combinations of genes that the child can receive: BB, Bb, and bb. Since the gene for brown eyes (B) is dominant, the child will only have blue eyes if he or she receives two genes for blue eyes (b).

In simple genetics problems, the Punnett square can be used to calculate the likelihood that certain traits will appear in offspring. For example, suppose that a man is **PURE** for blue eyes, which means that the genes from both of his parents call for blue eyes. His set of genes for eye color are written like this: **b b**. His wife is **HYBRID** for brown eyes. This means that she has one chromosome that calls for brown eyes, while the other chromosome has instructions for blue eyes. Her set of genes for eye color are written: **B b**. (Can you figure out what color her eyes are?) A Punnett square is used to determine what color eyes their children could have:

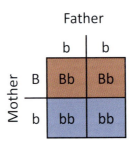

Father

	b	b
B	Bb	Bb
b	bb	bb

Mother

B = brown   b = blue

As you have learned, each of the colored boxes in the Punnett square stands for one of four possible combinations of genes which the father and mother can pass on to their child. To calculate the probability that the child will have blue eyes, find the number of combinations that will result in blue eyes and divide that by the total number of combinations. In this case, there are two combinations that will result in blue eyes and four combinations total. This means that there is a 50% chance that the child will have blue eyes. Can you calculate the probability of blue eyes if a man who is pure for brown eyes (**B B**) marries a woman who is hybrid for brown eyes (**B b**)? Don't forget to draw a Punnett square!

Worksheets:
25.1–25.7

Formal Lab:
25.8

Answer: 0 % probability for blue eyes.

Fr. Gregor Mendel

Gregor Mendel (1822-1884), the Father of Modern Genetics, grew up on his family's farm in what is now called the Czech Republic. In 1843 he graduated from the university and entered the Augustinian Abbey of St. Thomas in Brno; he was ordained a priest in 1847.

The work of the Augustinian Order includes teaching and scientific study, and Fr. Mendel's religious superiors quickly recognized his talent in these areas. Mendel's superiors supported his studies by sending him to study mathematics and science for two years at the University of Vienna. When Fr. Mendel returned, he was assigned to be a science teacher at a local high school, a job which he appears to have loved. Certainly his students loved him—he is remembered as an exceptional teacher who knew how to engage his students' interest.

Fr. Mendel taught high school for many years, during which time he also carried out his famous experiments with pea plants which led to his discovery of the basic laws of genetics. The Augustinian community where he lived had a huge garden set aside for scientific experiments, and in this garden Mendel patiently grew and tested nearly 30,000 pea plants. Unfortunately, Fr. Mendel's discoveries were not appreciated by other scientists until after his death.

In 1868, Fr. Mendel's fellow monks elected him as the abbot of the monastery. Mendel was a

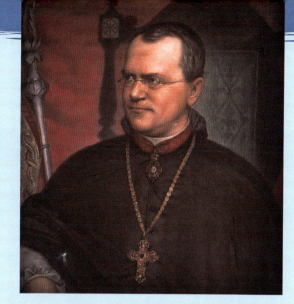

FIGURE 25.12. GREGOR MENDEL
While experimenting with peas in a monastery garden, Gregor Mendel discovered the mathematical rules of inheritance.

dedicated father to his religious community, and his official duties did not leave him much time for scientific research. Abbot Mendel insisted on faithfulness to the Augustinian Rule and did everything he could to promote the spiritual and intellectual development of the monks. During the last years of his life, Abbot Mendel's energy was absorbed by a fight for religious liberty against an unjust law which imposed special taxes on religious communities. The law was eventually repealed, but only after Mendel's death in 1884.

On the 100th anniversary of Gregor Mendel's death, Pope John Paul II praised him for combining "the wisdom of faith and the insights of reason." "During his life," Pope John Paul II explained, "prayer and praise sustained the research and reflection of this patient observer and scientific genius." Mendel was remembered for his kindness and patience, as well as for his sense of humor and common sense.

FIGURE 25.13. The grounds of the abbey where Fr. Gregor Mendel bred his peas. The foundation is all that remains of the greenhouse, seen in the near front of the picture.

ECOLOGY

When you do the common things in life
in an uncommon way, you will command
the attention of the world.

—George Washington Carver

FIGURE 26.1. ILLUSTRATION OF BRITISH REEDBED ECOSYSTEM
Animals shown include two marsh harriers (birds), an otter (center), a great
crested newt (left), eels (bottom center), dragonflies (center), and rudd (fish).
Microscopic life is shown in the inset.

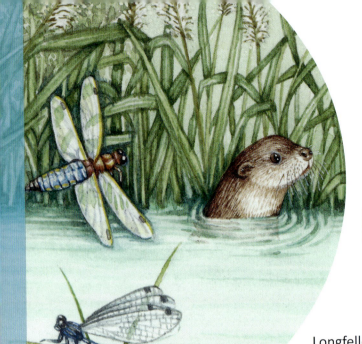

Ecology

Longfellow's "Little Hiawatha" goes out into the forest to kill his first buck. As he stalks his deer the rabbits, birds, and squirrels run out of the way. The "deer with antlers," feeding and drinking near a stream, senses danger. Instinctively it leaps, but Hiawatha's arrow sails true and the deer falls dead. Back at the Indian village, old Nokomis, the grandmother, makes a feast of the deer meat and a cloak from its hide. The bones of the deer are used to make needles, handles, and ornaments.

Now take our "Average Adam." He goes out into the stores on his first shopping trip alone. As he browses, the air conditioners, electric lights, and escalators run continually. When the pizza vendor calls out to him, Adam orders two slices of pizza and a large soda. Then he buys some things for himself and his cousin, Haphazard Harriet. Back at the house, Haphazard Harriet "munches out" on the artificially sweetened gum while Adam tries on his new shorts, which were produced with fibers manufactured from petroleum. The plastic wrappers and paper bags get tossed into the trash.

A tremendous change has occurred during the last two hundred years. A life in tune with nature was once the normal way of life. For most of us, that type of life style is gone. There is no going back. Of course, we wouldn't want to go back to a time when many people your age were disfigured or killed by infectious diseases that today are rare. We wouldn't want to go back to a time when foods could not be easily preserved or transported. Nor would most of us want to go back to using an outhouse on a cold winter's night! On the other hand, Harriet should want streams that are clean enough to drink from. Adam should be able to walk down paths "flecked with leafy light and shadow."

FIGURE 26.2.
"And a deer came down the pathway, / Flecked with leafy light and shadow." —"Song of Hiawatha," Longfellow

Humans are interrelated with all creatures, great and small, and with the non-living parts of the environment. Our habits and actions affect the **BIOTIC** and **ABIOTIC** things with which we share the earth. **ECOLOGY** is the study of the relationships between living and non-living things.

George Washington Carver

An outstanding example of using scientific knowledge to understand the relationships between organisms is the work of George Washington Carver (Figure 26.3).

Carver was born in 1864 to slave parents near Diamond, Missouri. He struggled to get an education (a lesson in itself) and later to carry out numerous experiments. Carver tried to convince poor farmers of the post-Civil War South to grow peanuts. Why peanuts? Everyone in the southern United States grew cotton or tobacco, but both of those crops deplete the soil, especially of nitrates. Without nitrates, plants cannot produce chlorophyll, so each year the farmers' crops were less and less fruitful.

George Washington Carver knew that the peanut plant, <u>Arachis hypogaea</u>, is a legume. As you learned in Chapter 6, nitrogen-fixing bacteria live in the root nodules of legumes. These bacteria take nitrogen gas from the air and "fix" it into nitrates. Carver knew that if Southern farmers planted peanuts in their cotton fields for a year, the next year's crop of cotton would grow better because the peanut plants would have enriched the soil with nitrates.

However, farmers could only grow peanuts if someone would buy them. To create a demand for peanuts, Carver developed not just ten, or twenty, or even a hundred uses, but actually hundreds of uses for peanuts and soybeans, another legume.

Against great odds, George Washington Carver learned and experimented. His understanding led to ecologically sound farming practices still used today.

FIGURE 26.3. GEORGE WASHINGTON CARVER

Carver discovered more than 300 uses for peanuts, including cheese, coffee, vinegar, cosmetics, dyes, soap, and nitroglycerin. When asked how he had invented so many peanut products, Carver explained:

"Why, I just took a handful of peanuts and looked at them. 'Great Creator,' I said, 'why did you make the peanut? Why?' With such knowledge as I had of chemistry and physics I set to work to take the peanut apart. I separated the water, the fats, the oils, the gums, the resins, sugars, starches, pectoses, pentoses, pentosans, legumen, lysin, the amino and amido acids. There! I had the parts of the peanut all spread out before me. Then I merely went on to try different combinations of those parts, under different conditions of temperature, pressure, and so forth."

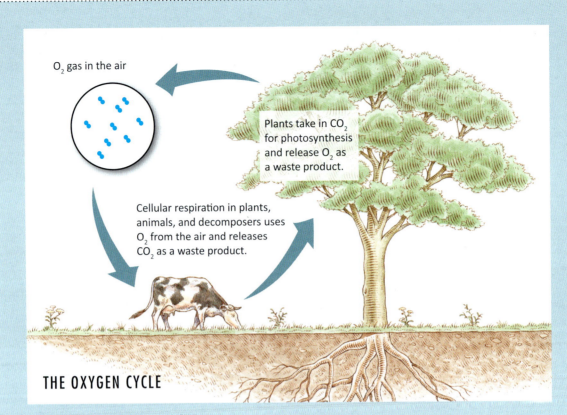

FIGURE 26.4. THE OXYGEN CYCLE
Almost every living thing takes in oxygen (O_2) from the air for the process of cellular respiration and releases carbon dioxide (CO_2) into the air as a waste product. Plants take in carbon dioxide (CO_2) for photosynthesis and release oxygen (O_2) into the air as a waste product.

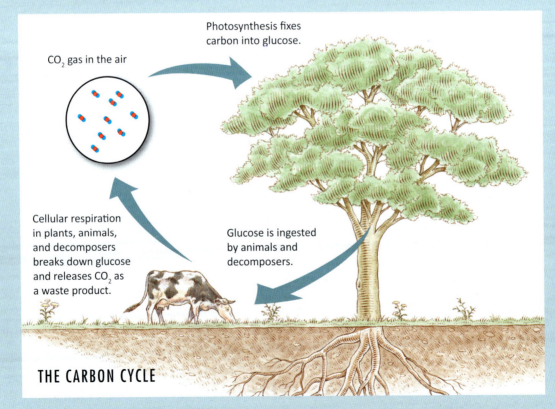

FIGURE 26.5. THE CARBON CYCLE
The process of photosynthesis in green plants fixes carbon from carbon dioxide (CO_2) gas into glucose. Cellular respiration in every living thing returns the carbon to the atmosphere.

Use and Reuse

Carver's understanding of the need to return to the soil what has been taken out—that is, crop rotation—was based on his knowledge that the elements on earth are used and reused many times over.

Imagine if an atom could tell us where it has been! The oxygen atoms you are breathing right now have traveled between the cells of animals and plants many thousands of times (Figure 26.4). The toast or cereal you ate for breakfast contains carbon atoms that plants absorbed from the air and converted into glucose through the process of photosynthesis (Figure 26.5). Similarly, the carbon atoms in the man-made fibers of your clothes came from petroleum which was formed from plants millions of years ago.

The oxygen cycle and the carbon cycle are fundamental to the study of ecology. A third important cycle is the nitrogen cycle. As George Washington Carver understood, nitrogen is used and reused many times over. Unlike oxygen and carbon, however, nitrogen gas (N_2), the most abundant element in the air, cannot be used directly by most organisms.

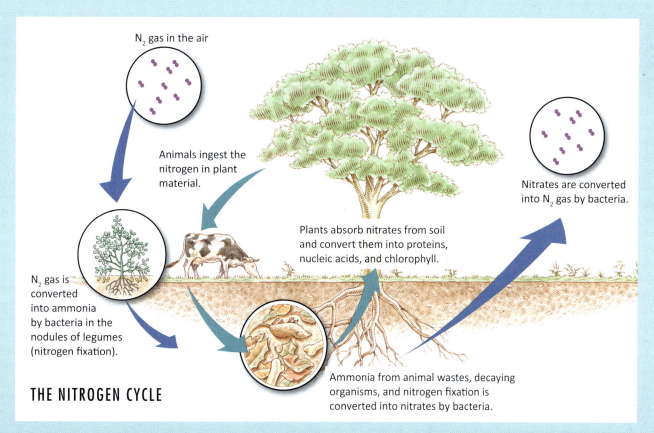

N₂ gas in the air

Animals ingest the nitrogen in plant material.

Plants absorb nitrates from soil and convert them into proteins, nucleic acids, and chlorophyll.

Nitrates are converted into N_2 gas by bacteria.

N_2 gas is converted into ammonia by bacteria in the nodules of legumes (nitrogen fixation).

Ammonia from animal wastes, decaying organisms, and nitrogen fixation is converted into nitrates by bacteria.

THE NITROGEN CYCLE

FIGURE 26.6. THE NITROGEN CYCLE
Nitrogen is found in the proteins of living things. When the proteins are digested, nitrogen wastes are produced. The wastes are decomposed and the nitrogen fixed into living things again. Bacteria are involved in three phases of the nitrogen cycle: converting nitrogen gas (N_2) into ammonia, converting ammonia into nitrates, and converting nitrates back into nitrogen gas (N_2).

Plants and animals depend on nitrogen-fixing bacteria to convert nitrogen gas into nitrates. Living organisms then use the nitrates to make chlorophyll, nucleic acids (DNA and RNA), and proteins. Refer to Figure 26.6 to trace the steps in the nitrogen cycle.

In nature, **DECOMPOSERS** recycle nutrients and the elements. Life could not go on without the fungi and bacteria which decompose the elements of life. The basic idea of cycles is one that humans can apply, also. Just as the oxygen, carbon, and nitrogen in organisms' bodies must be recycled in order for life to continue, so the things we make and use must be recycled eventually.

Energy and Food Chains

As you know, the source of energy for almost every living thing is ultimately the sun. The energy from the sun is not used and reused the way elements are, so the energy relationships between creatures are often described as a pyramid or chain instead of a cycle. We call these the food pyramid and the food chain.

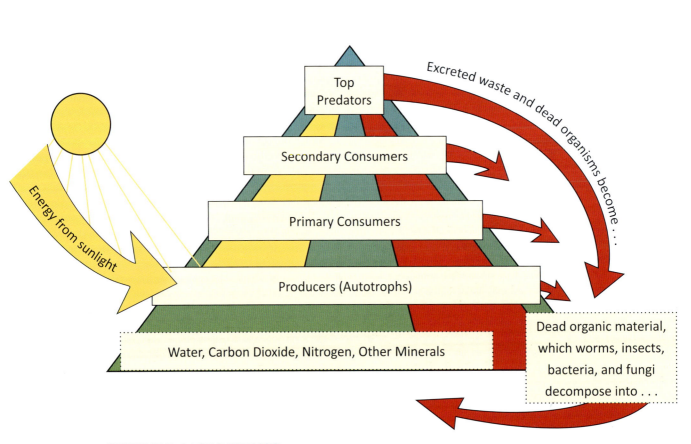

FIGURE 26.7. A FOOD PYRAMID
At each level of the pyramid, energy is used up as organisms perform the life functions and engage in activities such as collecting food, raising offspring, and building nests or dens. Because of this energy loss, there must be more secondary consumers than top predators, more primary consumers than secondary consumers, and more producers than primary producers. The number of producers is limited by the climate, including the amount of sunlight, and by the availability of soil nutrients.

Every day, energy from the sun pours onto the earth as sunlight. Much of the energy is lost back into space or used as heat to power the weather. Green plants, called **PRODUCERS**, use a small part of the sun's energy to make food. When **PRIMARY CONSUMERS**—that is, animals that eat plants—eat the food-energy stored in the green plants, they use some of it to power their life functions. The energy which they do not use right away is stored in their bodies. When other animals, called **SECONDARY CONSUMERS**, ingest the energy stored in the primary consumers, they use up some of the energy to power their life functions and they store the rest in their own tissues. Because energy is used up at each step to power each creature's life functions, there must be many more producers than primary consumers, and more primary consumers than secondary consumers. This fact is illustrated by the pyramid in Figure 26.7. Notice that the energy in the food pyramid is not recycled and used over again.

The last level in a food pyramid is the top predator, which is not ingested by another animal. Instead, when the top predator dies, the elements in its body are decomposed by decay organisms such as worms, fungi, and bacteria. These decomposers also recycle the wastes and dead organic matter produced at the other levels of the pyramid. The right side of Figure 26.7 shows how the elements of life, unlike the energy from the sun, are used and reused.

Examples of related organisms from each level of the food pyramid make a **FOOD CHAIN**. Every food chain begins with a producer and ends with a top predator. For example, the bald eagle, <u>Haliaeetus leucocephalus</u>, is America's national bird. The bald eagle does not have any natural predators, so it is called a top predator (Figure 26.8). The fish, small birds, and mammals that the eagle eats are primary consumers, and the plants eaten by the primary consumers are the producers. A favorite food of the bald eagle is the sockeye salmon, <u>Oncorhynchus nerka</u> (Figure 26.8). The sockeye salmon eats plankton and many other small marine organisms.

FIGURE 26.8.
In a food chain made up of plankton, a salmon, and a bald eagle, the plankton is the producer and the eagle is the top predator.

SOCKEYE SALMON
(<u>ONCORHYNCHUS NERKA</u>)

PHOTOSYNTHETIC PLANKTON

BALD EAGLE
(<u>HALIAEETUS LEUCOCEPHALUS</u>)

FIGURE 26.9. A SIMPLE FOOD WEB

Actually, a food chain simplifies the situation just a little too much. The plankton in Figure 26.8 may be eaten by any of numerous marine animals. The salmon, too, may be eaten by many other creatures, including bears and human beings. When we try to draw a diagram that shows more of these relationships, we get a big web of lines connecting the organisms. A **FOOD WEB** is a group of food chains that are linked together (Figures 26.9–10).

Biomes

A **HABITAT** is the special place where an animal or plant lives. The bald eagle's habitat is a wild, remote forested area. When different organisms share the same habitat, they often occupy different niches. A **NICHE** is the special role of an organism in its habitat. A bald eagle's niche includes its role as a top predator. Many insects fill the niche of pollinating flowers, and earthworms fill the niche of aerating the soil.

Any habitat that includes all of the factors needed for it to continue in existence forms an ecosystem. The habitat is only one part of the larger **ECOSYSTEM**. An ecosystem can be as small as a fish tank or as large as a state. The earth's surface is divided into six, very large ecosystems called **BIOMES**. The differences between biomes are caused mainly by the differences in climate and terrain.

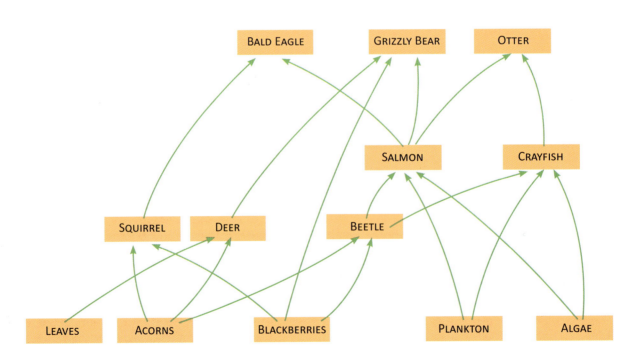

FIGURE 26.10. FOOD WEB

Servant of God Paul Xu Guangqi

Paul Xu Guangqi (SHOO GWAN-chee) was born in 1562 in rural China. A deep love for his country and a desire to use his talents for the good of his people led him to seek civil service. To support his wife and family, Xu Guangqi worked as a tutor until 1604, when he passed the final series of exams and entered the service of the emperor.

During the years when Xu Guangqi was studying for his exams, he met Fr. Matteo Ricci and other Jesuit missionaries to China. Xu converted to Catholicism in 1603, and was baptized with the Christian name "Paul." Paul Xu's family soon followed him into the Church, and their home became a center for evangelization and catechesis. Paul Xu himself instructed more than 200 catechumens in the faith. When Paul Xu served at Mass, he expressed his deep faith in the Real Presence by always dressing in courtly attire, just as if he were in the presence of the emperor.

Paul Xu's growing love for God increased his desire to serve his country, especially the poor who frequently suffered from famine. Paul Xu believed that better agricultural techniques could increase crop production and reduce starvation. He carefully experimented with different methods of farming. For instance, after three years of experiments with soil, water, and fertilizer, he discovered a way to grow wet-rice in northern China. Previously, it had been necessary to transport rice from southern China at great expense. Paul Xu also experimented with growing sweet potatoes and cotton and wrote the first complete book on agriculture, including topics such as water conservation, land reclamation, and forest preservation.

Paul Xu was devoted to God above all else. In 1616, when Catholics in China were threatened with persecution, Paul Xu defended the missionaries

FIGURE 26.11. PAUL XU GUANGQI
Chinese scholars credit Paul Xu Guangqi with beginning the Chinese enlightenment. In this picture, Paul Xu is wearing a typical scholar's costume and holding a Chinese-bound book. The emblem on his robe indicates his rank in the Chinese government. The Chinese calligraphy on the scroll behind Paul Xu reads: "There is but One God, Creator of Heaven and Earth."

and Chinese converts in a letter to the emperor. During the persecution, he even hid many of the missionaries in his own home.

When Paul Xu died in 1633, he held some of the highest offices in the Chinese government. Paul Xu's combination of scientific brilliance, moral integrity, and sincere love for God and neighbor has led one author to call him "the greatest glory of Chinese Catholicism." Paul Xu Guangqi was declared a Servant of God in 2011 and the cause for his beatification is underway.

The biome that includes the bald eagle is the boreal forest. The **boreal forest** is the coniferous forest found near mountain tops and in the northern parts of North America, Europe, and Asia. North of the boreal forest is a colder biome called the **tundra**. South of the boreal forest is the temperate, or deciduous, forest. Most of the eastern United States is part of the **deciduous forest** biome.

There are three other major biomes, each with its own unique plants and animals (Figure 26.12). The golden eagle, Aquila chrysaetos, lives in the **desert** biome. The bateleur eagle, Terathopius ecaudatus, feeds on snakes in a **grassland** biome. The Philippine eagle, Pithecophaga jefferyi, is a top predator in the hot, **tropical rainforest** biome. There are also various **freshwater** and **marine** biomes. All the biomes of the earth taken together form the BIOSPHERE. The biosphere is just what its name sounds like: the ball of life.

Because people have the ability to learn and to reason, human beings can be found in any of the biomes. Men and women can make clothing and shelters to keep themselves warm in the tundra. Medicines and buildings let people live in the swamps of rainforests. Humans live under the sea in submarines. Human beings even live in outer space where no other living things have ever been found!

FIGURE 26.12.
Eagles can be found in almost every biome, but different species of eagles make their homes in different biomes.

PHILIPPINE EAGLE
(PITHECOPHAGA JEFFERYI)

GOLDEN EAGLE
(AQUILA CHRYSAETOS)

BATELEUR EAGLE
(TERATHOPIUS ECAUDATUS)

**FIGURE 26.13.
THE HUDSON RIVER**

Mankind is different from every other species of animals. Human beings—you and I—have a special responsibility, a special niche, in the biosphere. Since we are able to understand the relationships that living things have with each other and with their environment, we must use our intelligence to care for our earth and the creatures that live on it.

In your study of ecology you have learned that all the organisms in the biosphere are interdependent. Smog, acid rain, and improper disposal of solid wastes are problems that strain the ecology of our habitats. They are problems we can solve.

For instance, several decades ago the Hudson River in New York state was very polluted. Today, there are more people living in the Hudson River Valley, but the river's waters are cleaner, thanks to extensive cleanup efforts and a better understanding of ecology. There is still room for improvement, but with effort we can make the changes necessary to put modern life in tune with nature.

The human foot print has as much right in the forest as the fox print or the deer track. But the fox and the deer are not named *"sapiens,"* the wise one. It is up to us, you and I, to conserve and manage the earth. An earth we share with all creatures great and small.

 Worksheets:
26.1–26.3, 26.5

 Diagram:
26.4, 26.6

 Test:
Final Review

 Experiment:
Miniature Ecosystem

Word Roots

Root word	Meaning	Examples
A OR AB	NOT	ABIOTIC, ANAEROBIC
ANTI	AGAINST	ANTIBODY, ANTITOXIN
AQUA	WATER	AQUARIUM, AQUATIC
AUDIO	SOUND OR HEARING	AUDITORY NERVE
BI	TWO	BINARY FISSION, BILATERAL, BICEPS
BIO	LIFE	BIOLOGY, BIOME, BIOSPHERE, BIOTIC
CARDIAC	REFERRING TO THE HEART	CARDIAC MUSCLE
CELLA	SMALL ROOM	CELL, CELLULAR
CENTI	100	CENTIMETER, CENTURY, CENTS
CHROMO	COLOR	CHROMOSOME
CYANO	DARK BLUE	CYANOBACTERIA
CYKLOS	CIRCLE	CYCLOSIS, CIRCULAR, CYCLE
DECI	TEN	DECIMETER, DECIMAL, DECADE
DERMA	SKIN	EPIDERMIS, MESODERM
DI	TWO	DIVIDE, DISSECT
EPI	UPON	EPIDERMIS
EX	OUT	EXIT, EXCRETION, ECTODERM
GASTRO	REFERRING TO STOMACH	GASTRIC JUICE, GASTROINTESTINAL
GEO	EARTH	GEOTROPISM, GEOGRAPHY
GLOTTIS	TONGUE	GLOTTIS, EPIGLOTTIS
GRADE	GRADUATION OR STEP	GRADUATIONS, CENTIGRADE
IN	IN	INHALE, INGEST, INSPIRATION
MACRO	BIG	MACRONUCLEUS
MARINE	OCEAN	MARINE, SUBMARINE
METER	TO MEASURE	METRIC, METER, THERMOMETER
MICRO	SMALL	MICRO-ORGANISM, MICROSCOPE
MILLI	1000	MILLIMETER, MILLILITER, MILE
MULTI	MANY	MULTICELLULAR
OLOGY	THE STUDY OF	BIOLOGY, ORNITHOLOGY
PHOTO	LIGHT	PHOTOSYNTHESIS, PHOTOTROPISM
PULMO	REFERRING TO THE LUNG	PULMONARY CIRCULATION
RE	TO DO AGAIN	REPRODUCE, REVIEW
SEMI	PARTLY	SEMIPERMEABLE
SOMA	BODY	CHROMOSOME
SUB	UNDER	SUBMARINE, SUBCUTANEOUS
SYNTHESIS	TO MAKE	SYNTHESIS, PHOTOSYNTHESIS
TRANS	ACROSS	TRANSPORT, TRAIN
VACCINUS	COW	VACCINE, VACCINATION
VIDEO	SEE	VISION, VIDEO

Plant Uses

FOOD

Almonds
Apples
Apricots
Asparagus
Bananas
Beans
Beer
Beets
Birch beer
Blackberries
Blueberries
Bread
Cabbage
Cantaloupe
Carrots
Cashews
Cauliflower
Cassava
Celery
Cereals
Cherries
Cider
Cocoa
Coconut
Coffee
Corn
Crackers
Cucumbers
Dates
Doughnuts
Eggplant
Figs
Garlic
Grapefruit
Grapes
Honeydew melon
Jams
Lemons
Lettuce
Macaroni
Nectarine
Noodles
Oats

Olives
Onions
Oranges
Peaches
Peanuts
Pears
Peas
Pecans
Pepper
Peppers
Pie crust
Pineapple
Pistachio
Plums
Potato
Potato, Sweet
Prunes
Pumpkin
Raisin
Raspberries
Rhubarb
Rice
Rolls
Root beer
Rye
Sassafras
Soybean
Spaghetti
Spinach
Squash
Strawberries
Sugar beet
Sugar cane
Syrup
Tobacco
Tea
Tomatoes
Turnips
Vanilla
Walnuts
Watermelon
Wheat
Wine

FIBER

- Cotton
- Cotton balls
- Pants
- Shirts
- Socks
- Towels
- Underwear
- Flax (linen)
- Paper
- Books
- Boxes
- Cups
- Dollars
- Looseleaf
- Napkins
- Newspapers
- Plates
- Toilet paper
- Wallpaper
- Plastics
- Boats
- Car parts
- Coats
- Furniture
- Gloves
- Pens
- Rayon
- Skateboards
- Surfboards
- Toys
- Helmets
- Motorcycle parts

WOOD

- Baseball bats
- Baskets
- Beds
- Boats
- Cabinets
- Chairs
- Cutting boards
- Decks
- Desks
- Doors
- Houses

- Lumber
- Paneling
- Pencils
- Picture frames
- Plywood
- Skis
- Straw
- Tables
- Wooden spoons

OTHER

- Acetic acid
- Acetone
- Coal
- Cork
- Decorations
- Ethanol
- Firewood
- Flowers
- Formaldehyde
- Gasoline
- Glues
- Gum
- Natural gas
- Oil
- Oxygen
- Propane
- Rubber
- Balls
- Boots
- Raincoats
- Rubber bands
- Sneaker soles
- Tar
- Tires
- Tubing
- Turpentine
- Shade
- Varnish

Glossary

ABIOTIC   non-living.

ABSORPTION   the process of passing through the wall of the intestine or through a cell membrane.

ADIPOSE CELLS   cells of connective tissue that store large amounts of fat.

ADRENAL GLANDS   endocrine glands located on top of the kidneys which produce adrenalin and cortisol.

ADRENALIN   a hormone produced by the adrenal medulla that prepares the body for emergencies.

AEROBIC   using oxygen gas from the air.

AGNATHA   the class of jawless fish in the Phylum Chordata.

AIDS   acquired immunodeficiency syndrome; a fatal infectious disease that destroys the body's ability to fight off other diseases.

ALLERGY   a condition in which the immune system overreacts to a substance.

ALVEOLUS   an air sac in the lungs where gas exchange between the air and the blood occurs.

AMINO ACIDS   nitrogen-containing molecules which are linked together to form proteins.

AMPHIBIA   the class of gilled then lunged vertebrates in Phylum Chordata.

AMYLASE   the enzyme that begins the digestion of starches.

ANAEROBIC   not using oxygen gas from the air.

ANAPHASE   the fourth stage of mitosis, during which the chromosomes move apart to either side of the cell.

ANGIOSPERMAE   the class of plants in Phylum Tracheophyta with seeds inside a fruit; the flowering plants.

ANIMALIA   the kingdom of multicellular, heterotrophic eukaryotes without cell walls.

ANNELIDA   the phylum of segmented worms in Kingdom Animalia.

ANNULUS   the ring on the stipe of some mushrooms.

ANTERIOR   front end.

ANTIBIOTIC   a chemical from molds or bacteria that can kill microbes.

ANTIBODIES   proteins produced by an organism to help phagocytes capture invading pathogens.

ANTISEPTIC	a substance that stops or prohibits infection.
ANUS	the opening in the digestive system through which wastes are excreted.
AORTA	the main artery of the body; exits the left ventricle.
ARCHAEA	a kingdom of prokaryotes which often live in extreme conditions.
AREA	a measurement, in square units, of the surface of a solid; area = length × width.
ARTERY	a thick, muscular blood vessel that carries blood away from the heart.
ARTHROPODA	the phylum of animals with jointed legs and exoskeletons.
ASCUS	a sac-like structure containing spores in some fungi; plural = asci.
ASEXUAL REPRODUCTION	the process in which a new organism is made from one parent.
ASSOCIATIVE NEURON	a nerve cell that connects sensory and motor neurons and processes impulses in the brain.
ATOM	the smallest part of an element with all the properties of the element.
ATOMIC NUMBER	the number of protons contained in the nucleus of an atom.
ATP	adenosine triphosphate; a high-energy molecule produced by cellular respiration and used to power the cell's life functions.
ATRIUM	either of the two upper chambers of the heart that receive blood from the veins and pump it into the ventricles.
AUDITORY NERVE	the nerve that sends electrical impulses from the ear to the brain.
AUTOTROPH	"self feeder"; any organism capable of making its own food energy.
AUXINS	plant hormones.
AVES	the class of warm-blooded, feathered animals in Phylum Chordata.
AXON	the long, thin part of a nerve cell which transmits impulses to other cells.
BACTERIA	the kingdom of organisms with no nuclear membranes or organelles; thrive in a wide variety of habitats.
BACTERIAL SPORE	a tiny, thick-walled structure of a bacterium which allows it to survive unfavorable environmental conditions.
BACTERIOPHAGE	a virus that infects bacterial cells.
BARK	thick layer of dead cells on the outside of woody stems.
BASIDIA	microscopic club-shaped structures on which spores form in some fungi; singular = basidium.
BEEF TAPEWORM	a parasitic member of Phylum Platyhelminthes which infects humans; found in beef.
BENEDICT'S SOLUTION	a blue solution used to test for simple sugars.

BICUSPID	a type of tooth with two points (cusps), for grinding food.
BILATERAL SYMMETRY	a shape which may be cut into two similar parts.
BILE	a digestive juice produced in the liver that emulsifies fats.
BINARY FISSION	a type of asexual reproduction in which a cell splits into two equal parts.
BINOMIAL NOMENCLATURE	a system of labeling which uses two names for each object.
BIOLOGY	the study of living things.
BIOME	a very large ecosystem with a specific climate and terrain.
BIOSPHERE	all the biomes of the earth taken together.
BIOTIC	living.
BLUE-GREEN ALGAE	a member of Kingdom Bacteria that gets its energy through photosynthesis; also called cyanobacteria.
BONE	cells of connective tissue containing hard calcium salts that support the body.
BRONCHIAL TUBES	the bronchi, bronchioles, and other branching air passages inside the lungs.
BRONCHUS	either of the two main branches that connect the trachea to the lungs; plural = bronchi.
BRYOPHYTA	a phylum of the Kingdom Plantae containing land plants with no vascular system.
BUDDING	a form of asexual reproduction in which the DNA is duplicated but the cytoplasm is not evenly divided between the parent and daughter cells.
BULB	a short underground stem with enlarged leaf bases for food storage; ex. onion.
CALORIE	a basic unit equal to the amount of heat needed to raise the temperature of one gram of water by 1 °C.
CALORIMETER	an instrument used to measure heat energy in calories.
CAMBIUM	a special area of cell division between the xylem and phloem in plants.
CAP	the umbrella-shaped top of a mushroom.
CAPILLARY	a microscopic blood vessel that connects arteries to veins.
CARBOHYDRATE	any carbon, oxygen and hydrogen compound with two hydrogen atoms for each oxygen atom.
CARDIAC MUSCLE	the involuntary muscle of the heart; made of branched cells with striations and a single nucleus.
CARNIVORE	meat-eater.
CARTILAGE	a rubber-like connective tissue that acts as a shock absorber and provides support in flexible areas.
CELL	the basic unit of structure and function in living things.

CELL MEMBRANE	the thin, dense film of protoplasm that surrounds the cell; also called plasma membrane.
CELLULAR RESPIRATION	the combining of oxygen and glucose in a cell to release energy with carbon dioxide and water as waste products.
CELL WALL	a stiff box of non-living material that surrounds plant, fungal, and most bacterial cells.
CENTI	the metric prefix meaning 1/100th of the basic unit; abbreviated "c."
CENTIGRADE	a temperature scale with 100 degrees between the freezing (0 °C) and boiling points (100 °C) of water; also called Celsius.
CENTRIOLES	a pair of spherical organelles in animal cells which assist in cell division.
CEREBRUM	the largest part of the brain; it controls thinking.
CEREBELLUM	the part of the brain that controls coordination and balance.
CHEMICAL DIGESTION	the process of chemically breaking down foods into simpler substances.
CHEMOSYNTHESIS	the process which uses energy from chemical reactions to produce food energy in the absence of sunlight.
CHEMOTROPISM	a plant response to chemicals.
CHITIN	an insoluble chemical forming the cell walls of many fungi; also in the exoskeleton of arthropods.
CHLOROPHYLL	the green pigment (coloring) that captures sunlight for the process of photosynthesis.
CHLOROPLAST	an organelle in plant cells and some protists which contains chlorophyll.
CHONDRICHTHYES	the class of cartilaginous fish in the Phylum Chordata.
CHORDATA	the phylum of animals with a dorsal nerve cord, an internal skeleton, and a notochord.
CHROMOSOME	a double strand of DNA, consisting of many genes, with the information to operate a cell.
CILIA	tiny hair-like structures; used for movement by some protists.
CLASSES	subdivisions of a phylum.
CNIDARIA	the phylum of animals with bag-like bodies, tentacles, and two tissue layers; ex. jellyfish.
COCHLEA	the snail-shaped part of the inner ear that converts vibrations into electrical impulses.
COLD-BLOODED	able to maintain its body temperature independent of the environment.
COLONY	a mass of bacteria large enough to be seen without a microscope.
COMPOUND	a pure substance made of two or more elements chemically joined in a definite ratio.

CONCAVE LENS	a lens that is thicker at the edges than in the middle.
CONDITIONED REFLEX	a simple, quick response which involves the brain.
CONE CELLS	specialized neurons in the eye that are sensitive to color; light receptors.
CONIFER	"cone-bearer"; any plant that has cones.
CONJUGATION	a type of sexual reproduction in which only some of the nuclear material in a cell is exchanged with another cell.
CONTRACTILE VACUOLE	a star-shaped organelle used for excretion by protists.
CONTROL	part of an experiment in which all variables are kept the same; provides a basis for comparison.
CONVEX LENS	a lens that is thicker in the middle than at the edges.
CONVOLUTIONS	bumps on the surface of the cerebrum which increase surface area.
CORNEA	the clear covering on the front of the eye that helps to focus light.
COROLLA	all the petals of a flower together.
CORTISOL	a hormone produced by the adrenal cortex that regulates sugar metabolism and reduces inflammation and allergic reactions.
COTYLEDON	a seed leaf; used for food storage in a seed.
CROSS-POLLINATION	the process in which pollen from one flower reaches the stigma of a different flower.
CUSPID	a type of tooth with one point (cusp), also called a canine tooth, for ripping meat.
CUTICLE	a waxy, transparent layer on a leaf used for protection.
CYCLOSIS	a circular movement of the cytoplasm in a cell.
CYTON	the cell body of a neuron.
CYTOPLASM	the protoplasm outside of the nucleus.
DECI	the metric prefix meaning 1/10th of the basic unit; abbreviated "d."
DECOMPOSERS	organisms that recycle nutrients and elements by breaking down dead organic matter.
DEKA	the metric prefix meaning 10 times the basic unit; abbreviated "da."
DENDRITES	the branch-like extensions on cytons which receive impulses from other neurons.
DEPENDENT VARIABLE	the variable in an experiment that changes because of the independent variable.
DERMIS	the layer of skin beneath the epidermis; contains capillaries, glands and nerve cells.
DIABETES	a disease in which the pancreas does not produce enough insulin, causing high glucose levels in the blood but glucose deficiency in cells.

DIALYSIS	the separation of substances in a solution by diffusion through a semipermeable membrane.
DIAPHRAGM	(1) a dome-shaped sheet of muscle which separates the chest from the abdomen and is important in breathing.
	(2) the part of a microscope which controls the amount of light reaching the slide.
DICOT	a flowering plant which has seeds with two cotyledons.
DIFFUSION	the movement of material from high to low concentration without the use of energy.
DIGESTION	the process in which complex foods are changed into smaller, simpler foods.
DIRECT CONTACT	disease transmission by touching a sick person or animal.
DISACCHARIDE	a complex sugar made of two sugar rings.
DISEASE	any condition in which an organism cannot carry out one of the life functions properly.
DNA	deoxyribonucleic acid; the chemical instructions in the nucleus of a cell.
DOMINANT	the form of a gene that is always expressed, even if an organism also inherits a different form of the gene from one of its parents.
DORSAL	top or back.
DROPLETS	tiny drops of liquid.
ECHINODERMATA	the phylum of spiny-skinned animals.
ECOLOGY	the study of the relationships between biotic and abiotic factors in an environment.
ECOSYSTEM	a community of organisms and the abiotic factors needed for its continued existence.
EFFECTORS	muscles or glands that put nerve messages into effect.
EGG	a large, nonmotile cell with only half the normal number of chromosomes; the female gamete.
ELECTRON	a negatively charged particle with almost no mass, located in the energy shell of an atom.
ELEMENT	a simple substance that cannot be broken down by ordinary chemical means.
EMBRYO	a tiny organism in an early stage of its development.
ENDOCRINE SYSTEM	a system of ductless glands that produce hormones.
ENDOPLASMIC RETICULUM	an organelle made of tube-like membranes which provide a surface for chemical reactions.
ENERGY SHELL	a region around the nucleus of an atom where electrons may be found.
ENZYMES	proteins that help specific chemical reactions to occur.

EPIDERMIS	the outer layer of skin made of closely packed cells.
EPIGLOTTIS	a flap of tissue that covers the trachea during swallowing.
ESOPHAGUS	the smooth muscle tube that connects the pharynx to the stomach.
ESTIVATE	to become dormant in hot weather.
EUKARYOTES	organisms that have a nuclear membrane and organelles.
EUSTACHIAN TUBE	a tube that connects the middle ear to the pharynx.
EXCRETION	the life function of eliminating waste products.
EXHALE	to breathe out.
EXOSKELETON	a skeleton on the outside of the body.
EXPIRATION	the process of exhaling, or breathing out.
EYESPOT	a light sensitive organelle in <u>Euglena sp.</u>
FAMILIES	subdivisions of an order.
FARSIGHTEDNESS	a condition in which light is focused too far from the lens and only distant objects can be seen clearly.
FAT	giant, high-energy molecules of carbon, hydrogen, and oxygen with many more hydrogen atoms than oxygen atoms.
FERTILIZATION	the process of an egg and a sperm nuclei fusing together to form a new individual.
FIBRINOGEN	a protein in the blood that forms fibers to help platelets form a clot.
FIBROUS ROOT	a root system made of many small roots; specialized for absorption.
FILICINEAE	a class seedless plants in the Phylum Tracheophyta; ex. ferns.
FILTRATE	the liquid that has passed through a filter.
FLAGELLUM	a whip-like protein fiber used for locomotion.
FOOD CHAIN	a simplified energy relationship that begins with a producer and ends with a top predator.
FOOD WEB	a map of energy relationships made of many, interlinked food chains.
FROND	the fan-like leaf of a fern.
FUNGI	the kingdom containing heterotrophic organisms with chitinous cell walls.
GALL BLADDER	a balloon-like organ that stores bile.
GAMETES	sex cells; sperm or egg cells.
GAS	the highest energy phase of matter, in which it does not have a definite shape and volume; ex. steam.
GENES	"pieces" of coded information found within chromosomes.
GENERA	subdivisions of a family; the first half of a scientific name; singular = genus.

GENETICS	the study of how traits are transmitted to the next generation by genes.
GEOTROPISM	a plant response to gravity.
GERMINATION	the process of a plant beginning to grow.
GILLS	(1) thin flaps on the underside of a mushroom's cap where spores are produced
	(2) a feathery organ, full of capillaries, for exchanging gases under water; used by fish, immature forms of amphibians, and some insects.
GLOMERULUS	the knot of capillaries in the capsule of a nephron where filtration occurs.
GLUCAGON	a hormone produced in the pancreas that controls the release of glucose from the liver.
GLUCOSE	a simple sugar, $C_6H_{12}O_6$, also called blood sugar.
GLYCOGEN	a starch made of many glucose molecules linked together; used for short-term storage of glucose in the liver.
GOLGI BODY	the part of a cell that transports, modifies, and stores proteins.
GONADS	the reproductive organs where gametes are produced.
GRADUATION	markings or degrees on a measuring instrument.
GRAM	the basic unit of mass in the metric system; abbreviated "g."
GROWTH	the life function in which cells increase in size or number.
GROWTH HORMONE	a hormone produced by the pituitary gland that stimulates tissue growth.
GYMNOSPERMAE	a class of the Phylum Tracheophyta characterized by plants with seeds not inside a fruit; "naked seed"; ex. conifers.
HABITAT	the special place where an organism lives.
HEAT	the amount of energy available for transfer.
HEART	the muscular organ in the chest cavity that pumps the blood.
HECTO	the metric prefix meaning 100 times the basic unit; abbreviated "h."
HEMOGLOBIN	an iron-containing protein in red blood cells that carries oxygen.
HEMOPHILIA	a genetic disease in which the blood does not clot properly.
HERBACEOUS STEM	the non-woody, green stem of annuals, biennials, and some perennials.
HERBIVORE	plant eater.
HETEROTROPH	"other feeder"; any organism that cannot make its own food energy.
HIBERNATE	to become dormant in cold weather.
HICCUPS	spasms of the diaphragm that force short intakes of breath.
HORMONES	chemical messengers that regulate body activity.
HOST	an organism that is attacked by a parasite or pathogen.

HUMUS	dark, decayed organic matter in topsoil.
HYBRID	an organism with two different types of genes for the same trait.
HYDROTROPISM	a plant response to water.
HYPHAE	thread-like filaments of fungal cells.
HYPOTHESIS	a suggested explanation for something that has been observed.
IMMUNITY	the ability of the body to resist disease.
IMPULSE	an electrical message carried by nerves.
INCISOR	a type of tooth shaped liked a chisel for biting off foods.
INDEPENDENT VARIABLE	the variable that is purposely changed in an experiment.
INDIRECT CONTACT	disease transmission by contact with objects touched by a sick person.
INFECTIOUS	able to be transmitted from one to another by direct or indirect contact.
INFERIOR VENA CAVA	the major vein from the lower part of the body that enters the right atrium.
INGESTION	the process of taking in food that is already manufactured.
INHALE	to breathe in.
INSECTIVORE	insect eater.
INSPIRATION	the process of inhaling, or breathing in.
INSTINCT	a built-in inclination toward a complex behavior directed toward a specific end result.
INSULIN	a hormone made in the pancreas which allows the absorption of glucose from the blood into the cells.
INTERPHASE	the first stage of mitosis, during which the cell grows larger and duplicates each of its chromosomes.
INVOLUNTARY	not able to be controlled by the conscious mind.
IRIS	the "colored" part of the eye that adjusts the size of the pupil.
IRRITABILITY	the ability to respond to stimuli.
ISLANDS OF LANGERHANS	patches of tissue in the pancreas that produce insulin and glucagon.
JOINT	the point where two bones meet; comes in four types: immovable, ball-and-socket, hinge, and gliding.
KILO	the metric prefix meaning 1000 times the basic unit; abbreviated "k."
KINGDOMS	the six largest taxons in our modern system of classification.
LACTEAL	a small lymph vessel inside a villus that absorbs fatty acids and glycerol.
LARGE INTESTINE	a short, thick section of the digestive system where water is absorbed.

LARVA	an immature form in many kinds of animals; larval insects are also called caterpillars.
LARYNX	the voice box, made of cartilage, that contains vocal cords.
LEARNING	using past experiences to determine future responses to stimuli.
LENTICELS	small openings in the bark of young stems for gas exchange.
LICHEN	algae and fungi growing together in a mutualistic relationship.
LIGAMENT	a fibrous connective tissue that connects bone to bone.
LIQUID	the phase of matter in which it has a definite volume but no definite shape; ex. water.
LITER	the basic unit of liquid volume in the metric system; abbreviated "l."
LIVER	the largest organ of the body; produces bile and takes part in other metabolic activities.
LUGOL'S SOLUTION	a brown solution containing iodine used to test for starch.
LUNGS	sack-like organs rich in capillaries; used by mammals, birds, reptiles, and mature amphibians to exchange gases in the air.
LUNG CANCER	a noninfectious, environmental disease often caused by smoking.
LYSOSOME	small, bubble-like organelles that contain digestive enzymes.
MACRONUCLEUS	a large nucleus in a paramecium that controls cell metabolism.
MALARIA	a protistan disease transmitted by an animal vector, the female <u>Anopheles sp.</u> mosquito.
MAMMALIA	the class of warm-blooded animals in the Phylum Chordata with mammary glands and hair.
MARROW	a soft substance in the center of some bones where red and white blood cells are made.
MASS	the amount of matter in an object.
MECHANICAL DIGESTION	the process of breaking down food into smaller pieces of the same material.
MEDULLA	the part of the brain that controls involuntary actions.
MEGA	the metric prefix meaning 1,000,000 times the basic unit; abbreviated "M."
MEIOSIS	special cell division that produces cells with half the usual number of chromosomes; these cells, called gametes, are used for sexual reproduction.
METABOLISM	the sum total of all life functions.
METAMORPHOSIS	the process of changing shape while developing to adulthood.
METAPHASE	the third stage of mitosis, during which the chromosomes line up in the middle of the cell.
METER	the basic unit of length in the metric system; abbreviated "m."

METER STICK	an instrument used to measure length that is graduated into 10, 100, and 1000 divisions of the meter.
METRIC SYSTEM	the common name for the International System of Units (S.I.), a system of measurement based on the number 10.
MICRO	the metric prefix meaning one millionth of the basic unit; abbreviated "µ."
MICRON	a unit of length equal to 0.001 mm; also called a micrometer; abbreviated "µm."
MICRONUCLEUS	a small nucleus in a paramecium which is used for sexual reproduction (conjugation).
MICROORGANISM	an organism too small to be seen without a microscope.
MILLI	the metric prefix meaning 1/1000th of the basic unit; abbreviated "m."
MINERAL	an inorganic element or compound needed by a living system in small amounts.
MITOCHONDRION	a cell organelle containing a folded membrane where energy in the form of ATP is released through cellular respiration (plural = mitochondria).
MITOSIS	normal cell division in which two new cells are formed, each with a complete set of chromosomes.
MIXTURE	two or more substances together in any ratio, each keeping its own characteristics.
MOLAR	a type of large, broad, flat tooth for crushing food.
MOLECULE	the smallest part of a compound with all the properties of the compound.
MOLLUSCA	the phylum of soft-bodied animals with a muscular foot, most with a hard shell.
MONOCOT	a flowering plant which has seeds with only one cotyledon.
MONOSACCHARIDE	a simple sugar made of one sugar ring; ex. glucose.
MOTOR NEURON	a nerve cell that sends impulses out to muscles or glands.
MUCUS	a sticky secretion that lines much of the respiratory, reproductive, and digestive systems.
MULTICELLULAR	many-celled.
MUTENESS	a condition in which a person cannot speak.
MUTUALISM	a close relationship between two organisms which benefits both organisms.
MYCELIUM	a mass of fungal hyphae.
MYCOLOGIST	a person who studies fungi.
NEARSIGHTEDNESS	a condition in which light is focused too near the lens and only nearby objects can be seen clearly.
NEMATODA	the phylum of round worms in the Kingdom Animalia.

NEPHRON TUBULE	the long, thin part of a nephron where reabsorption occurs.
NEPHRONS	the basic functional units of the kidney which filter wastes from the blood.
NEURON	a nerve cell; transmits information through electrical and chemical signals.
NEUROTRANSMITTER	a chemical that carries a nerve message across a synapse.
NEUTRON	a particle with no electric charge located in the nucleus of an atom; has a mass of 1 amu.
NICHE	the special role of an organism in its habitat.
NODULE	a small bump on the root of a legume containing nitrogen-fixing bacteria.
NONINFECTIOUS	not able to be transmitted from one to another by direct or indirect contact.
NOSTRILS	the openings in the nose.
NUCLEAR MEMBRANE	the thin, semipermeable film that controls what enters or leaves the nucleus.
NUCLEOPLASM	the protoplasm within the nucleus of a cell.
NUCLEUS	(1) the dense center region of an atom.
	(2) the dense round structure in a cell that controls cell activity.
NUTRIENT	any substance needed by an organism to live and grow.
NUTRITION	the process of getting and using food.
NYMPH	an immature form of an animal that undergoes incomplete metamorphosis.
OLFACTORY NERVE	the nerve that sends electrical impulses from the nose to the brain.
OMNIVORE	an animal that eats all kinds of food.
OPTIC NERVE	the nerve that carries visual information from the eye to the brain.
ORDERS	subdivisions of a class.
ORGAN	a group of tissues working together to perform a single function.
ORGANELLES	tiny, specialized "organs" within a cell, each with its own function.
ORGANISM	any living thing.
OSMOSIS	the diffusion of water through a semipermeable membrane from a higher to lower concentration of water.
OSTEICHTHYES	the class of bony fish in the Phylum Chordata.
OVARIES	the female gonads that produce egg cells.
OXIDATION	the process of oxygen combining with another substance.
PALISADE LAYER	a layer of tall cells in a leaf where most photosynthesis takes place.
PANCREAS	a glandular organ that secretes pancreatic juice, insulin, and glucagon.
PARASITISM	a close relationship between two organisms that benefits one organism and harms the other.

266

PASTEURIZATION	the process of heating milk or another liquid to kill bacteria.
PATHOGEN	any disease-causing organism.
PELLICLE	a stiff layer supporting the cell membrane that gives shape to some protists.
PEPSIN	an enzyme in gastric juice that begins the chemical digestion of proteins.
PERIOSTEUM	the lining that surrounds and nourishes a bone.
PERISTALSIS	rhythmic, wave-like contractions of some organs in the digestive system.
PHAGOCYTES	white blood cells that ingest pathogens.
PHARYNX	the region at the back of the nose and mouth above the esophagus.
PHLOEM	tube-like cells that transport food in a plant.
PHOTOSYNTHESIS	the process by which plants use light to make food energy.
PHOTOTROPISM	a plant response to light.
PHYLA	subdivisions of a kingdom; singular = phylum.
PIGMENT	any coloring substance.
PISTIL	all the female parts of a flower.
PITH	storage cells in the center of a plant stem.
PITUITARY GLAND	a tiny endocrine gland at the base of the brain that controls many other endocrine glands.
PLACENTA	a capillary-rich organ formed by mammalian embryos to allow diffusion of food and wastes to and from the unborn and its mother.
PLANTAE	the kingdom containing autotrophic organisms with cellulose cell walls.
PLASMA	the liquid part of the blood.
PLATELET	a colorless cell fragment in the blood that begins the clotting process.
PLATYHELMINTHES	the phylum of flat worms in the Kingdom Animalia.
POLLINATION	the process of pollen being transferred from the anther to the stigma.
POLYSACCHARIDE	many sugar rings fastened into a long chain to form a starch molecule.
PORE	a small opening.
PORIFERA	the phylum of pore-bearing animals called sponges.
POSTERIOR	rear end.
PRECIPITATE	a solid that forms and falls to the bottom of a test tube when two liquids react.
PRIMARY CONSUMER	organisms that eat producers.
PRODUCERS	organisms that use the sun's energy to make food; autotrophs.
PROKARYOTES	organisms without a nuclear membrane or organelles; bacteria and archaeans.

PROPHASE	the second stage of mitosis, during which the chromosomes organize themselves into pairs and the nuclear membrane dissolves.
PROTEIN	one of the nutrient groups; molecules made of long chains of amino acids.
PROTISTA	the kingdom containing unicellular or very simple multicellular organisms with nuclear membranes and organelles.
PROTON	a positively charged particle in the nucleus of an atom; has a mass of 1 amu.
PROTOPLASM	all the living material which makes up a cell.
PSEUDOPOD	a projection of the cytoplasm of amoeboid cells used for locomotion; "false foot."
PULMONARY ARTERY	either of the two arteries that carry oxygen-poor blood from the heart to the lungs.
PULMONARY CIRCULATION	the path of blood vessels from the heart to the lungs and back.
PULMONARY VEIN	any of the veins that carry oxygen-rich blood back to the heart from the lungs.
PUNCTURE	a small but very deep wound.
PUPA	an immature, resting stage of an organism that undergoes complete metamorphosis.
PURE	an organism with two identical genes for a given trait.
PYLORIC SPHINCTER	a ring-like muscle that closes the lower end of the stomach.
PYRENOID	a storage area for starch in algae.
RADIAL SYMMETRY	a shape which may be cut along the radii of a circle into similar parts.
REASONING	the process of using what one has learned to solve new problems.
RECEPTORS	the parts of sensory neurons that receive input from the environment.
RECESSIVE	the form of a gene that is not expressed if an organism also inherits a different form of the gene from one of its parents.
RECTUM	the storage area for solid waste at the end of the large intestine.
RED BLOOD CELL	a disk-shaped cell in the blood which contains hemoglobin for carrying oxygen.
REGENERATION	the process of regrowing a missing part of the body.
REPRODUCTION	the life function in which living things produce more of their own kind.
REPTILIA	the class of scaly-skinned animals with lungs in the Phylum Chordata.
RESIDUE	the solid caught in a filter.
RESPIRATION	external: the taking in of oxygen and release of carbon dioxide; also called breathing.
	cellular: the process of getting energy through the oxidation of food.
RESPONSE	the movement of a muscle or gland due to an impulse from a motor neuron.

RETINA	the light-sensitive tissue containing rod and cone cells that lines the back of the eye.
RHIZOIDS	thin, root-like structures on fungi, mosses, and ferns.
RHIZOME	an underground, horizontal stem that can produce a new plant.
RIBOSOME	a small, dot-like organelle on the endoplasmic reticulum where proteins are made.
RINGWORM	an infectious fungal disease that produces a ring-like spot in the skin.
RNA	ribonucleic acid; a chemical in the cytoplasm that contains the instructions for certain functions in the cell.
ROD CELLS	specialized neurons in the eye for black and white vision; light receptors.
ROOT CAP	specialized cells that protect the tip of a root.
ROOT HAIRS	elongated epidermal root cells used for absorption.
SALIVA	a secretion from the salivary glands in the mouth which contains amylase.
SAPROPHYTISM	a relationship in which an organism uses dead organisms as a food source.
SCURVY	a noninfectious disease caused by lack of vitamin C.
SECONDARY CONSUMERS	organisms that eat primary consumers.
SEED DISPERSAL	the scattering of seeds.
SELF-POLLINATION	the process in which pollen from a flower lands on its own stigma.
SEMICIRCULAR CANALS	three fluid-filled loops inside each ear that send impulses to the cerebellum for balance.
SEMIPERMEABLE	able to be penetrated by some molecules but not by others.
SENSORY NEURON	a nerve cell that receives data from the environment and sends impulses into the brain.
SEPTUM	the wall of cardiac muscle that separates the left and right sides of the heart.
SESSILE	attached by the base to one spot.
SEXUAL REPRODUCTION	the process of making a new individual from two parents.
SIMPLE GOITER	a swelling of the thyroid gland, often caused by iodine deficiency.
SKELETAL MUSCLE	voluntary muscles with striations and many nuclei per cell; used for movement.
SMALL INTESTINE	the organ in which digestion is completed and absorption occurs; the longest organ of the body.
SMOOTH MUSCLE	involuntary muscle found in the digestive system with one nucleus per cell and without striations.
SOLID	the lowest energy phase of matter, in which it has a definite shape and volume; ex. ice.

SOLUBLE	able to dissolve.
SOLUTE	the substance that dissolves, usually the smaller amount.
SOLVENT	the substance that does the dissolving, usually water.
SORI	clusters of sporangia on the undersides of fern fronds; singular = sorus.
SPECIES	subdivisions of a genus; the smallest taxons, containing only one kind of organism; second half of a scientific name.
SPERM	a small, motile cell that has only half the normal number of chromosomes; the male gamete.
SPONGY LAYER	a loosely packed layer of cells in a leaf where gas exchange takes place.
SPORANGIA	structures in which spores are made.
SPORE	an asexual reproductive cell that can produce a new fungus, moss, or fern.
SPORULATION	a method of asexual reproduction in which a spore produces a new organism.
STAMEN	all the male parts of a flower.
STIMULUS	anything that causes a sensory neuron to send an impulse.
STIPE	the stem-like part of a mushroom.
STOLON	a thin, often fan-shaped, sheet of fungal hyphae.
STOMACH	a digestive organ that chemically and mechanically digests food.
STOMATE	an opening for gas exchange in the lower epidermis of a leaf.
STOOL	the solid matter excreted from the rectum.
STRIATIONS	bands or lines; caused by organized, repeating units in skeletal and cardiac muscles.
SUPERIOR VENA CAVA	the major vein from the upper part of the body that enters the right atrium.
SWEAT GLANDS	tiny coiled tubes in the skin that form perspiration for excretion through pores.
SYNAPSE	the microscopic space between an end brush of a neuron and another cell.
SYNTHESIS	the process of making useful chemicals in an organism.
SYSTEM	a group of organs working together to perform a life function.
SYSTEMIC CIRCULATION	the path of blood vessels from the heart to the systems of the body and back.
TAP ROOT	a root system with one, very large central root; specialized for storage.
TASTE BUDS	bumps on the tongue and sides of the mouth that contain nerve cells sensitive to sweet, sour, salt, and bitter.
TAXON	group.
TAXONOMY	the science of classifying and naming organisms.

TELOPHASE	the fifth and final stage of mitosis, during which the cell divides into two parts, each containing a complete set of chromosomes.
TEMPERATURE	how hot or cold compared to a standard.
TENDON	a fibrous connective tissue that connects bone to muscle or muscle to muscle.
TENTACLE	a long, soft appendage, sometimes with suction cups or stinging cells (nematocysts).
TESTES	the male gonads that produce sperm cells.
TETANUS	an anaerobic bacterial disease called lockjaw that is spread by puncture wounds.
THIGMOTROPISM	a plant response to touch.
THYROID GLAND	an endocrine gland in front of the trachea that secretes thyroxin.
THYROXIN	the hormone produced by the thyroid gland which regulates metabolism.
TISSUE	a group of cells having the same shape and performing the same function.
TONGUE	a thick, muscular organ in the mouth.
TRACHEA	the wind pipe; a cartilage-reinforced tube connecting the pharynx and the bronchi.
TRACHEOPHYTA	a phylum of Kingdom Plantae containing plants with a vascular system.
TRANSLUCENT	anything that allows light to pass through but cannot be seen through clearly.
TRANSPIRATION	the process of water evaporating from a plant.
TRANSPORT	the life function that includes the absorption and distribution of materials.
TRICHOCYSTS	barbed projections used by a paramecium for defense.
TROPISM	a plant response to environmental factors which is controlled by plant hormones.
TUBER	a short, enlarged, underground stem specialized for food storage; ex. potato.
UNCONDITIONED REFLEX	a simple, quick response that does not require the brain; a simple reflex.
UNICELLULAR	one-celled.
UNIT	the part of a measurement that specifies the quantity being measured; for instance, meter, gram, etc.
UREA	a colorless nitrogen compound eliminated by the kidneys as waste.
URETERS	the two ducts that lead from the kidneys to the urinary bladder.
URETHRA	the duct that leads from the urinary bladder to the outside of the body.
URINARY BLADDER	a balloon-like organ in the lower abdomen that stores urine.
URINARY TRACT	all the parts of the body that produce and eliminate urine.
URINE	a mixture of water, nitrogenous wastes and other soluble compounds filtered from the blood by the kidneys.

UTERUS	womb; the organ in which mammals live inside their mothers before birth.
VACCINE	any substance used to give immunity from specific diseases.
VACUOLES	bubble-like parts of a cell that may contain air or food.
VASCULAR SYSTEM	the xylem and phloem tissues of a plant which form a system for transport of liquids.
VECTOR	an organism that carries a pathogen from one host to another.
VEGETATIVE PROPAGATION	a method of asexual reproduction in which a part of one plant is used to produce another plant.
VEIN	a thin-walled blood vessel with valves that carries blood back to the heart.
VENTRAL	underside or bottom.
VENTRICLE	either of the two lower, muscular chambers of the heart that pump blood into the arteries.
VERTEBRATA	a subphylum of Phylum Chordata containing all organisms with vertebrae forming a backbone.
VILLUS	a finger-like projection of the lining of the small intestine that increases surface area for absorption of digested nutrients.
VITAMIN	an organic compound needed by a living system in small amounts.
VIRUS	a DNA or RNA particle, usually with a protein coat, able to take over a host cell's metabolism.
VOCAL CORDS	two thin membranes in the larynx that produce sound when vibrated.
VOLUME	a measure in cubic units of the amount of space an object takes up; volume = length × width × height.
VOLUNTARY	able to be controlled by the conscious mind.
VOLVA	a cup-like structure at the base of a mushroom's stipe.
WARM-BLOODED	able to maintain a steady body temperature regardless of environmental temperatures (within limits).
WATER	a chemical made of two hydrogen atoms and one oxygen atom; also called hydrogen oxide.
WHITE BLOOD CELL	an amoeboid cell in the blood that engulfs and destroys pathogens.
WOODY STEM	a type of hard stem, covered with bark, found in many perennials.
XYLEM	straw-like cells that carry water and minerals upward in vascular plants.
ZYGOTE	the new individual produced by the fusion of a sperm cell and an egg cell.

IMAGE CREDITS

Line art illustrations: Michael J. Spear

Pg. 15: Bettmann/Corbis Images

Pg. 22: Public domain, Robert H. Mohlenbrock @ USDA-NRCS PLANTS Database

Pg. 23: Archives of the Congregation of the Mission, Paris

Pgs. 26, 28, 50: Universal Images Group/Getty Images

Pgs. 33, 35: © Carol and Mike Werner/PhotoTake, Inc.

Pg. 67: Gwenda Pini

Pg. 68: Photo and conk art by Sarah Lane. First published on InsideBainbridge.com.

Pg. 72: altrendo images/Stockbyte/Getty Images

Pg. 148: Used with permission of the Jérôme Lejeune Foundation: www.LejeuneUSA.org

Pg. 151: Used with permission of Tony Melendez Ministries: www.tonymelendez.com

Pg. 193 (two photos): Used with permission of Harvington Hall, Worcestershire: www.harvingtonhall.com

Pg. 204: LifeART Image ©2004 Lippincott Williams & Wilkins

Pgs. 210, 212: Imperial War Museums

Pg. 247: Used with permission of The Ricci Institute for Chinese-Western Cultural History, University of San Francisco

Shutterstock.com: Cover, pg. i: michaeljung; pgs. 1, 5: YanLev; pgs. 1, 144, 146: Sebastian Kaulitzki; pgs. 1, 248: Edwin Verin; pgs. 2, 4: KennStilger47; pg. 5: mtr; pg. 5: Maxim Blinkov; pg. 5: Pan Xunbin; pg. 6: Kzenon; pg. 12: Yaviki; pgs. 18, 20: Nathan B Dappen; pg. 23: Hung Chung Chih; pg. 25: Tom linster; pg. 25: Yongkiet jitwattanatam; pg. 25: Jost Stergarsek; pg. 25: Andre Goncalves; pg. 25: anekoho; pg. 25: Steve Byland; pgs. 31 (three photos): Magcom; pg. 31 (two photos): molekuul.be; pg. 42: Jubal Harshaw; pg. 42: vetpathologist; pg. 42 (two photos): Dimarion; pg. 42: Wilson's Vision; pg. 42: Pan Xunbin; pgs. 44, 54, 62, 70, 82, 92, 100, 116: cluckva; pgs. 44, 54, 62, 70, 79, 82, 92, 100, 116: nadiya_sergey; pgs. 44, 54, 60, 62, 70, 82, 92, 100, 116, 231: Lebendkulturen.de; pg. 47: Alila Medical Media; pg. 52: Coprid; pgs. 57, 103: Olga Bogatyrenko; pg. 58: Erik Zandboer; pg. 65: withGod; pg. 68: apple1; pg. 75: Birute Vijeikiene; pg. 75: Marbury; pg. 77: Jubal Harshaw; pg. 76: loflo69; pg. 77: Aleksey Stemmer; pg. 78: Madlen; pg. 79: PhotographyByMK; pg. 79: WDG Photo; pg. 79: Studio Barcelona; pg. 81: xpixel; pg. 81: Jubal Harshaw; pg. 84 (two photos): Jubal Harshaw; pg. 84: Pan Xunbin; pg. 85 (two photos): Richard Griffin; pg. 88: Dimarion; pg. 95: Lebendkulturen.de; pg. 96: epsylon_lyrae; pg. 97: BlueRingMedia; pg. 99: 3523studio; pg. 99: Bogdan Wankowicz; pgs. 100, 102: Vilainecrevette; pg. 103: StevenRussellSmithPhotos; pg. 103: Computer Earth; pg. 107 (three photos): Jubal Harshaw; pg. 107: Dray van Beeck; pg. 109: Rich Carey; pg. 110: robert cicchetti; pg. 110: Ryan M. Bolton; pg. 110: Jason Patrick Ross; pg. 113: BlueRingMedia; pgs. 114, 115: Stubblefield Photography; pg. 114: NatureDiver; pg. 115: Daryl H; pg. 115: Igor Sirbu; pg. 115: nicola vernizzi; pg. 115: Four Oaks; pgs. 116, 118: pr2is; pg. 119: Shane Gross; pg. 119: cbpix; pgs. 119, 122: Colin Edwards Wildside; pg. 119: Christian Musat; pg. 120: Nantawat Chotsuwan; pg. 122: Tobyphotos; pg. 123: Four Oaks; pg. 123: worldswildlifewonders; pg. 124: Micha Klootwijk; pgs. 124, 144, 153, 156, 158, 166, 174, 183, 188, 198: stihii; pgs. 124, 144, 153, 158, 166, 174, 183, 188, 198: Sedova Elena; pgs. 124, 144, 153, 158, 166, 174, 183, 188, 198: Alila Medical Media; pg. 125: Tyler Olson; pg. 125: KonstantinChristian; pg. 128: Magcom; pg. 129: molekuul.be; pg. 129: Tom Reichner; pg. 130: spline_x; pg. 130: Valentyn Volkov; pg. 131: Julia Ardaran; pg. 132: janecat; pg. 132: Evgenia Sh.; pg. 142: Prapann; pg. 143: Fotokostic; pg. 146: leonello calvetti; pg. 147: Jaimie Duplass; pg. 148: Denis Kuvaev; pg. 150: aslysun; pg. 156: Designua; pg. 161: Alila Medical Media; pg. 162: leonello calvetti; pg. 163: leonello calvetti; pg. 163: lila Medical Media; pg. 165: Alex Luengo; pg. 168: Tony Wear; pg. 169: Alila Medical Media; pg. 169: leonello calvetti; pg. 170: Blamb; pgs. 171, 180: Andrea Danti; pg. 173: ducu59us; pg. 173: Alila Medical Media; pgs. 174, 176: posztos; pg. 176: f9photos; pg. 177: Alila Medical Media; pg. 180: Alila Medical Media; pg. 185 (two photos): Alila Medical Media; pg. 186 (two photos): Alex Luengo; pg. 191: Denis Kuvaev; pg. 191: Alila Medical Media; pg. 195: Alex Luengo; pg. 197: Alila Medical Media; pgs. 198, 200: Portokalis; pg. 201: Alila Medical Media; pg. 203 (two photos): Alex Luengo; pg. 205: Felixdesign; pg. 206: Alila Medical Media; pg. 209: Oguz Aral; pg. 215: Shutterstock; pg. 216: Jari Hindstroem; pg. 223: pedalist; pgs. 226, 228: Four Oaks; pg. 229: Bradley Hebdon; pg. 233: Lucian Coman; pg. 240: Maksym Gorpenyuk; pg. 245: craig hill; pg. 249: Songquan Deng; pg. 252: Yeko Photo Studio; pg. 252: monticello; pg. 252: Egor Rodynchenko; pg. 252: gillmar; pg. 252: Valentyn Volkov; pg. 252: Olga Popova; pg. 252: matin; pg. 253: marylooo; pg. 253: Julian Rovagnati; pg. 253: gdvcom; pg. 253: Alex Studio; pg. 253: Iryna1; pg. 253: Chukcha; pg. 253: pterwort; pg. 253: Dmitry Kolmakov; back cover: oksana.perkins, ephotographer, oorka, Poznukhov Yuriy, markrhiggins, Valerie Potapova. **Workbook reference symbols:** Myvector, ekler, Fernando Eusebio, Vector Icon.

Science Source: pg. 5: Science Source; pgs. 10, 12: Frans Lanting, Mint Images; pg. 28: Martyn F. Chillmaid; pgs. 36, 38: Russell Kightley; pg. 38: Andrew Syred; pg. 40: John Durham; pg. 41: Biophoto Associates; pg. 42: Biophoto Associates; pg. 43: Merlin D. Tuttle; pg. 43: Dr. David Furness, Keele University; pg. 43: Christian Darkin; pgs. 44, 46: Tek Image; pgs. 44, 49, 54, 62, 70, 83, 92, 100, 116: Hazel Appleton, Health Protection Agency Centre for Infections; pg. 47: Medi-Mation Ltd; pgs. 48, 49: John Walsh; pg. 49 (three photos): Biophoto Associates; pg. 49: Juergen Berger; pg. 49: CNRI; pg. 49: Perennou Nuridsany; pg. 52: Dr. Jeremy Burgess; pg. 52: